DR. RANA AWDISH is the director of the Pulmonary Hypertension Program at Henry Ford Hospital in Detroit and a critical care physician. She was recently named Medical Director of Care Experience for the $6-billion, 24,000-employee Health System. She was awarded the Speak Up Hero Award in 2014 for her work on improving communication, as well as the Critical Care Teaching Award in 2016. In 2017 she was a finalist for the Schwartz Center's 2017 National Compassionate Caregiver of the Year (NCCY) Award and the Physician of the Year award from the Press Ganey National Client Conference. Dr. Awdish is board certified in internal medicine, pulmonary and critical care medicine.

Additional Praise for *In Shock*

"An extraordinary memoir." —*Daily Mail* (London)

"A brave, powerful memoir." —*The Times* (London)

"Tense, powerful, and gripping . . . Her writing style is often nothing short of beautiful—evocative and emotional."
—Adam Kay, *The Observer*

"Outstanding." —James McConnachie,
The Sunday Times (London)

"An enthralling page-turner and a haunting call to arms."
—Rachel Clarke, author of
Your Life in My Hands: A Junior Doctor's Story

"Should be required reading in every medical, nursing, and health professional school." —Andrew J. Shin, JD, MPH,
Senior Director, Policy,
The Schwartz Center for Compassionate Healthcare

"Remarkable." —Jeffrey Millstein, MD, Penn Medicine

"A very important book and the perfect antidote to the ever-increasing canon of rather self-congratulatory medical literature hitting our shelves. After reading this book, I feel like a different doctor." —Dr. Gabriel Weston, author of
Direct Red: A Surgeon's View of Her Life-or-Death Profession

In Shock

My Journey from Death to
Recovery and the Redemptive
Power of Hope

Rana Awdish

Picador
St. Martin's Press
New York

Dedicated to Randy

IN SHOCK. Copyright © 2017 by Rana Awdish. All rights reserved.
Printed in the United States of America. For information,
address Picador, 175 Fifth Avenue, New York, N.Y. 10010.

picadorusa.com • instagram.com/picador
twitter.com/picadorusa • facebook.com/picadorusa

Picador® is a U.S. registered trademark and is used by
Macmillan Publishing Group, LLC, under license from Pan Books Limited.

For book club information, please visit facebook.com/picadorbookclub or
email marketing@picadorusa.com.

The Library of Congress has cataloged the
St. Martin's Press edition as follows:

Names: Awdish, Rana, author.
Title: In shock : my journey from death to recovery and the redemptive
    power of hope / Rana Awdish.
Description: First edition. | New York : St. Martin's Press, 2017.
Identifiers: LCCN 2017022275 | ISBN 9781250119216 (hardcover) |
    9781250119223 (ebook)
Subjects: LCSH: Awdish, Rana—Health. | Physicians—United States—
    Biography. | Physician and patient. | Medical ethics.
Classification: LCC R154.A93 A3 2017 | DDC 610.92 B—dc23
LC record available at https://lccn.loc.gov/2017022275

Picador Paperback ISBN 978-1-250-29377-0

Our books may be purchased in bulk for promotional, educational,
or business use. Please contact your local bookseller or the Macmillan
Corporate and Premium Sales Department at 1-800-221-7945, extension
5442, or by email at MacmillanSpecialMarkets@macmillan.com.

First published by St. Martin's Press

First Picador Edition: October 2018

10 9 8 7

Contents

A Chance to Die

Medicine can be a magical lens through which to view the human body. Focus its light on an unsorted pile of symptoms and it will converge them neatly into a diagnosis. A swollen, red "strawberry" tongue in a feverish child will lead the doctor to examine the heart and affirm a diagnosis of vasculitis. A man's burning stomach pain transforms into gastritis, which has both a cause and a cure, whereas his nonspecific pain had neither.

Medicine does this by asking questions and listening for not just what is said, but what may be true. If empathy is the ability to take the perspective of another and feel with them, then, at its best, the practice of medicine is a focused, scientific form of empathy. Truly caring for a patient necessitates traversing borders and inhabiting the view of another with the humility of a visitor who knows he or she can choose to look away. They each possess the power to heal.

The first time I viewed the world through medicine's transformative lens I was five years old, listening as my mother offered a seemingly vague description to the pediatrician by phone. My brother was leaning forward in the crib, onto his hands, drooling, and seemed to be gulping the air rather than breathing. The doctor understood this to be epiglottitis, an often fatal swelling of the airway. He instructed her with a calm but firm urgency to bring him immediately to the emergency room, where he would be waiting. That ability to translate symptoms into diagnoses and treatments, the power to save lives through knowledge and listening, struck me as the most beautiful job description I could imagine.

Attending medical school was like entering a secret society, complete with its own language, uniforms, and societal norms. We learned to translate the genetic code and sequence genes that produced proteins that made up organs. We were granted cadavers to dissect and study, each structure's name rooted in ancient Latin or Greek. We spent a year immersed in the divine elegance of the human body, so that in our second year we could learn to recognize pathology. We were instructed by professors who spoke of the innate intelligence of disease. Parasites that exploited their host, small changes in genes that resulted in defective hearts, and endlessly replicating cancer cells. By learning the pathway to disease, we were taught, we could unlock cures. The knowledge was intoxicating. I followed the vectored curriculum, believing I would emerge transformed and able to heal.

I couldn't have imagined the circuitous form my training would actually take. The forward progression through residency and fellowship was nothing more than a comfortable lie my body would ultimately dismantle. My body somehow understanding that despite completing my training, despite being surrounded by every form and severity of disease, I had yet to learn what it meant to be sick. I would experience an illness—followed by a long, painful recovery—that took me apart, piece by piece, and put me back together in a conformation so different I questioned if I still existed at all.

The wish for the cure is seductive; it captivates and charms. Devastating illness, despite its ability to utterly transform, is not revered in the same way. Illness is viewed as an aberrant state. It is a town we drive through on a journey home, but not a place to stop and linger. We pass through with gritted teeth, as if it were a storm, with no regard for the illuminating beauty of the lightning as it strikes. But those shattering moments that break our bodies also allow us access to wisdom that is normally hidden, except in times of utter darkness.

From my new vantage point in an ICU bed, I would begin to sense a dark hole at the center of a flurry of what was otherwise highly proficient, astoundingly skillful care. I couldn't name it at first. I would have glimpses of clarity, only to have it recede out of focus. I had to train myself to see it, like negative space on a canvas. It took years of being a patient to understand that though the healing potential of knowledge is magical, it is also a lie.

Medicine cannot heal in a vacuum; it requires connection.

As a patient, it's upending to be confronted with the actual fragility of everything you once believed to be a constant. To inhabit that vulnerable space, and to have no one around you who is open to discussion of the devastation is patently surreal. We all desire to be seen, to be known, to share our experiences and feel heard. To have our life events given context and meaning, redirected back to us in a way that we can understand and integrate into our understanding of who we believe ourselves to be. This need is more acute in times of sickness. When organs and limbs function without fail, we can indulge notions of self-reliance and agency. We believe ourselves to be the narrators of our own lives. When we are sick, we are humbled by our dependency on others, the loss of control, the uncertainty of the ending. This change opens channels for communication we are hardwired not to tune into during the monotonous routines and spaces of normal life.

Recognizing those open channels and fostering connection in full view of the knowledge is what heals. Making the choice to be present for someone else's suffering requires a kind of anticipatory resolve. Because it does get hard, sometimes even unbearably so. The choice to be present means deciding at the outset that you will be there for the duration. That premeditated sort of intentionality may not resonate with the kind of effortless empathy we'd imagined, until we remind ourselves that all forms of love require work and a fierce commitment.

Had our training somehow taught us to avoid these channels? Did we know what to do when we recognized them?

I work at a large urban hospital, in the center of a busy and diverse city. We are sent patients, by helicopter and ambulance, who have run out of options elsewhere. The kind of clinical excellence, determination, and teamwork necessary to care for these uniquely complex patients far surpasses what I've experienced in other hospitals during medical school or residency training. I have the great privilege of working at an amazing institution. The shared purpose and the pride that comes from doing hard work well is one of the reasons I chose to stay on after my fellowship training.

The hard times, the times when I knew we missed the mark, can almost always be understood and rationalized. Health care is exceedingly complex. Errors will inevitably occur, at even the best hospitals. What seems different to me is our transparent willingness to acknowledge that we are a learning organization. This orientation causes us to look honestly at each lapse, whether it be in communication or drug delivery. Acknowledge it, determine the point the process broke down, and address it. Perhaps it is because of our awareness that all systems attempting remarkable things will at times fail that we've learned to cultivate resilience. We never allow a failure, however small, to be the end of the story. It's always the beginning of a better way of being.

It's how we heal.

I was recently rounding in the same ICU that I had once inhabited as a critically ill patient. I stood at the head of the team, as their attending physician, with a group of eager medical residents presenting the critically ill patients in sequence. The patient we were discussing was on the waiting list for a lung transplant and had been waiting in the same ICU room for months. I had first met her years earlier, when she was transferred into our hospital for evaluation of a leaky heart valve.

When the resident completed his presentation, the ICU nurse added her report on the events of the night. She had cared for the patient many times, and the longitudinal relationship provided a depth of understanding the resident couldn't hope to match. She wore seafoam green scrubs that bore her handwriting near the knee, a potassium value she'd jotted down when the lab called and she couldn't quickly find paper. Rounds required standing in place and so she fidgeted, a substitute for the constant movement she was more adapted to. Her brown hair was pulled into a ponytail, and she spoke with purposeful brevity, not referring to her notes.

"She had a setback overnight, and she's on high-flow oxygen now, fifteen liters," she began. "She's spent the morning listening to recorded sermons by her pastor. She's different today. If you ask me I think she is really scared."

The resident frowned, having just reported that she was stable clinically. He appeared tired, the whites of his eyes fissured by fine red cracks. There was a spot of hair at the crown that was sticking straight up, the only visible evidence that he had laid down at some point in the evening. It reminded me of my son's cowlick and I had to resist my maternal urge to smooth it down. He was wearing a hooded sweatshirt under his white coat. Residents often add this layer, sometime around hour twenty of their assigned thirty-hour call. Something about being awake for so many hours straight dysregulates the hormones that control body temperature, and we were all always cold on post-call mornings.

I had been through setbacks with this patient before; many of us had. They were usually a sign of worsening heart failure, and though she had always managed to recover, they took a severe toll on her emotionally. It was as if her body was insisting that she acknowledge the possibility of her death. Her resource in combating fear was hope and prayer, and she immersed herself in both.

"I asked her about her breathing, but I didn't get that," he said, apologetically.

"Every listener hears a different story," I reminded him. "The fact that she shares something different with her nurse than what she tells you or me is to be expected," I explained. I knew she had different answers for different people. We each had different relationships with her. "It doesn't devalue what she told you, it's just different," I added.

I saw a blank index card in his pocket.

"Did she give that to you?" I asked.

"Yes, she wants me to write a message of hope for her wall," he said, sounding defeated. "To be honest, I'm uncomfortable writing anything because I think she is going to die before she gets a transplant. Transplant says she has a lot of antibodies and it's going to be hard to find a matching donor." He paused. "It seems like I'd be lying if I wrote something encouraging."

I saw in his expression the same discomfort I often felt in the face of uncertainty. I saw the disillusioned fatigue, a by-product of the effort expended wrestling the facts to the ground so that we could stare at them and more honestly represent them. Not just to ourselves, but to our patients. Our feeble attempts to understand how to allow for optimism, when the truth seemed intent on blocking out the sun. It was so hard to palpate the borders of authentic hope, to know where falseness began.

"It's hard, right? When we don't know," I said, lacking articulate words.

"Listen, I get it," I continued. "You don't want to provide false hope. It's hard. What if we took our lead from her? What do you think she needs from us?"

"We have to coordinate her care so that she is ready when an organ becomes available, make sure the lab work is ordered and she has the IV access anesthesia needs for when it's time to go to the operating room, make sure her fluid balance in her body stays stable, and titrate her medications to ensure that," a resident answered.

I nodded. "That's all true, and we absolutely have to do all of that. But, is that what she is telling us she needs in this moment?" I asked.

They quietly shrugged, in a way that suggested they were doing what they knew how to do and were at least somewhat exhausted by it.

"Let's see what other people have written," I suggested.

We entered her room, leaving the lights off. She was sleeping, her body attempting to recover from the terrible night. Even when she was awake, her lung disease was so severe that she only managed to speak in small, choppy fragments, one or two words at a time. I had visited with her earlier in the morning, and had shared her fear that her difficulty breathing was escalating. Even sitting felt like a struggle lately. She was spending more of her day in prayer. Sitting quietly with her, I knew she was days away from death. I wanted to talk to her about that imposing reality. The "what-ifs" that were seemingly more likely each day than her undergoing a successful transplant. I thought it was time. She met my eyes and smiled. She expressed her disappointment that the new residents this month hadn't completed the cards. "I just want to know that they are hoping along with me," she said. I looked down, breaking our gaze and feeling guilty for anticipating her death.

She had glossy, framed, full-color pictures of her standing proudly with her family, personalizing the room. They were the first things that confronted the team, forcing everyone to acknowledge how she identified herself. *This is me, not what you see in the bed, but this,* they seemed to say.

I turned to the dark blue wall, peppered with white cards filled with messages of encouragement and read them quietly. "I am in awe of your resolve, your strength and your faith. Thank you for allowing me to be a part of this journey with you."

"You are the bravest person I know," said another.

"I have hope that I will see you on the other side of this, when you can breathe freely and be well," read another.

We walked out of the room and tried to process what we had read. Was it appropriate and just to provide hopeful support to someone on the cusp of death? Was it rational to prioritize hope, even as we struggled to provide the highly technical medical care she needed to survive? I believed it was. The cards gave her tangible evidence that each of us were going to acknowledge the primacy of her version of her patient story, that we saw her suffering and shared her fear. By writing something hopeful we were allowing ourselves to imagine with her the range of the possible: not just the likely outcomes but the expansively possible.

One resident began to formulate a thought, about how completing the card was essentially one side of a transactional exchange. "I see, so we give her something she needs, and in turn—"

He stopped himself short and the post-call resident began speaking.

"No, she needs us to see her, even as sick as she is, not just to see her as sick, but as being healed." His simple description of how our attending to her allowed us to better represent her was beautiful. He went on. "Those cards make the hope visible."

"Wow." I was stunned by his statement. "Think about that. If in the end, that's what we do today, somehow manage to make hope visible . . ." I couldn't quite complete my thought.

"That would be success," the nurse added, nodding.

"Well, that and she gets a transplant," a resident added with an edge of apathy. The others laughed quickly, like childish conspirators. I understood the discomfort they were feeling.

I knew we valued the cure, the goal, the win. We were far less comfortable in the gray, shadowed area of suffering. We excelled at providing complex, precision medicine in a way that appeared almost effortless, yet at times struggled clumsily when it came to empathy. I recalled a time when I had responded to a tearful patient's question, "But how could this have happened?" with explanations of the complex interplay between genetics and environment, behaviors and predispositions that had led to the terminal diagnosis. I had been trained to believe that all questions were a request for data. Because of this orientation, I recognized neither the fear nor the existential nature of the question. It would be years before I understood the subtext behind the questions. And even then, once I recognized them as an opportunity to connect, I still didn't believe in the healing power of just being present to bear witness to someone's struggle. I didn't value the intangible, the moments of shared understanding.

I had distanced myself from my patients the way I had been instructed to do in training, in the same way the team was doing now. I had subscribed to the paradigm of medicine set forth by my mentors, one that advised me to cultivate space, to be sparing of myself. I was taught that connection begets loss, which in turn begets disillusionment and burnout. As if I were made of some quantifiable measure of stuff that once given away would leave me depleted. I don't know if I fully believed in that model, but until my own experience as a patient, I didn't allow myself to envision an alternative where I was unguarded, receptive and freely giving of myself. I didn't understand that open channels would replenish my supply of self. That there was reciprocity in empathy.

Luckily, I had the chance to die.

One

Bled White

Death is the dark backing that a mirror needs
if we are to see anything.
—SAUL BELLOW

All pain becomes abstract in retrospect. It is a merciful truth
that no one is capable of summoning to the surface the
actual intensity of pain endured. As I sit now, reflecting on the
pain that first brought me to the hospital, I can sketch an outline, delineate the general size and shape, but it's become separate from me. A kind of sensory satiation occurs, in much the
same way repeating a word endlessly causes it to lose its meaning. I remember knowing the pain was not compatible with life.
I remember thinking I knew absolutely nothing of the meaning
of the word pain before that moment and that anything I had
labeled as pain prior to that was nothing more than a shadow of
a construct called pain. The pain that tore into me was excruciating and unsustainable.

I knew instinctively that if pain of that magnitude continued, it would kill me.

I was writhing miserably on a gurney in a triage room of Labor
and Delivery, the walls an institutional gray-green tile. Curled

on my right side, my face was close enough to the squares to pick up the scent of bleach embedded in the grout. My eyes tracked the tiles to the ceiling, designed to facilitate easy cleanup of blood splatter. I shivered, haunted already by what was yet to come. I found the premeditative aspect of those easy-to-mop wall tiles unnerving, the same way watching *Dateline* footage of someone at a hardware store purchasing duct tape just before a murder is frightening. The dull monotony belied the ensuing violence.

The pain had begun suddenly an hour prior, over a neglected dinner. It was the kind of featureless day I would easily have forgotten, had it not ended so disastrously. Instead, that bland day has become the beginning, a designation that can only be granted in retrospect.

"It was an entirely ordinary day."

I hear this often from patients or families, the survivors of devastating illness or tragedy. When they reflect upon the subsequent life-changing events of any one day, they inevitably comment on how bland and unremarkable the day had been up until that moment. The peaceful calm of the water the day of the drowning. The cloudless, clear blue of the fall sky the day of the plane crash. The absence of any premonitory clues, where we've been conditioned by Hollywood and literature to expect foreshadowing, leaves us feeling somehow cheated of a chance to anticipate the outcome. Cheated of a chance to change it.

It was an early spring day, bright with the promise of an approaching summer. The air in the shade was still bracingly cold, but in squares of sunlight, the sharp edges of the chill had been softened. I had a day off from work and planned to run some errands before dinner. I had a list of supplies I needed to purchase for a knitting class I had signed up for. The idea of knitting struck me as almost comically inefficient, which is probably why I was attracted to it. After so many years of each moment being assigned to reading, study and patient care, the idea that I might have time to knit felt gloriously liberating. And the nostalgia of making something for the baby by hand, that she could keep, was enchanting.

First though, I would take my swollen feet shopping for new shoes. I was into my seventh month of pregnancy, and my body was bloated and heavy. I had stopped wearing attractive shoes entirely, and even my flat brown orthopedic shoes now left deep indentations around the circumference of my feet by midday. I entered the large shoe warehouse and looked for the row of flats.

I had a vague sense of disequilibrium as I walked toward the aisle. I realized I didn't remember driving there. I looked around, suddenly unsure if someone had driven me. No, I was alone, I had driven. How odd that I had already lost that memory. I wondered if my sleep deprivation was catching up with me. I'd just come off a demanding ICU month, spending every fourth night on overnight call, and I was finding it difficult to stay awake if I sat down anywhere remotely comfortable. I wondered if I had lapsed into a microsleep while driving. I touched my pregnant belly, almost as an apology. I knew I had to be more considerate of my body, given the baby.

I found an area that had a series of unattractive, practical shoes and studied my options. A woman repeated, "Excuse me, excuse me," with increasing irritation as she attempted to pass me in the aisle. Apparently I'd failed to hear her the first four times. I shook off the fog and realized that I had been standing, blocking the aisle, while staring at the two shoes in my hands for far longer than necessary. I awkwardly pretended that I was just unable to choose between them and brought both pairs to the register.

I thought I should head home, but I stopped at the grocery

store, thinking I remembered needing something. It seemed larger and more difficult to navigate than usual. Walking only a few steps, my breath quickened as though I were biking up a steep hill. My mind slowed, with long stretches of cloudy silence distancing elusive thoughts. I was unable to remember what I had come for and left inexplicably with only a small jar of vanilla sugar. I was meeting my friend Dana, who was also a physician, for dinner. Perhaps she could help me brainstorm why I was feeling so bizarrely off.

When the pain began, it came in a breathtaking wave that receded just as swiftly as it approached. My first thought was, *OK, so there really is something wrong; I'm not crazy.* I looked across the table at her and said, "I don't think I can eat." The look on my face told her more than the words I had managed. I tentatively pushed away from the table, afraid any movement could bring on the next unwelcome wave, and walked out of the restaurant to anxiously pace the sidewalk.

The adrenaline surge from the explosive pain had cleared my mind. I knew I had to use this time well, before whatever was to come. After calming myself, I called my husband, Randy. "I'm not feeling well . . . my stomach . . . it's weird, there is this pain . . . I don't know . . . but don't worry, the baby is fine."

I cringed at the casual lilt in my voice. In attempting to reassure him, I had overcompensated and failed to convey an appropriate sense of urgency. I tried starting over. "I think you may need to take me to the hospital." I considered trying to explain my sense of displacement all day: the fugue state that I found myself in at the shoe store, the breathlessness and confusion I felt at the grocery store. Instead, I settled on adding, "I don't think I should drive," hoping that would suffice. That was at least a tangible fact. Randy, who was an attorney at a law firm in the city, answered something about leaving as soon as he responded to the mythical "one final e-mail," confirming to me that I had failed to convey the immediacy of my need.

Dana, from her view out the restaurant's window, recognized the elliptical and casual narrative I was constructing. She was well versed in my personality. She knew that I was not an alarmist by nature, that I generally assumed things would work out fine and I wouldn't want to worry him unnecessarily. My husband didn't have the benefit of that insight, having been married to me not quite a year. Dana thankfully prioritized action above reassurance and called him the moment I hung up: "I don't know what she just told you, but come home *now*. I'm going to drive her and we'll meet you there."

He did. To this day he insists it was without responding to the e-mail, although I am less certain of that. I imagine, knowing what he knows now about what would happen that day, he can't allow himself to imagine he sat at his computer a moment longer than necessary. In his retelling of the events, he may have even run to the car.

Dana drove me the short two blocks home. I saw the baking soda out on the counter when we walked in. It reminded me that my acid reflux had been terrible that morning, and I'd taken cold milk and baking soda to try to calm it naturally. I'd been trying to avoid any medication that could interfere with the baby's health, even very innocuous antacids. I wondered if the pain meant the acid had eroded through my stomach wall and into my abdominal blood vessels. All doctors were prone to attempts at self-diagnosis, though the results were seldom reassuring. Recognizing that a perforated ulcer could potentially explain the corrosive pain did not actually help the situation, because I could easily list fifteen other possible causes in order of decreasing severity. Being able to pick the one that suited me in the moment left me nowhere.

We walked to the living room, which is where Randy found me ten minutes later. I was on the floor, kneeling, compressing a pillow tightly against my abdomen. It was the latest effort in a series of awkward contortions aimed at reducing the pain. I eventually found that if I laid horizontally across the arm of the leather sofa on my right side with my right hand on the floor bracing me, the pain would just slightly quell. I had no way of knowing then that the pressure I was placing against my liver with the sofa arm was slowing the blood gushing from my liver, and that I had less than two hours before that blood loss would empty my arteries, veins, and heart entirely. I reasoned, poorly, that if the pain was manageable in that position, perhaps we could wait before going to the hospital.

"When I lay like this, it's not so bad," I announced, proud to have finally found a position that worked.

They shook their heads at me, unimpressed, while debating between them if we should drive to the hospital or call an ambulance. An ambulance seemed the safer choice, but would eliminate the ability to control which hospital I'd be taken to. I wanted very much to go downtown, to my own institution. It wasn't that I thought I'd receive better care because I worked there. We were an enormous system, with far too many doctors for us to all know each other. But having worked in the intensive care unit for the past three years, I'd witnessed on a daily basis the quality and safety of the complex care we delivered. I knew we could do things no one else could. I trusted us.

Presenting to any hospital as a patient struck me as a radical decision. I still wanted to think the situation was potentially manageable, although I didn't actually believe that it was at all manageable. Somehow I felt if I admitted it wasn't, then it would become incontrovertibly real. I would just stay there, lying across the couch in our living room in an inverted U-shape, until the pain passed.

For years to come, I would complain endlessly and irrationally about that couch. I disliked the orange tone of the brown leather, the bulkiness of it. Randy would defend it, having paid far too much for it and having special-ordered the leather, believing it needed to be that particular shade of brown. He interpreted my dislike of the couch as an indictment of his bachelor years, as symbolized by an abundance of brown leather furniture. I realized the stupidity of endlessly expressing my dislike for the couch, without honestly discussing why it bothered me, what memories it brought back. I would instead begrudgingly attempt to embrace the couch until I found I just couldn't anymore. Just this year, in a fit of transference, I pushed the heavy sofa into the garage and declared I never wanted it in the house again, haunted as I was by my memory of that night. Randy, finding it in the garage, shook his head and said, "Please tell me you didn't move it yourself," followed by, "Why didn't you tell me you hated it that much?"

"I did tell you," I'd reminded him. "I've always hated it," although it wasn't entirely true. There was that one night, when I was eviscerated by pain, that it had provided much-needed comfort.

I moaned, which was interpreted as an invitation for them to proceed with their plan. "Enough. You can't just stay here strewn over the couch forever; you're going to the hospital," they both said in their own exasperated way. Possibly this was communicated by one of them entirely with a look. In the time it took them to reach for me, to help me stand, the pain changed. I became nauseated and began vomiting profusely. I experienced what others have described as seeing stars. But to me it seemed rather that most of my vision had fallen away, leaving only pockmarked circles of light. The beams advanced and retracted in time with the sharp stabs that began in my right side and radiated in a band across my body. I closed my eyes and could still see the light, as if it were burned into the dark backing of my eyelids. I doubled over, gagging, unable to stand upright. I braced hands on my knees and moaned, incredulous. What was this? There was no more wait-and-see. Dana pragmatically found Tupperware containers to put on the floor of the car, knowing the vomiting was unlikely to cease. I was laid in the back of the car and never saw that house again.

Electing to go to the emergency room became racing 100 miles per hour to the hospital, praying we'd get there fast enough. I was certain something inside of me had burst. I couldn't be sure if the pain was indicative of a perforated ulcer as I had thought or something else. I recalled in medical school hearing a description of how the digestive enzymes of the pancreas, if unleashed, could erode through the internal organs like battery acid, destroying any architecture within the body. I took the torturous, spreading burn to mean my organs were being reduced to that sloppy pulp. I knew I needed surgery. At the door to the emergency room as I was loaded into a wheelchair, Randy asked if I wanted one of the Tupperware containers in my lap.

A security guard saw me, a pregnant woman who was clearly nauseated, and asked exactly how pregnant I was. "Seven months?" I replied, not seeing the relevance of disclosing this personal fact to hospital security. We were calmly redirected to Labor and Delivery and away from the Level 1 Trauma Center that I was targeting. It was policy, he explained. "Anyone over six months pregnant goes to L & D." I knew there was no point in arguing. Our hospital valued policies. It was in large part how we ensured the safety of our patients. Reliably providing excellent care required standardization. And yet my years of medical training, my own assessment of my abdomen as being a surgical emergency, my understanding of the need for evaluation by a surgeon was in this case all negated by a hospital policy. I'd been triaged by hospital security who, in the space of five seconds, had made a determination of who I was and what I needed. I looked at my husband with an expression that said, *Just so you know for later, that decision may well be the one that kills me.*

When I arrived in Labor and Delivery, I was briefly made to stand in order to be gowned, and immediately appreciated how much had already changed. My vision tunneled, leaving only a central focal point in view. My mind felt bubbly, as if it had gone without me on an effervescent New Year's Eve binge. A morbid curiosity allowed me to transiently focus my attention, as I realized that I was experiencing shock firsthand. I knew the stale drunkenness was indicative of a lack of sufficient blood flow to my brain. The blood vessels in my body could redirect the flow well enough when I was lying flat, by allocating more to my brain by squeezing down in other areas. But upright, they couldn't compensate against gravity. The small amount of blood that remained within my vessel walls would pool at my feet, depriving my brain of adequate flow.

A hand shoved a small orange-capped specimen container into my field of view. Did I think I could give them a urine sample? I imagined the coordination involved in fulfilling that request. I shook my head no. I was unceremoniously turned over to the OB nurses with the single-minded intention of evaluating the baby.

"The baby . . . is fine," I grunted, breathless from pain and speaking in choppy fragments, "but something . . . is wrong . . . with me. Please . . . call surgery." They responded by clocking fetal heart tones and attempting to strap a fetal heart-rate monitor around my tender, swollen abdomen. I couldn't bear any additional pressure and attempted to wriggle out of the constricting belt. I was shot a stern disapproving look each time they caught me. "Leave that on! What's wrong with you?" a nurse clucked her tongue in disbelief. A catheter was placed in my bladder, an indictment of my failure to provide urine the "easy way." An IV line was placed in a difficult vein that was reprimanded for its defiance.

There were myopic smiles directed toward the then reassuring fetal heart tones. Nurses hummed while they charted. The blood pressure cuff cycled and recycled tightly around my arm, struggling to register my very low pressure. A single IV line in my arm allowed a slow trickle of saline to enter, inefficiently expanding my blood volume. I reached across with my other hand and furtively adjusted the roller mechanism, allowing for the faster rate of IV fluids that I knew I needed.

As I stared at the hideous wall tiles, I silently worked backward, terrified by the velocity of my deterioration and somehow searching for reassurance in the utter ordinariness of the day. I wanted to buy yarn. I had gone to the store and had bought two pairs of shoes, a size bigger than I normally wore because of the swelling. All pregnant women swell, that's not interesting. I went to the grocery store and bought vanilla sugar. I went to dinner, I thought I'd have the salmon. Salmon had high levels of omega-3 fatty acids that were supposed to be good for the baby's brain. Then the pain started. It was a beautiful spring day. The sky was cloudless.

Several men arrived, first a resident, then the attending obstetrician.

"She's a doctor here," I heard one of them alert the others. "ICU I think," he added.

I took his cue, channeled my adrenaline, and attempted to

engage them as a hybrid physician-patient, providing my relevant history in the concise medical vocabulary that was just barely still accessible to me. I struggled to convey urgency, but the pain made me dysfluent. Each spasm engulfed my intended words. I looked to their faces for a sense of identification, but instead found grimaces of pity. I was an abstraction—a sick patient, a mother. My pain was interpreted through the distorting lens of my pregnancy. They were united in the orientation of their concern—the baby.

The attending doctor ordered morphine, which caught my attention. *Oh my God, they are giving me morphine.* We almost never gave pregnant women heavy intravenous narcotics, understanding that it put the baby at risk. How had I gone from not wanting to take an over-the-counter antacid to getting intravenous morphine in the space of a day? I tried to reframe my fear about morphine's possible effect on the baby as evidence that they were appropriately concerned about the seriousness of my illness. As they pushed the morphine, I waited, wondering if it could even work against the crushing pain. It did nothing. So, they pushed more.

Surgery was called. They sent the intern.

He walked in, young and earnest, with a blank template he was expected to fill with my comprehensive history and physical examination prior to reviewing his work with his senior resident. I didn't understand how he could think for a moment there was time for any of that.

He set his paper template down on the tray-table and clicked his pen open. He compared the name and medical record number on his paper to my wristband, before addressing me. "Can you tell me when the pain started?" he asked.

I felt I had no words left. "Call your attending," was the only answer I would give him.

He attempted to stick with the ritualized formality of the paperwork. "Does anything make the pain better or worse?"

He was met with silence.

He sighed, frustrated. Sensing he was going to get nowhere, he paged his resident. While only twelve months his senior, she had just enough experience to know when she saw me rigid from the pain, with unstable vital signs, that there indeed was no time. That was all the insight I needed her to have. "Who is your attending?" I asked her.

The trauma surgeon on call that night was someone I had worked with in the Surgical ICU. I'll call him Dr. G. He was thoughtful, meticulous and incredibly skilled. I asked her to please page him and tell him it was me, and ask him to come up to L & D. She did just that, with the limited information she had. He was told only "I don't know what's wrong but you know her and she's really sick." Surgeons are, as a rule, not usually tolerant of such incomplete reports from their resident teams. They are not accustomed to "I'm not sure" and "I don't know." Their field demands certainty. They expect to be summoned to the bedside of a patient when the work has been done, the labs and imaging complete and interpreted. They expect to be given a diagnosis, an assessment, a plan and even an operating room time. They would rather you be wrong, but take a principled stand based on conviction, than to say, "I don't know." While another surgeon might have berated her, he simply sensed her fear and humbly showed up.

Dr. G checked my lab results, winced, shook his head and began listing the possibilities. He listed the differential of possible diagnoses: "Fulminant liver failure, perforated ulcer, ruptured appendix . . ."

I heard those possibilities and thought, no, I'm dying faster than any of those can kill you. This is worse. I don't know what it is but it's something worse. And although none of the proposed diagnoses captured the gravity of the situation, I felt a relief that there was at least a list of possibilities. I wanted to know what was causing the pain and to fix it; I didn't want to pretend it wasn't there, silencing it with morphine as it killed me. I worried, being physically located in the OB triage area, that the baby would be prioritized over my own well-being.

Ten years into my training, I'd seen enough to know the possible outcomes. I had seen women lose pregnancies; I had seen mothers die and babies survive. I feared the latter. I feared the uniquely awful incongruity of a baby entering into the world through a portal of death. Muted celebrations of birthdays, superimposed onto anniversaries of deaths. Motherless children. Balloons and gravestones. I shook my head deliberately to release the vision of gravestones.

I looked up and my mother was at my side, her face betraying her worry. Her lips were pursed, brow furrowed, a result of receiving the call that all mothers dread. During her perfectly normal evening routine, the phone had rung. She heard the fear in my husband's voice. She had driven thirty miles in the dark of night to an inner-city hospital.

"You called my mom?" I accused Randy. I couldn't remember him even leaving my side long enough to make a call.

"Of course he called me," she replied for him.

I sunk into the gurney, feeling defeated. I was upset not because I didn't want her there, but because it confirmed that I could not confine the pain to my body. I was sick enough that the people I loved would be hurt by it.

"I don't know what's wrong," I apologized, feeling useless in my inability to reassure anyone of anything.

The tube draining my urine filled with blood.

"Maybe it's just a kidney stone," my mom directed her statement to the doctors. "Her dad had horrible kidney stones."

They pushed more morphine. It didn't touch the pain. The nurse reported back to the obstetrician in charge of triage that night, and he replied, "If she wants more, give her more. But that baby's going to have a hard time if we have to deliver her. Whatever she wants."

Whatever I wanted. What a curious thing to say.

I had never specifically wanted morphine. I wanted the pain to stop because they had found the cause and fixed it. I was struck by both the flippancy of his reply and the stupidity of him volunteering me as the physician in charge of my care. I knew I was not in any condition to direct my care. But I did understand what he was implying when he said the baby would have a hard time. All of the morphine that entered my system would also enter the baby's small system. Theoretically, if the baby were delivered that night, the baby probably would not breathe effectively on its own. My pain, or rather, my unwillingness to endure it, was compromising the baby.

I had received 50 milligrams total in 2- and then 4-milligram increments. It was enough narcotic to kill me had I been well, by shutting down my center of respiration, but due to the ferocity of my pain, my body barely acknowledged it. It couldn't and hadn't touched the pain.

"Isn't that bad for the baby?" my mom asked, as the nurse pushed another syringe into my IV.

"Probably," I conceded. I was just frankly no longer able to prioritize the baby in any of this. I felt as if I had awoken in a house engulfed by flames, and my first instinct was just to get out. Let someone else worry about the others.

• • •

There were arguments over whether I should be sent down to radiology for a CT scan to help delineate the source of the pain. Radiologists were reluctant to perform a CT, concerned about the radiation risk to the baby. Dr. G was hesitant to operate without a CT, as it rendered them unable to anticipate, and therefore to plan. Nothing was happening, but that inertia seemed preferable to being transported away from the doctors and down to radiology. I knew, the same way one could sense an approaching thunderstorm by the air going thin, that I was too unstable.

"I think it's a mistake . . . to let me travel. I think I'll die if you send me down," I implored them, breathless from the pain.

My intuition was validated by my second set of lab results. I had lost nearly my entire blood volume somewhere in my abdomen. I felt momentarily vindicated, like an eager medical student who had nailed the diagnosis her superiors had dismissed. I believed they would now see the necessity of operating, of identifying the cause of the intractable pain. Rather, in a squall of black irony, I watched as the values only served to amplify their concern for the baby, and they wheeled a portable ultrasound machine to my bedside.

"Bear with me," the obstetrical resident warned, his foot tangling in the cord. "I'm not great at these yet."

He didn't need to be. Here I could still be a physician. From the first grainy images I could see the small ventricles still and pulseless—like a four-chambered pool filling with slowly falling snow. "There's no heartbeat." The words cascaded out of me on a torrent of agonized breath.

"Can you show me where you see that?" he asked.

The words reverberated in the suddenly hollow space behind

my eyes. I heard my own gasp, and shuddered in a shock of pain. It was as if the subtle movement of my diaphragm with the breath had spread open some barely healed gash, freshly exposing the injury. As my breath caught, I stared at him, incredulous. Could I show him how to interpret the ultrasound images of my dead baby? The baby whose impossibly small dresses were still hanging expectantly in the guest room closet. I hadn't gotten around to setting up the baby's room, but she had belongings. Small socks and onesies. I'd just begun to prepare.

I felt an emptiness begin to envelop me from the inside, a kind of meditative panic. The baby we'd imagined—that was at least, transiently, very real and tangible—was dead. I was dying as everyone watched, a roomful of doctors and none of them able to grab the yoke to save me from crashing into the sea.

"Can you show me where you see that?"

I realized the resident's perspective in that moment was aligned squarely on himself. I imagined an alternate reality in which I would reach up from the gurney to trace my index finger around the outline of her perfectly elliptical, and utterly motionless, heart, delineating the anatomy the way he requested. The insensitivity of what he was asking struck me hard. I felt invisible to him.

His detachment reveals an unsettling, largely unspoken reality. We aren't trained to see our patients. We are trained to see pathology. We are taught to forage with scalpels and forceps for an elusive diagnosis buried within obfuscating tissues. We excavate alongside our mentors in delicate, deliberate layers, test by test, attempting to unearth disease. The true relationship is forged between the doctor and the disease. This bond is disclosed when we reencounter these diseases: we greet them respectfully as the worthy adversaries they are. Their reappearances evoke devastating losses, past insults when they prevailed. The patients carrying the diagnosis are at risk of becoming an accessory to the whole affair, just another vector.

As his question echoed, I discerned a tone in his voice that I hadn't initially noticed. It was genuine curiosity. I realized, with an uncomfortable tug of recognition, I was indeed not a person to him, but a case. And an interesting case at that. I was Abdominal Pain and Fetal Demise to him. I affixed my eyes onto his, willing him to see me.

I needed him to see me. I instinctively felt that if he didn't see me, if he didn't connect with me, he might not care enough to do what it would take to help me to survive. The baby had already died inside of me of a placental abruption, a grave and deadly situation where the placenta separates completely from the uterine wall, and the baby is deprived entirely of blood flow. They would later explain this was likely caused by lack of blood flow due to lack of blood volume from the massive internal bleeding I was experiencing. I was well on my way to dying as well. I saw two possible versions of the night that lay ahead of the resident. One, a sleepless night, with transfusion orders, countless pleas to the blood bank for more blood products, the micromanaging of lab values, ventilator settings, and expectations. I saw too how easy it would be to concede instead under the burden of it all. The alternate possibility: *She was very sick, and she died. I'm sorry.*

The baby, having declared her own distress, meant the surgery I'd been begging for came easily now, briskly even. I was pulled so quickly into the operating room, my IV pole struck the obstetrical resident in the face. He had never met my gaze. He was still attempting to decipher the ultrasound images on the screen.

Although by all accounts I'd been begging for the surgery, I never actually believed I would survive it. I had heard my lab values recited, gravely. I knew I had almost no circulating blood volume with a hemoglobin of 3 grams/dL. I knew I had almost no platelets, the component of the blood responsible for clotting. There hadn't been time to arrange for cross-matching and transfusion, so there was no hope of the numbers improving any time soon. I knew I was already in shock, with a blood pressure so low that it was barely detectable. Patients like that don't survive a surgery.

I had long regarded deathbed conversions as a self-indulgent shortcut to absolution, but I suddenly understood the temptation. I was dying, with still inchoate beliefs, having always planned on having time to be surer of something. Though there were times I had sensed the grace of something truly holy in my life, it wasn't tangible enough that I could build a physical structure around it and engage in worship. Like a soft wind, it just didn't have a substantial enough mass for me to wrap myself in it.

As a physician, I fully expected to die in the operating room, and as a physician I didn't think it would do anyone any good to disclose my conviction via some emotional good-bye. I believed people would be hurt when it was time for them to be hurt, and there was no sense anticipating the pain for them. So rather than frighten or warn my family, I simply said, "Ugh, such drama." And with that I was wheeled through the open steel doors into a harshly lit operating room.

Memory, the recall of specific events into the forefront of our minds, requires a reimagining of the event. And recall is far from passive. Unlike retrieving a mug from a cupboard, the simple act of recalling a memory changes the synaptic framework of the memory itself. It is retrospectively molded as we attempt to fill in the gaps. As if the cup is made of still pliable clay, and the warmth of our hand indents the surface. When we next retrieve that memory, we are recalling our last memory *of* the memory; we are in effect retrieving the indented mug. It's with this necessarily flawed data that we construct the narrative of who we are. And so the endlessly iterative process of rewriting ourselves goes on.

I remember the frigid operating room and the blue blur of scrubbed bodies moving briskly, voices muffled by masks in a way that recalled scarved children in winter. The square, snow-colored tiles covering the walls. The cool smell of volatile alcohols. The steel of the table, the drain in the floor to hose the still-warm blood into. The scrub tech pouring Betadine on my abdomen as a quick prep for the incision. It was as cold as gasoline. As they began sedating me, I heard the anesthesiologist's voice: "We're losing her . . . her systolic is 60."

I was drawn back into myself, from failing consciousness, by those words. *Are they losing me?* I attempted to survey the situation. *Focus,* I told myself.

"We're losing her."

Words echoed, or were they repeated this time?

"Guys! She's circling the drain here!"

You know I can hear you, I thought.

I struggled to maintain consciousness, trying to surface against a submersive force, a weighted pull into an obliterative darkness. My arms were so heavy and stiff. A movement of a millimeter was an impossible effort. My eyes darkened. My throat tightened. I sank below the still surface of the water. A heavy water that was dense as mercury, the crush of it accelerating my descent.

All at once, I felt a sudden release and lightness. I could see the operating room clearly, although I struggled to orient myself. The view was deceptive, in the way pilots staring for too long at the horizon can sometimes suffer sensory illusions that cause them to mistake the sea for the sky. My orientation was inverted. I was falling up. I could see the frustrated anesthesiologist who was working on placing IV access as I crashed. I could see the monitoring equipment surrounding me, the obstetrical team readying with instruments to extract the baby. I could see myself on the table.

It struck me that they were right; they were losing me. If I could see myself, perhaps I was already lost.

I felt nothing. The pain miraculously gone. The panic surrounding the pain was gone. An anodyne peace. I felt weightless, buoyant and very small. I watched the events unfold before me, unattached to any outcome, with an easy stillness.

I had died.

It would be a year before the surgeons who were present described to me in reverential tones the series of catastrophic events that occurred in that operating room. I had what was referred to in trauma as the "Triad of Death," the combination of hypothermia, acidosis and coagulopathy. In simple terms the phrase describes a self-perpetuating process in which the blood is too cold and too acidic to allow clotting, which means more bleeding, which requires more transfusions, which results in more hypothermia and acidosis. A sort of unremitting, suicidal spiral of the blood. They described the gallons of blood lost, the gallons frantically replaced, some run through a warmer to mitigate the hypothermia. The moment my kidneys shut down. The rapid accumulation of potassium in my bloodstream. The deterioration of my vital signs. The gradual acquiescence of my heart, irritated by the toxic milieu, beating aberrantly, then not at all.

With each disclosure, I'd share what I remembered. The location of the anesthesiology resident in the corner, by the computer. The harried requests for surgery to be called back to place a larger trauma line when the need for rapid infusion of blood products became apparent. The frantic search for the source of the blood loss.

You couldn't possibly remember that, I was told. *You've reconstructed the memories from what you've heard, or read in the chart.*

No, I was there. I can't explain it, but I was there.

That coldness, which I equated with the feeling of having been dead, remained for months. I was incapable of getting warm. Engineering would be called to my ICU room to adjust the heating apparatus until everyone entering the room would remove a layer of dress and comment on the warmth. Blankets were piled upon me, fluids warmed before hanging, but nothing touched that unshakable coldness. Years later, the Midwest was privy to a weather phenomenon termed the "polar vortex," and wind chill estimates reached thirty below in Michigan. Standing outside in the snow that winter, I thought it odd that people referred to that feeling as *cold*. How strange we only had the one word for both feelings. Cold to me was internal and unremitting and came with no promise of a spring.

Two

A Hollowness

I resurfaced, overtaken with a sudden fear. I felt a breath delivered, without having drawn it myself, and shuddered at the sensation. It was like trying to breathe with your head out the car window; the force of the air made movement of breath impossible. I was wholly dependent on machines; I understood the magnitude of catastrophe this signified. I resolved to breathe independently and tried to pull a breath against the gush of the machine breath, setting off sensitive alarms. I fatigued quickly. I found I couldn't maintain the intense vigilance that breathing required. Over time, there was a resignation to the reality and a gradual dampening of the waveform that was panic. I fell out of consciousness.

The cycle repeated: I regained consciousness, suddenly aware of my surroundings and filled with terror. I struggled to breathe and panicked that I couldn't get enough air in to ease the feeling that I was suffocating. I gave up trying to breathe and accepted the breaths the machine offered instead. After struggling on my own, the mechanical breaths became a welcome relief, despite their peculiar uniformity. I heard the artificial puff of my exhalation, every six seconds. I would again tire and lapse out of consciousness.

I later recognized these periods as weaning trials, brief routine episodes every morning when nurses turn off sedatives and pain medications to allow respiratory therapists and physicians to assess whether the patient may be able to breathe independently, with minimal support from the ventilator. This protocol isn't generally communicated to the patient. They are instead left to awaken to abrupt pain and anxiety precipitated by withdrawal of the medications that had quietly sustained them. Cyclic episodes of panic and darkness.

During the day, the sedating effect of the medications was thin and porous enough to allow the sound of voices to occasionally permeate the black silence. The words fell toward me, sinking to meet me where I lay. The drugs clouded my thoughts. In my muddied consciousness, I struggled to maintain alertness long enough to piece together clues: the warbled texture of speech, the bloat of my body, the gurgle of fluid in my lungs. In those days before my memories were coherent, I believed I had been drowned— drowned by bags of other people's blood, with insultingly shut- down kidneys that couldn't excrete the excess volume. The fluid had turned my lungs into heavy wet sponges. My body, with its fixed capacity, swelled with an additional forty-five pounds of fluid over the course of a night, in an effort to make up for the massive amounts of blood lost. Pale and turgid, I looked and felt as if I had been dredged up from the bottom of a lake.

During periods of alertness, my eyes darted around the room, silently imploring those present to explain what had happened. Eyes diverted. I attempted to talk, but the breathing tube in my throat prevented me. I attempted to make a gesture with my restrained hand, wanting to write questions.

"Just rest," I was told.

Hmm—unlikely.

I had suffered a stroke that affected the area of my brain responsible for vision and balance. I saw everything in duplicate, and people oscillated before me in nauseating waves. The stroke would later make walking terribly difficult, but we wouldn't know that for weeks. The congestion caused by the fluid resuscitation left my hearing impaired, with speech muddled and difficult to decipher. I heard phrases I had once spoken to families: "Her body has survived, but we're not sure at what cost." It was unclear if the words were floating up from my subconscious or sinking to me from above.

There were no mirrors in the ICU. Instead, I gauged my appearance by the reaction of the people entering my room. Physician colleagues—who were masters of the reassuring, permanent half-smile—gasped and cried instead. I understood what it took to generate that kind of a response, and I realized it was probably best that my vision was impaired and that there were no mirrors.

When I was deemed no longer at risk of pulling out necessary tubes and lines, my wrists were freed from restraints. I would palpate my own body, in a sculptor's attempt to see. I found it unrecognizable to the touch. The integrity of my skin was violated by thick tubes that accessed every available large vein. My face and neck expanded into new territory closer to the periphery of the pillow's landscape. My thighs were serpentine, with flat flaps on either side of the rounded center. My skin was an ashen shade of yellow with large swaths of blue and purple bruising. Twenty-nine sharp staples held my abdominal wall closed. I could indent my skin around my knee with a gentle poke of my index finger and it would remain for hours.

A man who looked like my brother walked in, but upon seeing me abruptly turned and left the room. I thought it couldn't be him, not just because I didn't trust my vision, but because he lived in Boston. But then time was so elusive, I had no idea what day it was. Had enough time passed for him to get here from Boston? I didn't know.

I awoke to the voice of my childhood priest as he made the sign of the cross on my body. As an ICU physician, I had only ever seen priests enter patient rooms when last rites were being administered. I hurriedly surveyed the room for more evidence that I could be actively dying. My brother was there, with others, heads bowed deferentially in prayer. I read the room as sad but not gravely solemn. I surveyed my body for evidence I was dying, and though I was very cold, my fingers didn't appear blue or mottled, which would suggest poor blood flow. Nurses were adjusting drips that they wouldn't have bothered with if there were no hope of recovery. I noted the head of my bed was at thirty degrees rather than the flat position we usually allocated to terminal patients, and I accepted that I was probably not dying in that moment. I allowed myself to once again drift out of consciousness.

I opened my eyes and it seemed my entire department was in my room at once. They were arguing about some aspect of my care. Something about the ventilator and fluids. One was discussing possible strategies, while others stared at the floor or out the window.

"We shouldn't be here. Looking at her when she's like this. It's not right," one of them said to everyone and no one.

"Have you told her yet?" I recognized my mentor's voice. The question seemed directed toward my right side, which I knew from the feeling of his hand on mine is where Randy always sat.

"No, I want to wait until she's off the breathing machine, so I know she'll remember," Randy said, with a tone of resignation.

"I'll tell her if you don't think you can. I'm used to giving bad news."

They don't think I can hear them.

I directed my gaze squarely in the direction of the colleague who had suggested everyone leave. He'd been ill, and I knew from his discomfort that he understood the indignity of exposure that comes with a critical illness.

"Come on, let's leave her alone." He ushered everyone out.

My mentor didn't follow the others. He leaned over and reassured me, "You are going to get better now. It's not your heart, we looked at your heart. I have to go to Argentina tomorrow. When I come back you'll be fine." There was something in his tone that revealed his last statement to be more of a wish than a promise.

He then turned to the surgical team and began giving instructions on how to get me off the ventilator.

What were they waiting to tell me? I couldn't fathom what I didn't know.

I watched silently as dusk fell outside my ICU window. The nursing shift changed, and the night nurse came in to do her assessment. She listened to my heart and lungs, checked each of my IV lines for signs of dysfunction or infection. She drained and measured what small amount of urine had collected in the bag draining my bladder. She administered medications and asked me questions I couldn't answer. I would wince or withdraw when some movement worsened the pain, but I had no other means of expressing myself. I gagged as she passed the suction catheter down the breathing tube, trying to clear my lungs of secretions. I wanted to somehow communicate to her how unbearably cold I was, but couldn't seem to coordinate my body to replicate a shiver. I just looked as though I was shaking my head and shrugging my right shoulder.

I knew it was officially night when Randy fell asleep in the chair at my bedside. I envied his ability to sleep despite any noise. The absence of even a full minute of silence combined with the constant pain made sleeping difficult for me. Every other moment an alarm would sound, a monitor would beep. This bag was out of fluid, that IV was kinked, my heart rate was too high, my blood pressure too low. Near-constant noise, activity in the hall, codes called over the PA system. Time passed one slow second at a time, punctuated by constant beeps and the dull hum of machines. After a thousand beeps the nurse would collect blood, so that the results would be available by morning rounds. A few alarms later and a sleepy surgical resident would enter and do a cursory exam, then report to the team how my night had been. At daybreak the radiology techs would try hopelessly to rouse Randy in order to take my morning X-ray without irradiating him. It brought back memories of his alarm clock at home, which was marketed for the deaf, vibrating his pillow in waves of larger and larger amplitude.

The breathing tube was removed in the morning. Though I still required oxygen, this was the first tangible success. Breathe on my own again. Check. Though I found I needed to remind myself to breathe; the time spent with the machine bearing that burden had reset my mind to believe it was someone else's responsibility. As long as I did nothing else I could breathe, but I quickly found I couldn't combine tasks. Shifting positions in the bed left me breathless and exhausted.

"I'm really cold," I said with great urgency and an inexplicable sadness.

The nurse left to get more blankets from the warmer.

Randy squeezed and attempted to warm my hand in his. A pained expression clouded his face.

"I need to tell you something," he began.

This must have been what I had overheard them discussing. I looked at him and realized it was about the baby. They didn't think I knew yet that the baby had died.

"The baby didn't make it."

My eyes welled, not with sadness for the baby, but with empathy for him. I recognized that he was trying really hard to break this news to me gently. They had discussed who should tell me and when, probably even how.

It had never even occurred to me that the baby was anything but dead. Of course the baby hadn't survived. I had barely survived. But seeing his face, I somehow understood it was best to play along. I nodded, solemnly.

"I'm really sorry," he added.

I had little voice from the irritation of the tube in my throat, so I whispered instead, "Yeah. It's OK. We can have other babies. But only if I'm not dead."

He smiled at me, appearing relieved.

"I'm really cold," I repeated, as the feeling recalled the events of the first night. I knew I had to tell Randy what had happened. In case I forgot, or died.

"I could see myself," I attempted, wanting to explain the moment in the operating room when the pain stopped and I was dying. I cleared my throat, wanting to have a voice. "There wasn't any pain; it all went away. And it was like I knew if I wanted to, I could always feel that way. I didn't have to go back to the pain. I don't know how I knew, but I knew there was a choice I had to make, you know?" I was trying so desperately to explain something to him that I had no words for. I searched his face for evidence that he understood and that I should go on. I paused to just breathe, not able to both breathe and talk at the same time.

"But you chose not to die," he smiled, as if we had conversations about out-of-body experiences every day.

"Yes." I was grateful that he seemed to be understanding despite my painfully vague description. I gave him my left hand to hold and warm. "Only I didn't know that was what I was choosing between. It's weird. It was almost like an invitation to leave the situation and the pain, but I knew if I left I was leaving everything. But I don't know how I knew, I just did."

"How did you feel?" he asked.

"Just completely safe. I wasn't scared of anything. I felt as if I were so expansive, like the edges of me were fuzzy and blurred and I was part of everything, but I also felt really small at the same time. I had absolutely no fear." I paused, wanting him to know the absolute peace I had felt. "Really, there isn't anything to be afraid of." I stopped, knowing how crazy I sounded. I glanced at my IV pole, with the various pumps and drips, thinking I could always blame the narcotics I was on for my magical thinking.

"Thank you," he said.

"For what?" I asked.

"For deciding to come back to me," he answered, tucking the additional blankets the nurse had brought around me.

I overheard myself being presented by the surgical resident in the hallway. It was time for morning rounds. "Thirty-three-year-old female with HELLP syndrome, post-op day four, status post-crash C-section for fetal demise. Intraoperative observation of a large subcapsular hematoma." The acronym he used, HELLP, stood for Hemolysis, Elevated Liver enzymes, and Low Platelets. It is shorthand for a poorly understood, often fatal condition that affects less than 1 percent of pregnant women. A condition in which the blood is shredded into useless shards, the liver fails, the platelets responsible for clotting the blood are consumed and women bleed to death. In addition to understanding that they thought I was suffering from HELLP syndrome, I also learned that I had bled into the space around my liver. Until that moment, I had no idea what had caused the excruciating pain. The diagnosis was disproven later, when the tumor was surreptitiously identified on a CT scan, but for now it would do.

"Hemoglobin is 7 after 26 units. Up 45 pounds, low urine output," he went on. So by rough math, I calculated I had received enough blood products to replace my entire blood volume three times, and my kidneys weren't functioning. Perfect.

"She's been trying to die on us."

Um, no, I thought, becoming angry.

No, I was not actually trying to die on anyone. Though perhaps not manifest by outward appearances, I was trying desperately *not* to die. And though I might not have had a lucid enough mind to articulate it, by blaming me I felt he was positing me as an adversary. If my care team didn't believe in me, what possible hope did I have? I felt the ice I was balancing on detach and begin to float me away.

Then I cringed with the discomfort of an uncomfortable memory. I had used that phrase, often and thoughtlessly, in my training: he was "trying to die on me." Oh my God, we all said it all the time. And inherent within that phrase is the reality that we attribute intention to patients, rudely hurling themselves toward death. We construe ourselves as barriers between the patients and their transparent though unstated goal. We subconsciously construct a narrative in which the doctor-patient relationship is somehow antagonistic. I recalled the relief I would feel in the ICU after a night of being alone on call, when the day team would walk in. "I kept them all alive, my work here is done." I would congratulate myself and sink into a chair. Others might gloat: "He may die today, but at least he didn't die on my shift." That was often what sign-out rounds devolved into, one doctor telling his or her colleagues how difficult it had been to prevent someone from dying.

My identification with the rounding team was short-lived. The attending looked at me from the doorway and shrugged. "So, give her Lasix."

His answer, to give me a medication to offload my body of some of the fluid, addressed only one small issue in the pile of problems facing me. And while it may have been the most obvious choice, it was the wrong choice. What wasn't immediately apparent to the team was that because my kidneys had been deprived of blood while I was in shock they were intent on not functioning, which was why I wasn't producing urine. This medication, Lasix, would challenge them, and they simply weren't up for it. Instead they would shut down further, propelling me into overt kidney failure. In some ways, this was something that could only be known in retrospect, when the micro-experiment produced results. The choice, to give me that drug at that particular time, represented a kind of casual negligence afforded to physicians practicing an imperfect science. A seemingly benign effort to effect change, that when scrutinized would only have resulted in harm. Casual choices sometimes come to horrific ends. And it's not only casual choices. Often, physicians will scrutinize a choice intensely, debate and discuss endlessly before deciding on the most seemingly sound course of action. These decisions are often punctuated by hesitation: "But what if we're wrong?" To which I myself have replied, echoing my mentors, "The only person who can tell us that now is the patient. He will declare himself."

As physicians, poor outcomes that are the result of well-intentioned choices are harbored under the safe umbrella term "the principle of dual effect." As the name implies it refers to one action with two distinct outcomes. One effect is intended and anticipated; the other is unintended and undesirable. It is often evoked in situations when a drug administered to help with one symptom causes another. For example, when a patient suffering severe pain is given morphine, the patient could suffer terrible nausea and itching as a side effect. The morally good effect, relieving suffering, is the focus. The discomfort of nausea and itching is the unintended consequence of the morally sound choice. If one had given the morphine with an intent to cause the uncomfortable side effects, that would have been morally wrong, but as an unintended but foreseeable side effect, it was forgivable. As a physician, I could accept some element of risk. In a sense, we all had to, or risk being paralyzed by fear and indecision. As a patient, I found it much harder to accept the risk each decision conferred. Ultimately, for me, the attending's choice to give me that drug at that precise time resulted in my kidneys failing.

I knew I couldn't afford for things to get worse. I needed a steady trajectory of forward progress, however slow, with no setbacks. In a misguided attempt to reassure myself, I performed a rough risk evaluation with the new data. It was something we routinely did in the ICU to give families a gross estimate of prognosis. Each organ failure increased probability of death by 20 percent. I counted silently: liver failing one, kidneys made two, then lungs three, blood four. Shit. I had reached 80 percent faster than I had expected and tried to forget that there were any other organ systems remaining, lest I count them and get to 100 percent.

I was already predisposed, as a physician, to imagine the variety of possibilities that could potentially result in my own death. Would it be a medication error, a complication of a procedure, a hospital-acquired infection, or some unfortunate combination? As I began to see the potential for error, each imagined possible ending suddenly felt more likely. I expected my death to come as the adjunct of some trivial oversight. It was in those moments that I came closest to understanding the illogical nature of true anxiety. A parade of seemingly plausible possibilities marched over reason and judgment. Anything seemed possible because nothing was preventable.

I worried that I might die. And then there were the times, just as terrifying, when I was worried I might not get to die. In those early ICU days, what I feared most was that transition space between life and death: The purgatory where someone connects a bag of liquid nutrition to a feeding tube and comes to suction your secretions every four hours, rolling you shift by shift so that the pressure ulcers don't form. One long, permanent night, punctuated only by beeps and hums. I feared the small complications, the missteps, knowing they led directly to that non-space. I feared decisions that were made without looking at the whole picture. I feared errors that led to dialysis.

I explained to my mother that I might require dialysis, and she nodded, having mastered the quiet art of accepting such setbacks. I wondered if she'd ever seen someone suspended permanently in limbo. I felt plainly that death would be preferable. I doubted my mother would agree. I wondered if Randy would be more practical.

I felt obligated to warn him what he could be in for. On our one-year wedding anniversary, I had him bring in a card I'd purchased "before" and asked a nurse to help me add an inscription. We left the prewritten nonsense intact, but in the margins explained that most marriages don't survive the death of a child and wished him luck. My nurse reviewed the card and frowned at me. I shrugged and took it from her. I knew I was not my most romantic self, but I believed it stated the situation perfectly. And it had value—it was a warning fashioned out of love.

I was pointing him guiltlessly to the door that led out of the ICU, out of the world of chronic care facilities and relationships that deteriorated from husband and wife to caretaker and invalid. I knew love and pain and sorrow could keep us together, but it could also reduce his life to waste.

I handed it to him and his face melted, believing it to be incredibly sweet that I wanted to commemorate our anniversary despite the circumstances. He opened the envelope and studied the card silently. He'd spent every night resting in a chair at my bedside. He was so profoundly sleep-deprived that the radiology techs eventually accepted that they couldn't wake him when they came to do my morning chest X-ray. My attempts at hitting him with the hospital remote didn't wake him. So in the end they resorted to throwing a leaded apron on him and letting him sleep through. His blind devotion made mapping his exit strategy my responsibility.

"The wetness is drool," I added, trying to make a point. I was betting that body fluids were the key to disgusting him away.

He smiled, unwavering. "We're not most people. We can get through anything."

Have it your way, I thought. *But don't say I didn't warn you because it's not going to be pretty.*

He was never repulsed by anything that happened to my body. In fact, the things I assumed would repulse him only served to increase his compassion toward me. My bruised and discolored body was proof to him of what I had endured to stay with him. The line of crusted staples traversing my abdomen were a testament to my ability to endure pain. I watched him move past compassion into deference. He honored my body and spirit even as it failed miserably. He was awed by its capacity to heal, albeit in its own time frame. He marveled at my strength and allowed me to see myself from his position of compassion and awe. Regardless of how I looked from the outside, or how weak and helpless I felt, he saw through to a core of fiery, molten strength. When I saw myself reflected back the way he saw me, I wanted to be more like that person. That person was resilient and was clearly going to recover.

There was a continual stream of doctors and nurses in and out of my room in those days. Often I would recognize them, from what felt by that point like a past life, but there were new faces as well. The surgery resident whose presentation I had overheard came in one morning to check on me after I had developed worsening kidney failure, which I blamed on the poorly timed Lasix. He was ambitious but soft around the edges. He wanted to become a plastic surgeon, an ultracompetitive field within the already competitive field of surgery. He worked hard to ensure his attendings viewed him favorably and hoped, against any discouragement, that they recognized his skill and dedication. He needed their support to apply for the few, coveted plastic surgery fellowship spots available each year. I picked up what was closest to me, a small plastic device meant to encourage me to take deep breaths so my lungs would stay optimally inflated, and threw it at him. He ducked, though he needn't have: I had terrible aim in the best of circumstances. With double vision and muscle weakness I had no chance of hitting him.

"How could you have thought giving me Lasix was a good idea?" I asked him.

"It wasn't my call." He attempted to skirt the blame and pro- jectiles I was directing at him.

"You wrote the order," I reminded him, knowing the struc- ture of rounds well enough to know that even if the attending was the one to state the plan, the resident wrote the order.

"I know I did, he told me to, but I knew it was a bad idea. I didn't want to," he explained.

I wanted to ask why he didn't say something if he had disagreed, but I knew the answer. It was the structure of the rounding team that had stopped him. Rounding teams usually consist of a medical student; an intern or two who are just out of medical school and serve as the workhorses for the more se- nior residents; the residents, maybe as many as five or six years out of medical school, depending on the length of the training program. There might be a fellow on the team, a sort of super- resident who though still in training has completed residency and has additionally declared a sub-specialty such as cardiothoracic surgery. In my case, I had completed a combined three-year fellowship in pulmonary and critical care medicine after my three years of internal medicine residency. All of these train- ees are supervised by one attending physician. The attending is there to direct and supervise the care, teach on relevant topics, and grade each member of the team on his or her performance. These team-based rotations usually last a month, during which time "good" residents aim to learn the relevant content, demon- strate their knowledge and impress their attending physician.

I knew that though I believed the resident had a say in the Lasix order, ultimately it went through uncontested because the resident was outranked. When discussing medical errors, the con- cept is referred to as the authority gradient, and it is essentially a barrier to communication due to a differential in status. He per- ceived a gradient in which he did not feel he could question the judgment of his attending surgeon, because of their roles and the excessively hierarchical rounding environment. And because in this case, the rounding attending wielded influence over even the resident's potential career advancement, the gradient was especially intrusive.

"It's OK," I said, my anger deflating. "I believe you," I added, understanding the position he had found himself in.

I thought about the training system we were each a part of. A system that had evolved over decades with norms, patterns and expectations that were so pervasive that residents in geographically diverse programs had nearly identical experiences. And though the expectations were never explicitly articulated, you just knew that there were some things you couldn't say and couldn't do. You knew it by watching how everyone around you handled similar situations, and how behavior that was deviant was dealt with. It was a training system that required that we defer to authority. The value of experience and position were impressed upon us, value that was meant to supersede even our own judgment. I wondered about the reliability of a system that was set up to ensure obedience rather than an honest exchange of information. Was it possible we'd been socialized to allow medical error rather than prevent it? Had we somehow inadvertently set up a system that obstructed good communication and allowed errors to occur unchecked?

I knew in that moment my kidneys had been set up to fail.

One day a woman in scrubs came in and perched herself casually on the window ledge. I couldn't see her clearly, both because of the stroke, and the way the light from the window shrouded her face in shadow. She identified herself as a nurse from the neonatal ICU team who had been in the operating room the night of my "delivery." The word *delivery* seemed a misnomer, as it was so far removed from my experience. Initially I thought she had the wrong patient. But then she began describing the events from her perspective, and I understood—she'd indeed been on the receiving end of a delivery of a baby and wanted to provide me with a firsthand account. She had ostensibly come to provide me with closure.

The baby, she told me, was evacuated from my uterus still encased within the amniotic sac, and the placenta fully separated. A complete abruption, which has the distinction of being the worst-possible scenario. The connotation was that at some indeterminate point earlier in the evening, the placenta had detached from the uterine wall, depriving the baby entirely of any blood supply. The baby was delivered already dead. They attempted to place a breathing tube, and were successful, which she appeared to be proud of, but the baby didn't respond to their efforts. The baby weighed less than a pound. She spoke with precision and an intentional gravity. She reminded me of the military officers that would arrive on the doorsteps of widows.

"Do you want to see the baby?"

I recalled the last time I had seen the baby, with her motionless heart on the monitor in the triage area.

Did I want to see the baby?

"No," I replied flatly.

"Well, I think that's really sad," she stated, visibly disappointed.

I was surprised by her reaction. It hadn't occurred to me that there was a right answer.

I attempted to explain that I knew the baby had died prior to entering the operating room. I also felt that as a physician, I had some working concept of death, and I didn't believe that I needed to see the baby to be able to grieve the loss. I stopped there, not understanding why I even felt it necessary to justify this choice to a stranger. It struck me as unnecessarily cruel to ask me to hold a baby that had been dead in my mind for days already.

"Well, you won't get another chance."

Interesting tactic, I thought, resorting to threats in an attempt to provide her version of compassionate closure on a failed pregnancy. As if to further drive home her point, she added, "You know, I don't want to be too graphic, but after a few days, their skin, it's very fragile and it starts to . . . um, break down, so you won't be able to change your mind later."

I was rendered speechless by her apparent need to provide a description.

I wasn't going to change my mind, I assured her, wishing she'd leave.

She looked at me with an expression of pity, the way one might look at a child who has broken his favorite toy in a fit of spite. "A baby deserves to be held by her mother at least once."

I stared back at her, silently imploring her to leave. I thought I would have done quite well to have avoided this whole encounter entirely. I agree, in principle, that a baby should have the experience of being held by her mother. But in my mind, that baby would ideally be alive. This baby was not alive. This baby stood to gain nothing from this imagined interaction with its mother. I felt as if she were asking me to submit to some act of self-abuse that she bizarrely construed as constructive. As if she were asking me to bare a wound she had neither the intention nor power to heal.

Randy had held the baby that first night. His wedding band would have fit around her leg, he said. Or maybe it did fit around her leg. I don't know if the image I have of him sliding his ring up her thigh was manufactured from his telling of it, or if he actually slid off his wedding band and assessed her impossibly small being in that way. My mom had held the baby while waiting to hear if I would survive. I thought we'd been through enough. Hearing about their time with the baby in the sad waiting room was really all I needed to hear for closure. I didn't need to hear the bit about her skin.

Ironically, in her attempt to provide me with closure, all she had left me with was an image of my decomposing baby.

I know that wasn't her intention. I believe she meant well. I believe that she came into that room with a plan. She genuinely thought it was imperative that I hold the baby. She believed she was intervening on behalf of some future version of me, a person who would regret a missed opportunity. She had been taught, and clearly held as dogma, that it was important for the mother to hold the baby at any cost. In her desire to help, she needed me to conform, to accept her predetermined plan. But there was no room in her plan for my needs or values. Presupposing what was right for me was ultimately her mistake.

Medicine has a long history of presupposing what is right for our patients, though it is changing. The paradigm had already shifted from the paternalistic model of doctor-knows-best to one of shared decision making by the time I reached medical school. But the new construct still weighted the doctor's recommendations heavily. As young physicians we were taught that we possessed knowledge that would allow us to delineate the possible paths for our patient, and that ultimately the choice was theirs to make. Implicit in this was that there still remained one "best" choice, and if the patient didn't select that choice, perhaps you hadn't done the best possible job selling them on it. It's impossible to be agenda-less when one believes one knows what's best.

We weren't trained to listen.

We were trained to ask questions that steered people to a destination. We were not wise enough to know that questions generate answers that are formulated in their likeness. We were trained instead to use the questions as fences, meant to constrain the answers and eventually corral them into manageable pens. In turn we were given answers that fit neatly into checkboxes.

"I've been having this feeling in my chest," the patient begins.

"Would you describe the pain as a pressure or a stabbing sensation?"

"I guess it's more of a pressure . . ."

"And how long does it last?"

"It depends. If I rest it goes away quickly, but if I don't—"

"Seconds or minutes?"

"Well, a few minutes sometimes."

All so that we could report back to our attendings, in a standardized manner, that "the patient describes a chest pressure that lasts several minutes and is alleviated by rest." Bland data, entirely devoid of context, quickly obtained. We were cautioned against generous, open questions that were posed from a position of true curiosity. We were trained to value efficiency over cultivating a relationship through trust and disclosure. We weren't trained to value the patient's story.

What else might we learn from an uninterrupted narrative, rich with context? "I've been having this feeling in my chest. I have been doing more lately, since my husband's Parkinson's disease has gotten worse. He just can't do what he used to. I've had to help him with so many more of his tasks, like showering and getting dressed or out of the car, and he's just heavy. When I've been bearing his body weight I start to feel this pressure in my chest, and it scares me, because if something happens to me, what will happen to him? We don't have children. I've nearly dropped him out of fear I'm having a heart attack."

To listen to our patients with a generous ear does require a willingness to relinquish control of the narrative. And like all loss of control, there is an element of risk involved. And risk carries with it an inherent degree of vulnerability. Our questions allow for the possibility that we do not already know the answers. By not dominating the flow of information, we allow the actual history to emerge. This kind of humility in listening requires that we abandon our assumptions to make room for truth. A truth that could be messier, but that will allow us to see the patient in the context of their values and their life. It requires that we value the question in a culture that values answers.

The real secret, though, is that the honesty elicited from genuine, reflective questions is also a reprieve for the physician. Imagine you are tasked with whether to recommend chemotherapy or radiation or a plan for hospice care to a newly diagnosed cancer patient. You may know the risks and benefits of each path, the side effects and the complications that lay ahead. You may know that the chemo will be terribly difficult to tolerate and may add three months of life in the best of circumstances. You may know that radiation will be far easier to withstand, and confer an added month at most. You may know that the death will be of respiratory failure, and a slow torture unless managed expectantly. You may feel genuinely conflicted, unsure what to recommend, given what you know. It's very easy as a physician to default to that practical knowledge base and begin with a cognitive question: "I know this is a difficult diagnosis, so do you want to discuss options for treatment that will extend survival?" Then every patient, regardless of what they value, will hear the odds of survival are better with chemo.

If the discussion instead begins with, "I'm so sorry that this is the diagnosis, and I know we've discussed the prognosis already, and it's difficult to face. Would it be alright if we talk a bit about how you envision spending your time, from now until whenever the end may be?" One patient may reply, "I want my family to know that I did everything possible to beat this cancer. If there is a clinical trial that gives me a one percent chance of another day, sign me up, I don't care how rough it is." Another may say, "I watched my mother die of cancer. The treatment made her so sick, I often wished she had just let go. It's important to me to be calm and at peace, and not have my family see me suffer." With the right question, each patient can be given a recommendation that fits their values. This way of questioning, this recommendation built on empathy and a patient-centered narrative, has the potential to heal everyone involved.

In lieu of the baby, we left the hospital with a small box containing three items: a black-and-white photograph of the impossibly small translucent baby posed beside a miniature stuffed teddy bear; the teddy bear itself, small enough to be a Christmas ornament; and the slightest smudge of a footprint. An anthology of her nonexistence offered as evidence of her almost existence. The bear offered something tangible that one could hold, if one wanted to appreciate the impossible smallness of our premature baby.

Two years later, sitting in the neonatal ICU with my premature son on a ventilator in the incubator in front of me, his nurse said, "You know, I was there that first night, with your first baby."

I looked at her and was immediately back in that ICU room with her perched in the window, the daylight silhouetting her and obscuring her features in shadow.

"That was a bad night," she said.

Yes, I thought, *it was a bad night.*

"This is going to be better," she reassured me, with a deep exhalation that made it sound like she was making a wish over birthday candles.

I certainly hope so, I thought, willing my premature infant son's lungs to start functioning. I had yet to hold this baby either. It was nearly Christmas, and hanging on his incubator was a tiny stuffed Santa. A Christmas ornament, just slightly smaller than his struggling three-pound body. I stared at the cheery red figure, wondering if it would be a cherished memory that one day hung on our tree, or if it would be become another prop in a remembrance box.

This declaration of the "badness" of that night for others became a theme. A shocking number of people entered my room after that with the express purpose of telling me what a bad night it was for them. The night I died. I didn't recognize the OB resident immediately. It had been over a week since I last saw him, and the right side of his face was now distorted by a purplish-black eye. Then the image of the IV pole striking him in the face surfaced and I remembered.

Can you show me where you see that?

He took a seat in the corner.

"You know, that was a really difficult night . . . for me," he began, haltingly. Looking at him, it was clear his pauses were measured attempts to keep tears at bay. As he bit his lip and sniffled, I wondered how it was possible that of all the people in the room, he was the one fighting back tears.

"I was in a different residency program. I started off in Neurology, but I switched into obstetrics because I thought, you know, delivering babies, I thought it was a happy field," he admitted.

I sighed and pushed, defeated, on my PCA button to self-

administer a dose of morphine. I somewhat hoped it would dull
the pain of the impending conversation. In those first few days,
I was not feeling at all sorry for myself; rather, it seemed to me
a tremendous good fortune to have survived the catastrophic
hemorrhage relatively intact. I had, by that point, seen a world's
weight of suffering come through the doors of the hospital and
I could use it as a sort of camera obscura to shrink the image of
my own suffering. I felt genuinely lucky. But I also had a quick
actuarial mind that could tally the suffering of the person before me and inevitably found they came up short.

They were violating the basic rule of the Ring Theory, which
I first encountered in a *Los Angeles Times* article by Susan Silk
and Barry Goldman. The concept is an etiquette lesson in complaining during times of crisis. Imagine concentric rings. The
center ring represents the sick person, in this case me. The next
circle is composed of the closest family, people who are also
affected by the illness or loss, in this case Randy and my mom. The
next circle, less close family, friends and so on, until eventually
random acquaintances conceptually inhabit the outer rings. The
person at the center, by virtue of being the most vulnerable, gets
to say anything she wants at any time to anyone. That is the sole
benefit of being encased in that awful central ring. That person should not be the recipient of complaints from people in the
outer periphery. They can say how they feel, how the trauma is
affecting them too, but only to people in larger rings. The rule, as
described in the article, is simple: "comfort IN and dump OUT."

For example, I was entitled to blatant outbursts of self-pity
and could say, "I feel like I failed everyone; everyone was so excited about the baby."

However, if a random family member said, "We were so looking forward to the baby coming; it's just been horrible news for
us," that would not be OK.

Everyone in those days seemed intent on dumping in.

"It wasn't just your case," the resident elaborated. "We had a really bad outcome the night before too. That mom died. You were lucky."

I looked at Randy, who, without the benefit of the narcotic fuzzing of his emotions, looked ready to fight. He explained later the only way he managed not to strike him in the face was that the disfiguring bruise suggested he had already been punched.

"It won't always feel like this. The happy outcomes will outnumber the bad," I offered, helpless but to comfort out. It wasn't that I was being unselfish, it was just that looking at him, I felt as if I were looking at a dumbstruck deer that had wandered out into the road. He had left us no choice but to collide. And I knew the look of abject defeat. I too had experienced bad outcomes as a physician, and they had rightly gutted me. I had certainly dumped in. I recalled admonishing a patient, "You really scared me last night." Recalling that memory was like watching a fabric quilted of self-centeredness rip open before me at the seams.

You really scared me.

That was a bad night for me.

I will never say those words again.

He nodded and left, shoulders just slightly less slumped than when he had entered. Randy vented, incredulous at his audacity. "How dare he think he was justified complaining to us?" I shrugged and shook my head.

It took time for me to feel genuine compassion for him. Improbable though it seemed to me at the time, it would come. Before I connected to it, I scheduled meetings to complain to his superiors about this particular resident's lack of insight. One physician who was the unlucky recipient of my tirade was a kind, middle-aged man with energetic eyes. He listened attentively and nodded. I would believe that by nodding, he was agreeing. I believed he would understand how poorly suited this young physician was to the role he was in. Instead of that, I got a reflective dissertation on a flawed system and the shame it cultivates, and the untold burden of suffering on the trainees. The pressure we place on them and the unseen toll of our collective expectations that they function on some superhuman level. I thought he had completely missed the point. I wanted to see indignation, an indictment of this particular resident's capacity. Instead, he demonstrated nothing but compassion toward him and encouraged me to do the same. I left his office with books on mindfulness and the power of gratitude. I didn't understand his position at the time. Of course medicine was high pressure; that was how we were shaped and molded. Medicine was a place for people who thrived under that pressure. It was no place for self-pitying doctors who cried to their patients. We didn't have the luxury of being broken. Our patients needed us to be strong. Or so I believed at the time.

The traits we revile in others are often the ones that remind us most of our worst selves. And we react most strongly to the faults and flaws we see in others that we are most ashamed of in ourselves. The OB resident had allowed himself to feel his sadness, something I had denied myself. In coming to our hospital room to cry, maybe he hadn't chosen an appropriate outlet for his grief, but he was searching for one. He was broken, and he was admitting it far before I allowed myself to do the same. I didn't have the insight to see myself in him then. But as these things usually go, life saw fit to keep him at my side until I did understand that we were far more alike than we were different. And that I owed myself the same compassion I owed him.

He resurfaced repeatedly through the next three years, like a buoy marking some distance we'd traversed in a vast sea. He was the resident rotating when we met with the high-risk maternal fetal medicine doctors to plan our next pregnancy. He was the resident rotating on reproductive endocrinology when we thought perhaps a surrogate would be the safest route. He never sank. He sometimes pretended not to recognize us, but more often he reflected on the sheer awfulness of that night, or his resolve to see his training through to the end. Had he appeared as a social worker at the adoption agency we visited, I don't think either of us would have been surprised. And when he failed to appear at the delivery of our son, we felt blissfully free. I had earned our uncoupling.

A curse was undone.

Three

Waiting to Fail

There is a saying in surgery: "All bleeding stops eventually." I first heard this in an operating room, as a medical student, uttered by a colorectal surgeon as he addressed a squirting blood vessel. I interpreted it as an abbreviated pep talk, a reminder to the surgeon from himself, of his own skills and ability. The subtext, like the wry smile beneath his surgical mask, was not accessible to me, his verdant student. It wasn't until I repeated the phrase myself, as the doctor responsible for stopping a patient's blood loss, that I understood the morose connotation. The bleeding will stop, because either you will gain control of it, or the patient will die because you couldn't. And then it will stop.

One week into my ICU stay, I was reminded there is a third way that bleeding stops: tamponade. I had bled into a relatively fixed space—the fibrous capsule surrounding my liver. As volume increased in the space, pressure proportionately rose, the blood politely obeying the laws of fluid dynamics. Pressure here was both a blessing and a curse. A blessing, in that it caused the bleeding to stop, or tamponade, when the pressure in the space exceeded the pressure in my arteries. A curse because that static column of viscous blood had displaced my liver, and the weight had compressed it to one-tenth its size. Crushed and confined, the cells of my liver began to die. The liver unfortunately bears responsibility for the manufacturing of blood products responsible for clotting. Without these clotting factors, all blood loss becomes unstoppable. Despite the horror of this condition, it has a rather poetic name: compressive hepatopathy with consumptive coagulopathy. They are beautiful phrases, with the quantitative meter of iambic pentameter. Their lyrical cadence melodic, until one considers their meaning: my liver was failing and I could bleed to death in a moment.

A doctor entered the room early in the day, in rumpled clothing and an ink-stained coat. He was still chewing whatever food he'd put in his mouth while on the way to my room.

"Hi, I'm from transplant." He introduced himself through what smelled like an onion bagel. He wiped his hand on his coat before offering it to shake.

I offered a feeble wave from my bed instead. He awkwardly attempted to give purpose to his outstretched hand and redirected it to push his glasses back up his nose with his index finger. A ridiculous circular gesture that only added to his informality. His pale, gangly frame backed up until it found a surface to rest against.

"So, listen. Your surgical team consulted us, because of your liver failure. Sounds like we're going to have to find you a new liver, unless you want to live here forever." A weak attempt at humor, which fell flat. Except for his own half-hearted snort.

Randy was incredulous. "What are you talking about?"

He attempted to explain the damage being wrought by the sheer weight of the blood. Then began saying, mostly to himself, "I guess we could try to drain it. I don't know if we'd thought of draining it." He glanced backward, as if to look outside of my hospital room for someone from his team who might know the answer, might rescue him.

"I thought . . . that the reason I'm alive is that the capsule around my liver stayed intact?" The panicked oscillations in my voice surprised me.

He paused for a moment, seeming to take my fear seriously. "Nah, you're right. I think draining it would mean certain death," he offered.

"Perhaps you could not offer options that would result in her certain death," Randy suggested, in an authoritative tone.

"Well, I'd discuss any plan with the transplant team, of course, prior to really solidifying the plan. I mean, what I'm talking about are really just possibilities," he stammered.

I glared at him. He began to back out of the room, pulling the other half of his breakfast out of his pocket.

"I'll be back later. You know, with the team, we'll talk more," he said. He waved the bagel hand in the air, in a sort of bizarre salute. And with that, he was out of the room, leaving us to consider his poorly formulated plan.

I recalled in residency, after a particularly poor decision by a resident, the attending ICU physician stating simply, "These patients deserve your full attention. They are the sickest patients in the hospital, possibly the entire city, and they deserve our best efforts. You must not accept anything less of yourself, because they cannot afford anything less of you. We owe it to them." Our patients deserve our best efforts.

Onion Bagel's senior, and eventually his attending, later came in to apologize for him. It seemed he had gone a bit rogue, discussing a plan that the team had never endorsed or vetted. I was assured if I needed a transplant, the discussion would occur at a far higher level and with far greater consideration than what we'd seen that morning. Though we understood this cognitively, it was difficult to absorb the shock of the miscommunication even within the same team. I was relying on them to keep me alive, and yet I was left feeling as if they were not entirely worthy of my trust.

Less than an hour after they had left my room, a fountain spray of blood arced out of my left wrist, toward the door, as if to punctuate the declaration of my liver failure. The nurse moved quickly, placing a bucket underneath my suspended arm. The plastic line dwelling in an artery in my wrist had fractured and was rhythmically spraying blood with each heartbeat.

A friend who was an older physician entered with a cheerful balloon, only to find me pale and hemorrhaging. He was in charge of a number of innovative initiatives for the health system and cared deeply about patient safety. The nurse darted in front of him with a WET FLOOR sign in his path and left to notify the on-call physician. I took one look at my friend and reminded him, "These are the new arterial line kits you approved, aren't they?"

"I'm sorry, we'd heard some reports that they fracture more, but the hospital was looking for less expensive . . ." he trailed off, staring alternately at the bloody ground and the balloon, feeling visibly stupid.

From my new position of vulnerability, everything had taken on a different weight. I felt the impact of even the smallest choices. I was secretly glad he had decided to visit at precisely that moment, so he could watch my blood spill.

"I didn't know you were this sick. I wouldn't have brought a balloon, I'm sorry." Despite my anger, he sat beside me, abandoning the balloon in the corner.

"I have to tell you something. Because no one else will be honest with you," I said. Sentences that began this way were usually the benefit of some disinhibition by narcotics. I could see him steel himself, prepared for some indictment of his medical decision making. His prioritization in this instance of cost over patient safety. Instead I surprised him by saying, "You have to stop wearing these awful ties with cartoon characters on them. You are too old and you look ridiculous."

I was dead serious, but we both laughed at the absurdity of my making this declaration while I was bleeding into a bucket. We were amused by the equal gravity I had given to both accusations. We talked about the obvious problem with the new lines. He listened intently, appearing chastened. He took my case back to the hospital administration and they agreed to go back to stocking the more expensive lines. My frustration was venerated. He announced this proudly to me, wearing a new bow tie.

It might seem an impossibly naïve position to suggest that everything matters, always. But when one considers that regardless of the seeming insignificance of a choice, it will affect a patient, then everything does matter, always. We often get the big things so perfectly right only to fall apart on the smallest detail, like the four cents saved per line.

There are items left at the door when one enters the hospital, chief among them comfort, a bit of dignity and any semblance of control. Decisions are often made with little input from the patient. Rather, the patient is informed of the plan and left to reconcile it with their best understanding of what could be. Patients rarely have the advantage of a comprehensive understanding of the array of available choices from which the proposed plan was selected. Even with the knowledge I had amassed by the time my liver failed, I was unable to contribute to the discussion. I was dependent on the efforts of others.

At the intersection of a lack of control and absence of rigorous attention is distrust. I couldn't trust the transplant resident, or the choice of arterial line kits, precisely because I *had* to trust them, and both presented me with just cause to doubt their worth.

When faced with a difficult decision, such as whether a patient requires a transplant, there is an inordinate amount of discussion and deliberation. For the sake of brevity, physicians sometimes make the mistake of distilling this down for the patient. One sentence is presented—*You may need a new liver*—rather than the cohesive narrative. In my case, it is likely that a number of experts from several different disciplines reviewed my case, conferring about the implications. There would have been a multi-disciplinary meeting, with discussion of the arc of the lab results and contingency plans made for every possible scenario. The risks and benefits of the various options, like draining the hematoma by creating a defect in the liver capsule, would have been carefully weighed and sorted.

When I reflect back upon times when I confidently declared a singular course of action the best route, I know at the core of that posturing was insecurity. I disliked the optics of admitting how many opinions I had elicited. I worried that to a patient, modesty would be read as indecisiveness, caution would be reinterpreted as a lack of authority. I was trained in an era when an edge of arrogance was considered an essential character trait of a truly skillful physician. I calibrated my confidence to match that of my mentors. Ego, the conscious portion of the psyche that is so concerned with external perception, wants to be fed. It will slyly interject itself as a wall against self-doubt. But allowing ego to dominate, coddling it as a mechanism of self-protection, is nothing more than allowing weakness to masquerade as strength.

As my distrust of the surgical team grew, I found myself relying more heavily than ever on my nurses. They truly knew how I was doing, having the advantage of spending a larger part of the day with me than any physician team could. There was a humility, too, that I came to favor. They didn't seem to have an agenda for what they would find when they examined me. They were objective, and reconciled their findings with what the team had laid out. When things didn't fit, they pushed back, forcing closer scrutiny. My favorite ICU nurse called me "hon." Normally, I'd recoil if a nurse or physician used that sort of diminutive endearment, but with her I didn't mind. I felt the warmth of her intention. And because she worked the night shift, and I slept most of the day, we had lots of time to spend together. She'd help me to bathe, confined as I was to the bed, referring to it as "spa time." She could deftly change the linens on the bed, with me still in it, a skill I still can't comprehend. She rolled me onto my right side and had me hold the handrail while she spread out the sheets. She reached up to the monitor to silence the alarm. My oxygen levels were falling with the slightest movement.

She looked squarely at me. "You shouldn't be so short of breath just rolling onto your side, hon. What did the doctors say today?"

"Nothing, really. My labs were about the same. My incision looked OK. I don't know. I guess there wasn't much to say."

"Hmm. Did they *see* your breathing?" she asked.

I shook my head. "I was just sitting when they came in, so my breathing was OK," I offered.

She'd tell the on-call team but urged me to discuss it with the rounding team the following day, as she doubted the level of ownership that the covering intern would have at night. I agreed. I asked if she would call engineering to turn up the heat in the room. She smiled at me and said, "Hon, it's so hot," as she mimed mopping sweat off her forehead. Then, "Of course I will."

By morning my difficulty breathing was worse, and the team

ordered a chest X-ray in response to her concerns. It showed a significant amount of fluid had accumulated around my right lung, my body's response to the trauma.

"We'll monitor it," they said. They didn't feel the risk of putting me through a procedure to drain it with a needle, given how poorly my blood was clotting, was worth the potential benefit. "Your breathing is still OK at rest. If we need to drain it, we will, but let's wait for now." They reminded me of how difficult it had been to stop the fountain spray of blood out of my wrist. "Imagine if that happened internally, and we couldn't apply pressure," they added ominously.

We weren't able to wait for long. The next morning a new nurse came in, preparing to do her assessment. She adjusted my bed so that it was flat, and then looking at the supplies she brought in, must have realized she had forgotten something and left the room.

Left flat, the excess fluid that had been held in other parts of my body suddenly began to redistribute. It moved through unseen channels, lymphatics and veins, toward my heart and lungs. Minute by minute, my lungs became heavier and heavier as they slowly filled with fluid. I gasped and gagged, feeling as if a garden hose had been placed in my mouth. I gulped in useless breaths, a breathing pattern referred to as guppy breathing, and felt I was getting no air at all. I tried to pull myself up to sit but didn't have the strength. My flailing movements propelled the remote with the call button onto the floor. *Well, there goes that option,* I thought. I heard my monitor alarm and felt momentarily hopeful. But by this point in my stay, the nurses at the station had alarm fatigue, a condition familiar to anyone who has spent time in an ICU. The alarms are always going off. It becomes impossible to differentiate an urgent alarm from a nuisance beep.

My alarms were always going off for either a high heart rate or low oxygen and were rarely an indication of an actual change in my clinical status. The nurses knew that, just as they knew me. No one was coming.

As I drowned, my vision tunneled, until all I could see was a small circle above the head of my bed. My eyes focused on a small blue square button, labeled CODE BLUE. The universal alarm would activate the code team in the event of a dying patient. I struggled to raise my arm and pressed it. Within seconds, the team rushed in. They had been rounding just feet away, oblivious to my distress. The first two to arrive looked at each other, and one of them asked, "But who called the code?" before quickly realizing that was, in fact, not the most pressing issue.

They worked quickly, almost wordlessly, with a grace that suggested it had been choreographed. A tube was placed to decompress my stomach, a higher level of supplemental oxygen was supplied. A portable chest X-ray was shot. A wordless decision was made to drain the effusion surrounding my right lung, and a thick needle entered my chest wall like a dart. They attached a catheter to a vacuum bottle and I watched as liters of foamy red liquid drained.

My nurse reentered, a look of shock spreading over her face. She joined the efforts without asking questions, drawing blood for labs and assisting where she determined she might be needed.

Within minutes, I could breathe again.

"I called the code," I said, addressing their forgotten question. "I couldn't breathe."

"You called a code on yourself?"

I nodded.

They smiled, incredulous. Their work done, they began filtering back out to return to rounds.

"I nearly died," I said to myself as much as anyone. It seemed like there was more to say. That we should discuss what had happened and how to prevent it from happening again, and that bit about how I had nearly died.

"But you are OK now. Just rest," was the sentiment offered by the last straggling physician.

I asked if he could stay. I was terrified to be left alone.

"No reason to worry. Your nurse is here. And look, you're connected to all of these monitors. We know everything that's happening every second. Even if we're not in the room." He smiled as he left.

I did not feel reassured. *The monitors were of zero use thirty minutes ago, why should I believe them useful now? You had no idea what was happening.* I couldn't say if it was a result of the surge in adrenaline, or some rapid-onset post-traumatic stress disorder, but I was certain I was not safe. I studied the monitors, inspected each of my IV lines and obsessively wondered what would happen next.

"What is my platelet count today?" I asked the nurse.

"It was around 50, I think," she replied, as she sat down to log in to the computer. Pulling up my lab results she confirmed, "Yes, it was 45."

But that's too low. They just tapped my chest with my platelets at 45? Did anyone check them first? I visualized the oozing blood that was probably filling my chest cavity as I sat there. I checked the monitor again. My oxygen level was OK, but I was certain it would fall at any moment.

"Is the oxygen working? I don't feel it coming out." I took the nasal cannula out of my nose and felt for flow. "It's barely coming out, feel this." I tried to hand it to the nurse.

She dutifully walked to the wall and turned the dial, increasing the flow so that I could feel it. "See? It's working fine. Just rest."

I couldn't rest. I was far too busy being preoccupied, imagining every impending disaster.

I asked for my labs to be printed. My vision didn't allow for me to read the numbers, but I needed to have them in some tangible, concrete form. Then, unsatisfied by the idea of isolated data points, I asked for a printout of the trend in my labs over the past week. I stacked the pile of papers neatly on my tray table. I put my face close to the papers, inhaling the scent of printer ink on freshly printed paper. Closing my eyes, I could imagine I was at a clean, organized desk in an office somewhere far from blood and catheters filled with urine. I imagined how good it would feel to hold a cold, heavy stapler. To use staples to hold important papers together, rather than my abdominal wall.

The emotions of patients are encoded in their behavior. It's an easy task to recognize a crying person as sad. But a compulsively attentive patient, documenting every lab result and asking well-formulated questions about antibiotic choices, is less easy to decode as anxious. I myself didn't recognize my own anxiety at the time. I believed I was appropriately adapted to my environment. An environment that required intense vigilance and anticipation of some impending cataclysm. The casual complacency I observed in others struck me as horribly naïve. Every solicitation to "just rest" filled me with contempt. I knew what would happen if I left the watchtower untended. I would die. I believed it was entirely up to me to ensure my own safety.

In an ICU in a world-renowned hospital, with around-the-clock care by highly skilled medical teams, I felt responsible for myself. That is the power of anxiety.

I took to surveying my body frequently. I believed the cursory examinations the team performed were unreliable. I found a deep-blue stain discoloring my right inner thigh. Like ink dropped onto wet paper, it was spreading, a thin ominous storm cloud. The blood that had been confined in my liver capsule was finding a way out. It was quietly forcing its way between planes of my tissue, squeezing itself between thin sheets of sinew called fascia, dissecting me like a liquid scalpel. I stared at it, gauging its intent. I had anticipated and sought evidence of some looming disaster, but having found it, promptly covered it with my gown. I was unable to face it. I pressed my fingertips to my lips, as if to hold the news in.

When the rounding team arrived, the attending ran through the preformulated plan for the day. He was bright, methodical and articulate, and I knew he had considered every lab result carefully before formulating a plan. We had worked together in the ICU before, and I had a vivid recollection for how hard he had been on himself when he had made an error. It was the only error I ever saw him make, and it changed how he talked about decisions to the teams. It changed the set of his jaw, and the way he listened to patients. My blood count was lower, but no cause for alarm. Likely just a result of frequent lab monitoring. They were considering giving me a unit of blood, just to "tank me back up." My chest X-ray looked better following the drainage. I sat silently. When he finished, I uncovered my mouth and whispered, "There is something I need to show you," and pushed off the covers and raised my gown.

"When did you notice that?" he asked, with a pitch that did little to conceal his worry.

"Just now," I lied. I had spent an hour at least in wordless shock.

He sighed and frowned, and nodded. Plans would have to change.

The day was hastily rearranged to accommodate a stat CT

scan. Individual images shot at two-millimeter intervals through-out my body, reconstructed into a virtual image of my chest, abdo-men and pelvis. They had been piecing together an impression of the chaos that resulted from the catastrophic bleed as best they could from lab results and glimpses of the edge of my liver in the operating room, but I had yet to be stable enough to travel for any scans. The actual images revealed the situation to be far worse than they had imagined.

The blood collection was the size of one of those globes el-ementary schools had in each classroom. In the process of ex-panding, it had reorganized my abdomen. My liver was pushed into a thin crescent on the opposite side of my body. My stom-ach's capacity was reduced to a tablespoon. My right lung was less than half the size it had been, and the space around it had al-ready refilled with a murky fluid. Worst of all, the contrast they had injected into my bloodstream could be seen not only in my veins, but leaching out of my vessels, into the still-expanding hematoma. A blush of white against the old dark blood. I was still bleeding.

The energy of the room changed. Nurses moved quickly and more purposefully, with economized steps. The hall outside the room filled with specialists and anxious chatter. Opinions were sought, entertained, and rejected. It felt as if a deck of playing cards had been thrown into the air, and everyone was scrambling against the clock to make a hand.

When my attending eventually reentered the room, he did so with a tense, solemn expression and reverential tone. I recog-nized the look as well as the tenor of his speech. It was how I spoke to people I knew were going to die regardless of what we did. The plan was outlined for us. If the bleeding continued, I would be taken back to the operating room, they would reopen my abdominal incision, evacuate the hematoma, try to find the source of the bleeding, pack thick gauze pads around my liver and leave me open. *They would leave me open.* As in, they would not close the incision at all but cover my exposed organs with a plastic-wrap-like layer of film and wait. Wait for the surgery to declare itself a success or a failure. Wait for me to re-bleed, wait for the bleeding to stop, wait for infection to set in, whatever. They would wait, and then they'd take me back again. Fix what needed to be fixed and regroup.

No one liked that option. No one would have even suggested it if there had been a single better option. No one thought this was an option that ended with me leaving the hospital intact. But they would do it if they had no other choice. They would do it to say they had done all they could. They'd done it before in similar situations. Those girls were all dead.

Everyone believed I was bleeding diffusely from the surface of my liver, which was a feared complication of HELLP syndrome, a condition that only affects pregnant women. That diffuse oozing being the presumptive diagnosis, they couldn't simply go in and block a bleeding vessel, a procedure called embolization. No one knew at the time that there were two very vascular tumors in my liver, one of which had ruptured, gushing blood into my abdomen. We couldn't cut off their blood supply because we couldn't see them. They couldn't be seen because like a pair of chameleons, they had blended in and matched the shade of the liver surrounding them. Later, when we knew to look for them, we timed the injection of dye just right and caught them blushing. Then they could be embolized. But that wouldn't be for another year. In the meantime, I was hemorrhaging without any mechanism to stop the flow.

They allowed for the possibility that the blood loss would somehow just stop. Then they could augment my body's supply of clotting factors with transfusions. Assuming my liver somehow began to recover, despite the pressure of the weight. They'd give me blood as well, and hope that my kidneys could take on the difficult task of expelling some of the extra fluid.

The fuse had been lit. We would wait and see.

The fluid around my lung reaccumulated at a faster rate, a byproduct of all of the transfusions. I had such poor nutritional status, having been unable to eat more than a tablespoon at a time, that the protein content in my body had fallen. This made all of my tissues boggy, as water leached out of my veins, following the principle of osmosis. I'd learned to sense the weight of the fluid in my chest, and when it reached two or three liters I would ask my team to drain it. It seemed a simple enough solution and provided me some measure of control. That plan proved sound for about two weeks, until one day when they placed the needle and only a small amount of fluid was evacuated. I felt a sharp pain.

"Something's wrong," I warned them. It had never hurt like this before. I felt certain they had collapsed my lung with the needle.

"I'm not getting much fluid out. Someone get the ultrasound machine," the pulmonologist asked.

As the ultrasound probe was placed on my back, I watched the screen. I knew there was a large amount of fluid; I could feel it. And on the screen, I could see the fluid surrounding my compressed lung, but there was something new. Strandy fibers, like seaweed at the coast, waved in the fluid.

"It's loculated," he said, seeing the same strands I was.

The protein in the fluid had coalesced around itself and grown into hard ropes, like a rock sugar growing along a string in some childhood science experiment. The strands separated the fluid into discrete pockets, each one a separate compartment, and they were no longer accessible by a single needle.

"We can't drain it, I'm sorry."

I struggled to grasp the implications. If we couldn't drain it, then I would always be unable to breathe. I would always be dependent on oxygen. There'd be no trajectory of recovery, only unremitting chronic illness.

"That can't be," I countered. I had been confronted by the limits of therapeutic options as a physician, and cognitively I understood that it was possible to run out of options. But as a patient, I just couldn't accept that we had hit that wall. My heart raced. I dug my nails into my palms to keep from crying.

"So what do we do?" Randy asked.

"To clear the loculations would require surgery. And even surgery doesn't guarantee success. Anyway, she's not well enough to have surgery. She just has to live with the fluid."

I'd have to live with it. Live with the fluid and wait to re-bleed. I couldn't fathom how I could possibly do that and stay sane.

I felt the kind of panicked desperation and disbelief I had seen in the faces of my patients with terminal conditions. I recognized it as the same feeling that drove people to embrace unproven alternative treatments. It felt distinctly as though I had nothing to lose. I thought of my patients who had spent their final days away from their children, traveling for experimental therapy only offered at distant cancer treatment centers. The patients who had spent their life savings on vitamin infusions, purified herbs and tonics. I thought of my patient who had unwittingly overdosed on a toxic Chinatown tea, brewed in pursuit of fertility after a series of miscarriages. And in that moment, it all seemed perfectly rational.

Four

Sequestered Words

Visitors came in the afternoon, so I learned to feign sleep. Some brought flowers, which were unceremoniously discarded by nurses. Gifts that carried any risk of infection were not permitted in the ICU, they explained. Others brought magazines I couldn't read, or food I couldn't eat. Everyone brought with them questions. And every question led down a circuitous path to more unanswerable questions. First we placed signs on the door: PLEASE CHECK IN AT NURSING STATION PRIOR TO ENTERING or PATIENT IS RESTING, DO NOT DISTURB. Naturally, no one thought the signs applied to them. So I enlisted Randy to man the waiting area and politely apologize to each person individually that I was resting, that today was a hard day and I was not up for visitors.

On particularly bad days, I'd beg him to turn everyone away.

"Don't worry, honey. I will be a pit bull." And he would. Alienating family and friends alike.

There was the rare visitor who was capable of just sitting in stunned silence with me. Those who explained later they just needed to see me, to have independent confirmation that I was alive. They would enter and leave quietly, silently proving that they needed no more than to share that physical space with a breathing version of me.

I declined phone calls, even as cell phones were held up to my ear. I'd shake my head no.

It wasn't that I wanted to be alone, or that I was ungrateful for the support. It was just that there was no longer such a thing as an effortless word. To speak I had to time my breath so that it passed through my vocal cords during an exhalation. This meant contracting my abdomen despite the staples, and aggravating the fiery pool of blood beneath my diaphragm. My difficulty breathing was a constant now due to the fluid compressing my lung. Assuming I was willing to endure the pain and shortness of breath, I then had to actually find the words. They darted just out of reach, like children in a game of tag. The more I grasped for them, the more aggressively they dispersed.

"What do you need from home?" my mom asked me. "I'll bring it in the morning."

I made a gesture for a pen. I would write a list. Far easier than speaking.

I held the pen, suspended over the paper, and the three of us stared at the page waiting for words to emerge. I realized I was unsure I had retained the ability to write. I wondered if there was some validated standard for how long was it acceptable to contemplate a word before it was labeled problematic. I suspected the limit was somewhat less than the long minutes that had already elapsed.

"I don't need anything," I declared, putting the pen down.

"Just tell me what you need," my mom offered.

I looked at her and realized I couldn't do that either. I just didn't know what I was trying to say. There were large pieces of me that were still submerged. I had been a person who loved words. I had rolled them like ball bearings in my head, until the ideal choice fell through the perfect miniature hole. I had been bright and articulate. I had not yet reclaimed enough of my identity to recognize myself. I began to cry.

"Why are you crying? Just describe what you need."

I could picture what I was trying to say. I saw them clearly, sitting at the bottom of my closet, but they were lost to me. I had surfaced only to be left hollow. What other core pieces of myself were to remain permanently submerged?

Then the word appeared, fully formed. *Shoes.* It was more than a word. It was imbued with all the context and subtext of a long-term relationship.

"Shoes," I whispered. "I want my shoes." I exhaled deeply.

She nodded. She understood that though I didn't know yet if I had been approved for physical therapy, I wanted to be prepared.

"I think they will help me to walk," I added. I silently hoped she wouldn't ask for direction as to which pair.

"Sure. I'll bring the brown flat ones, I think they'll fit."

I was grateful to not have to explain.

The odd thing about being completely terrified is that it cannot be maintained as a constant state. Though I certainly tried. The body primes itself with hormones, adrenaline and cortisol, readying it for some defensive action. When no true threat or cause for action is identified, the body's interest in remaining on high alert wanes. I became tired of being scared. Tired of imagining every worst-case scenario, running imagined contingency plans. As days passed without my worst fears coming true, I began to feel that perhaps all the anxious worry was, in fact, actually useless. After all, it wasn't really preparing me for anything, except to die. And if I did die, well, that would be how the story ended. I divested from any outcome. I stopped believing worry could change anything. I learned to wait and see. More often than not, the following day brought with it some small but tangible measure of improvement.

I had been looking forward to physical therapy. Having been entirely bed-bound for weeks, I was sore and miserable with weak, wasted muscles. The doctors knew I'd have to regain my strength slowly and weren't expecting much from me. They requested some basic range-of-motion exercises to keep my joints from stiffening. In my mind, the fact that the doctors ordered it at all meant that they believed I had potential for recovery. I wanted to prove to them they were right to believe in me. I would push myself and accomplish more than anyone expected.

The physical therapist was young and fit in a way that suggested she drove straight to a rock wall to practice climbing after work. She was so completely, unobjectionably pretty that I could have easily set her up with any one of my single male friends. Her disposition was so brightly optimistic, I felt she wouldn't become easily discouraged with me. She asked a few questions aimed at identifying our goal for the day.

"So, tell me a little about what you were able to do prior to being sick?" she asked.

I told her I had been practicing a form of Vinyasa yoga most days. And immediately thought, *Oh my God, that was a million years ago.*

"When were you last able to walk?" she asked.

It was the day I got sick. I remembered I had walked into the backseat of the car and entered a wheelchair when I got out at the emergency room entrance. That was the last time I had walked.

"I think I want to try to do the stairs," I confessed to her, avoiding her question entirely.

"Stairs, huh? OK, well, let's see where you're at. Why don't you first try to swing your legs over to this side of the bed?"

I placed my palms beside me on the bed and attempted to bend my knees. I found I couldn't rely on my abdomen to pull my legs in, and I had to manually grab the back of each thigh and slowly pull it toward me. Any movement that compressed my abdomen tugged on the sharp staples and aggravated the pain of both the long incision and the blood collection. I accepted the pain as inevitable, and dug deep for untapped pockets of strength. I inched my heels across the width of the bed until one slid off.

"Good," she said. "Now, try to bring the next one over."

Soon I had both legs dangling off the bed. I was breathless.

"This is hard, I know. Take a break. We'll stop soon."

Clearly she was just saying that to encourage me to keep going. I couldn't imagine we'd stop, as we had yet to accomplish anything.

"Let's try to get these socks on." She handed me a pair with traction stripes on the bottom. The bright yellow color, I knew, silently alerted nurses and physicians that I had been deemed a "fall risk."

I reluctantly took them from her and attempted to reach my feet. I could angle forward maybe thirty degrees, but no farther, which meant my hands couldn't reach below my knees.

"Here, take this." She handed me a long stick with an S-shaped hook at the end.

I stared at her quizzically.

"It's a hook. We'll use it to help you get your socks on. You want to be independent, don't you?"

Not especially, actually. I was beginning to think she was not as angelic as I had initially believed. I silently wished she would let someone else put my socks on, so that I could get on to the real task at hand of climbing the stairs. I was still unaware of the extent of my disability.

She demonstrated how to load the sock onto the hook at the end of the stick and then deploy it. After a few failed attempts, I had my right sock nearly entirely on my foot. I longed for a time when I was blissfully ignorant of the existence of sock-hooks.

The left went a bit smoother, though it still took far longer than I could believe possible. I looked up at her with pride and anticipation of my next task.

"Good, OK. So tomorrow we will try standing."

"Tomorrow?"

"Well, we don't want to wear you out. You've been at this for over an hour, so that's enough for one day. Let me help you get back into bed."

Over an hour.

Once situated, I realized she had wisely allowed for how difficult and time consuming getting me back into bed would be as well. "Thank you?" I offered, feeling defeated.

"You bet!" She nodded and slid through the ICU door as it closed behind her. "See you tomorrow!" she called out over her shoulder.

I sat sore and exhausted, staring at the stupid yellow socks on my feet. I tried to integrate what had just happened into who I believed myself to be. I was apparently now a person who took over an hour to put on socks using a sock-hook. And I was a person who found it incredibly difficult. I shook my head. I didn't recognize myself. I tried to access the last time I had found something so physically difficult to accomplish. It was a yoga position, flying pigeon pose, that required upper-body strength to balance the weight of the body as the legs lifted to the side. I'd never had much upper-body strength. But I chipped away at it, each day, until eventually it appeared effortless.

How had I done that? And more important, what could the person who had managed to do that teach me as I sat, unable to stand?

I had to learn to soften; I had to learn to accept my body's limitations. I had to value humility and choose to surrender when my first inclination was to force. I had to work each day toward a goal that seemed unreachable at times. I had to believe I could become a person who could meet herself in flying pigeon pose. I realized that the only difference now was my starting point. I was in pain, I was defeated, I couldn't stand, much less walk, but I still had agency. An agency that allowed that I could inhabit my broken body with a reverence for what it was capable of in the past and what it was able to do in this moment. I could honor its difficulty engaging in what I was attempting to do as entirely right and fair. This was where my body was now. I would choose to relabel discomfort as transformation. I'd regain my strength, slowly. I would recognize and celebrate small victories. Today I was a person who could put my socks on by myself.

I felt oddly grateful.

All at once, my kidneys started working again. The dormant little beans woke up and got to work ridding my body of liters and liters of excess fluid. I lost five pounds in a day, sometimes more. As my tissues consolidated, it became easier to move. I had peaked somewhere around two hundred pounds on a five-foot-two-inch frame. If someone saved me the effort and put my socks on for me, I could stand and walk a few unassisted feet, until the tether of the oxygen hose suggested I return. I would awkwardly veer to the left, and sometimes into the wall, a result of the stroke in the part of my brain responsible for balance. And though I learned over time to resist the pull and straighten my gait, doing so required a tremendous amount of reinterpreting of sensory input. In the light, I managed all right, but if I attempted to walk in the dark, I was guaranteed a bruised left shoulder. Even now, it creeps into my days. Randy smiles knowingly whenever the car repair shop calls and tells him that they couldn't identify any issue with my car's alignment. I've learned to shrug and say, "OK, fine. I won't take it in again. I was just convinced this time it really was pulling to the left." I can't go down escalators easily; my vision just won't converge the separate images from each eye into a cohesive whole when looking down. I stand at the top, as people pile up behind me, thinking I'll step on at any moment.

Back then, there was one ambitious day when the nurses and physical therapists conspired and had the respiratory therapist bring an oxygen tank, which they placed in a sturdy, heavy wheelchair.

"Here you go," they said. "Hold the handles like this, and see how far you can go. If you get tired, you can always just sit down in the chair."

I must have looked terrified.

"I'll come with you, don't worry," Randy said.

I grasped the black plastic handles and leaned forward, redistributing some of my weight onto the chair. I pushed forward and took a first tentative step. It led graciously, without rolling away. It was heavy and secure. Randy put a second gown on me so I'd be covered, a clear indication he believed I would go far enough to encounter other people. I took a few more slow steps and was suddenly in the hallway. I turned a corner. I was walking. I was outside of the room for the first time in weeks.

I felt confident enough to look up, rather than watch my feet. I met the gaze of a surgeon I recognized and his face went white.

"Wow," he said.

I assumed he was impressed by my progress, as he rightly should have been.

"I-I thought you were dead," he stammered.

I cocked my head to the side, paused for a moment, and silently walked past him.

I'd learn with time to recognize that characteristic I-just-saw-a-ghost look. Physicians and nurses who had encountered me early in my hospitalization, stopping in their tracks, truly shocked to see me alive. I found it insulting at first. It felt as if they were passing judgment on my strength and resilience without knowing me. But I came to regard it as a compliment—a tacit expression of how sick I had been, and how unimaginable it was that I was actually still here.

I followed the signs to the waiting room, surprising everyone.

I began to imagine I might one day leave the hospital. I began asking questions, trying to define the road markers and hurdles between the ICU and home.

"Whoa, there are a lot of steps between here and there," my attending physician began. His desire for an impossibly safe discharge signaled to me the presence of a ghost in the room. Some regret of some past mistake was there, influencing our conversation. "We'd need to repeat the CT scan, to be sure the bleeding stopped. I'd like to see your blood count be stable for at least three days without transfusion. I'd like to see you consistently be steady when you walk. I'd like to see you weaned from oxygen. You are needing a lot of electrolyte replacements, that has to decrease in frequency . . ."

He sensed his anxiety was evident and attempted to justify his statements to me. "Remember, you have a large blood collection within a very fragile, stretched liver capsule. Have you thought about what will it mean to drive in a car? To hit a bump? What if another car hits you? What if it ruptures and you are thirty minutes away from the hospital?"

"Well, I'm not going to live here. So order the CT scan. I have only needed oxygen if I'm walking and not at rest," I countered, attempting to orient him to the true risk rather than the imagined fears. It was as if I had transferred all of my anxiety onto him. "I'll get labs drawn every day at the satellite hospital near home if you want me to," I offered. And so began negotiations.

One doctor, the generous obstetrician who would later endure my tirade about the floundering, self-doubting resident, understood. "Tell you what," he said. "I know it is hard being stuck here. I'll write an order that you can go down to I-3. We'll find an unoccupied room. They have nice big bathrooms there, with built-in shower chairs. You can try to take a proper shower. Take some of the sticky glue off from all the monitor leads and tape. How about that?"

I thought it sounded as good as a Popsicle in the summer.

He failed to mention I-3 also had mirrors.

I hadn't seen myself in weeks. I stood naked in front of the mirror. My skin was a Day-Glo yellow, a by-product of the liver failure. My breasts were engorged and veiny in a way that reminded me I was supposedly postpartum. My abdomen was protuberant and discolored by large, ugly blue streaks that ran the entire width of my body. The staples were yellow and crusted, with dried blood at each puncture site. Sticky glue strips were everywhere, with lint and hair stuck to them. My arms and neck bore fist-sized yellowish-purple bruises. My inner thighs were a dark blue-black from the tracking blood. I looked myself in the eye and felt overwhelmed with self-pity.

I felt sorry for myself that I'd been through all of this and there was no baby to even show for it. I felt sorry for how long and hard I knew my recovery would be. I felt angry that my body looked as though it had birthed a baby, and people would unknowingly ask me about the baby, but the baby was dead, and I'd have to tell them that, and then they'd feel bad about asking, and then I'd feel bad that they felt bad. I felt angry that the pregnancy had nearly killed me. I felt overwhelmed by the knowledge that a diagnosis of HELLP syndrome meant it would never be safe for me to become pregnant again. This was almost certainly the closest I would ever be to delivering a baby, and this baby was dead. I felt ashamed that I failed so miserably at being pregnant. I hated everyone.

"How's it going in there?" Randy asked from outside the door.

"Fine," I answered and moved out of view of the mirror. "I look terrible," I admitted through the closed door and tears.

"Not to me you don't. You're alive," he said, his voice steady and reassuring. Then, after a breath: "If you had died, I promise you, I'd still be on the floor."

His unwillingness to identify with me was a kind of deliberate non-empathy. But his assurance in that moment was exactly what I needed. I didn't need my shame and disgust reflected back to me, I needed to see myself through his eyes. His love and perspective graciously eased the pain, and left only a self-pitying sadness.

I sighed and sat in the shower, allowing the water to dilute my tears.

The repeat CT scan required being transported down three floors and halfway across the hospital. Transport arrived while my nurse was occupied in another room, and so I was taken without my usual pain medications. I thought it would be fine. A test of how

I would handle bumps in the actual road, without such strong medications to dull the pain. It was awful. Each small bump over a ridge or an elevator ledge sent a piercing stab through my abdomen. I arrived in radiology pale and panting.

A nurse took the chart and thanked the transporter. Finding a small plastic hospital wristband inside, she asked cheerily, "Oh! What did you have? A boy or a girl?"

"It was a girl. But she died," I managed, as the tears came.

"Oh, I am so sorry," she said, putting her arm across my shoulders. "I didn't know."

"Uh-huh, I know. You couldn't have known." I shook my head, feeling as badly for her as I did for myself.

The radiology tech fiddled with something in the corner, pretending not to know what was happening. "OK, just let me know when you're ready," he said.

The nurse helped me to slide over to the CT scan table, where I sat, waiting for direction. He walked over.

"OK, lay flat, and we'll tell you when to hold your breath," the radiology tech said as he fastened a belt across my waist.

"I can't lie flat." I hadn't lain flat since the day of the code blue.

"You have to try. It's only for a few minutes. I'll put a pillow under your head," he said.

I dutifully lay back, wondering when the drowning sensation would come.

He and the nurse went into the control room, leaving me alone.

I suddenly realized I was not on oxygen. I instinctively padded around with my hands to see if I could feel the oxygen tubing. No, there was none.

"Try to hold still," he said through the speaker.

When transport had come, I must have been off it, and so they had transported me without it. I began to panic.

"OK, now hold your breath." His voice through the speaker from the control room made him seem a million miles away.

Are you insane? I could hardly breathe. I tried to sit up but the belt restricted my movements. I looked around for a monitor to reassure myself that my oxygen saturation was fine, but found I was not attached to any monitoring equipment.

"Almost done, please try to hold still so we get good images for the doctor to look at," he pleaded.

They walked back into the room.

"OK, all done," he congratulated me. "That wasn't so bad, was it?"

"I need oxygen. I'm supposed to be on oxygen." I pointed at the wall where the gas outlet was.

"OK, we'll get you hooked up," he assured me, as the nurse opened a clean bag of tubing to connect to the wall.

I grabbed on to him and tried to pull myself up.

"Whoa there, let me help you," he said as he pulled me up to sit.

Sitting up, with oxygen on, I began to calm down. It was just a CT scan. I thought of how many scans I had ordered on my patients. How many everything I had ordered. It was shocking how little thought I had given to what it meant to leave the safety of the ICU, to be bumped and jostled and made to lie flat with lungs filled with fluid from heart failure or pus from pneumonia. How pathetically arrogant that I thought only of how clinically useful the images would be, or how necessary the test. I saw the patients leave and I saw them return, and what happened in between was unknown to me. How thoughtless I had been.

As the transporter wheeled me back to the unit, he asked, "So, they gotta send you for any more tests?"

"I think one more," I sighed.

He was there when it was time to take me to the next test, whether through randomness of scheduling, or personal ownership, I can only guess. As we arrived in radiology, he marched directly to the tech with my chart and advised her, "Do *not* ask her about the baby." She looked shocked initially by his tone, but then her expression softened and she nodded.

I smiled, then quickly neutralized my expression. It was clear he didn't intend for me to overhear him. She didn't ask about the baby. Nor did anyone else for the rest of my hospitalization. It seemed every transporter now knew the expectation was to protect me from well-meaning questions while I was off the floor. In an eight-hundred-bed hospital, they had united to form a protective enclosure around one patient.

Back in the relative safety of the ICU, we waited for the results of the testing. I had asked repeatedly each day when I would be well enough to leave. Now I sat, acutely aware of each and every person I was dependent upon to provide assistance, supply supplemental oxygen or administer some treatment necessary to keep me alive. They constructed a lattice of support beneath me so deftly and discreetly that, like a teenager, I had mistaken security for self-sufficiency.

The repeat CT scan showed improvement, the fluid around my lung unchanged and my labs stable; they were running out of rational reasons to keep me. There were plenty of fear-based reasons, the what-ifs still haunted us, but they were easily identified as worries rather than risks. I was to be discharged. I sat in a wheelchair, cradling a box filled with the sympathy and get-well-soon cards that had papered the walls. The elastic maternity pants and T-shirt I was wearing defined my body's perimeter so explicitly, I felt more exposed than I had when draped in the handkerchief-like hospital gowns. I was reidentifying as myself and it was uncomfortable. In the gown, I was a sick patient, depersonalized and part of a larger community. By clothing myself, I was in effect reintroducing a version of me. A bloated, scarred, disabled and inferior me. What should have felt like a victory felt instead like a resignation. I had lost something in this battle, something more intangible than the concrete loss of the baby. I had lost my sense of myself as a strong, capable, independent person.

"The pharmacy will deliver your prescriptions shortly, and remember our motto, 'Drugs not Hugs'," the attending doctor joked. I had been warned to avoid every possible threat to my liver capsule including, comically, contact sports, car accidents and hugs.

Randy brought the car around and I was wheeled to the door. I had entered the hospital in spring and was leaving in the full heat of summer. We wouldn't be returning to our house. I had just regained the skill of walking, and couldn't have ascended the stairs to get to our bedroom. I'd be moving instead into my childhood home, where one floor of the split-level graciously accommodated a rented hospital bed, a shower with a shower chair, and the upholstered rocker and ottoman we'd bought for the baby. I would be cared for there by my mom, who had been schooled by nuns and understood the transformative nature of hard work and good deeds. She would find a way to transfigure her thoughts and worry into physical manifestations of helpfulness: helping me to shower, positioning me with pillows, counting out my pills and endless attempts to entice me to eat. Feeding your child obviously being the highest form of prayer.

The old house had been packed up while I was still critically ill, Randy intuitively understanding that we couldn't ever again live in a house where he watched me slowly die in the living room. I would not remember anything about the eventual move; I'd only recall turning up one day at the new house after I'd healed enough to leave my mom's care. The deficits in my memory later became a convenient pretext for my inability to find whatever I might be looking for. Randy, having worked feverishly to prepare our new home, would comically sigh when I'd wonder aloud, "Whoever put my stuff away could have at least left notes." Eight years on, I still blame the imaginary movers when I can't find the tea.

Breathing in the fresh summer air, I found I had an intense nostalgia for everything I saw.

"Wow, that's your car," I said, stating the obvious.

He indulged me. "Yeah, remember it?"

"I do. Wow, I haven't been in your car . . ."

"In a long time," he said, finishing my sentence.

I settled into the front passenger seat before stealing a quick look over my shoulder at the backseat. I looked at Randy as he buckled himself in. "Wow. Here we are again," was all I could manage.

Five

Increments and Impediments

I've found that it is sometimes easier to inhabit a space when not faced with the additional challenge of actually having to be there. I had fantasized for so long about going home, it had come to represent success to me. Instead, being in such a familiar space only seemed to accentuate every loss. The house felt filled with memories of a thousand days that had been easier than the current one. Even if I had been strong enough to make it up the stairs to my rose-colored, childhood bedroom, I couldn't lie flat, so sleeping in my own bed was out. The hospital bed that the discharging team had sent was placed in the lower-level den. And though I had longed for quiet, away from the constant beeps and hallway chatter of the ICU, the dull silence of that half-underground room, with no one to monitor me, felt like a crypt. I moved to the rocker in the family room.

The dark blanket of illness that enveloped me was an easy distraction from the lack of a baby, and I found I wasn't mourning that loss most days. I was mourning something, but it was more intangible. I was mourning the imagined and unmet future. A vision of what I had thought lay ahead, but couldn't quite bring into focus. When I tried to bring it into view, it was like watching grainy footage shot in 16 millimeter projected onto a white sheet. It was subject to disruption by the slightest shift in the wind. Randy, to his credit, acted as though I were the only living thing that had ever mattered and that he'd gladly live out the rest of his life with just me in tow. Most days I thought he should have married someone else. Someone as healthy as a thirty-three-year-old was supposed to be. I thought he got a raw deal.

When we knew we wouldn't be bringing home a baby, we'd asked a friend to call and cancel the furniture we'd ordered for the baby's room. We'd not need the crib or dresser, but we elected to still take delivery of the rocker and ottoman we'd had upholstered in a neutral pattern of off-white swirls. I am not sure why we made this choice, except that we probably thought we'd have a use for it in the new house, and it wasn't entirely obvious it had been intended for a baby's room, so the sight of it wouldn't necessarily gut us.

That rocker defined the new border of my small world. It was the only place I could find any measure of comfort. In the rocker, I was able to elevate my legs, pack myself in with pillows and sleep upright, with an airline neck pillow for support. It allowed me to stay upright twenty-four hours a day, which proved necessary because if I lay back at all it felt as if a heavy bowling ball were crushing my heart and lungs. When I found it difficult to explain why I couldn't lie flat, I calculated the volume and estimated the mass, like the scientist I had once been. I announced I thought the hematoma weighed roughly ten pounds. "Imagine a ten-pound ball crushing you from the inside," I would say. I stopped telling anyone that after hearing the response: "Wow. It's just like a baby." *Let me tell you all the ways this is not at all like a baby.*

I sat, or slept. When I slept, I dreamt of drowning. Dreams where the water is murky and heavy, and no light penetrates the surface. I'd flail and struggle to ascend while feeling crushed by the weight and pressure of the vastness above me. Awake, I was in constant pain. The pill form of the pain medication was no match for the intravenous version I'd been receiving at the hospital. And, unlike at the hospital, if I were to fall asleep, no one dared wake me, so I would miss a dose and get behind the pain, unable to catch up for hours.

Visitors came and drank coffee near me. I couldn't stomach it. I couldn't stomach much. Two spoonsful of anything and I was hopelessly nauseated for hours. I had flashes of cravings, some childhood memory of a sticky sweet. My mom spent hours carefully trying to recreate the dish from memory. I'd take a bite, maybe two, to honor her efforts, but nothing had the taste I was hoping for. Nothing fit right. I showered sitting on a plastic bench with someone always just outside the door, in case of *something*. Something like passing out, or something like getting claustrophobic and panicking in the enclosure, or something like just not being able to clean myself. When had I become claustrophobic? In the CT scanner, when I thought I would drown again, or in that first shower in the hospital, trapped with my disfigured body for the first time? I didn't know. I couldn't turn the water temperature past lukewarm. If any steam at all accumulated, I'd feel suffocated by it. I needed to feel the coolness of the air entering my lungs to believe I was even breathing.

When I could stay awake, I passively listened to the conversations happening around me. Like sitting in a hotel room, with loud voices next door coming unbidden through the wall. I just wanted quiet. Attempts to cheer me with stories, gossip or idle chatter were unwelcome. For some reason, it all made me angry, and then sad. Or sad, then tired. I just didn't get it. Like a stranger from another world, I didn't understand what they were doing. Was this how we were going to spend our time? I felt displaced and unsure of exactly what my part was, or how I was intended to play it. Fortunately, no one seemed to expect much of me, except to be on the stage and to answer that I was doing much better whenever asked. Then the performance would continue without me.

When my favorite uncle visited, I noticed how his skin tone had the same yellowish hue mine did. It was subtle enough then that anyone had yet to acknowledge it and had not begun the testing that eventually led to surgery and chemotherapy. I couldn't access the repository of diagnoses the discoloration implied, but I knew we'd be trading positions soon. I would one day be well and I would visit him during his recovery, as he struggled to get comfortable in his recliner. I would not know what to do, so I would attempt to cheer him with silly stories. He would learn to feign a smile, despite how acutely miserable he felt. He would sense the charade around him and play his role accordingly. He would do it for us.

I would be driven frequently for blood work and imaging studies, and once for the baby's burial. I hadn't thought there would be a burial. I'm not sure exactly what I had thought would happen to her body. In the hospital when I was told they would keep her body for us in the morgue until I managed to get home, I thought it was an odd place for the remains. I had imagined that the very premature baby, being only twenty-seven weeks, would perhaps be sent to the pathology lab to be examined in the same way they would examine the placenta, sliced and sectioned so the pathologist could issue a report that covered every microscopic abnormality, like an autopsy. Brain tissue demonstrates ischemia, evidence of lack of blood flow, and lungs are not adequately developed, eyelids remain fused shut, no cardiac defect noted. And after she was examined, I didn't know what would happen next. I thought of surgical terminations of pregnancy I had seen performed in the operating room as a medical student. Those remains went to pathology, not a cemetery. I recall the term "medical waste" entering my mind before I reprimanded myself.

When I was told there would be a service, a burial in a portion of the cemetery reserved for stillborn babies, I thought it seemed an excessive response, but I had no idea how to rein it in. I had the sense there wasn't another choice, or perhaps worse, that the ritual was intended to help me somehow. Or maybe it was for Randy; he was Catholic after all . . . perhaps there was some rule. My mom elected not to join us for the small funeral, a choice that revealed the sharp edges of her own personal grief over the loss. I sat and stared silently at the miniature coffin, numb from the extra doses of oxycodone I'd had to take in preparation, just to tolerate the road. I looked at our priest, the only other person invited to be present besides Randy, and understood he expected some outward manifestation of sorrow. I suppose mothers did cry at burials. From the front of the small chapel, he contorted his face into a comforting worried expression, enticing emotion. There was nowhere to hide from his gaze, so I met it. I looked back from the pew and thought, *Well, I'm not technically a mother, am I? So who are you to tell me how to feel?* I bit my cheek and dug my fingernails into my palms for the duration of the service, like a petulant child in a contest of will.

Acknowledging the loss in that formal, ritualized way hurt far worse than I had expected it to. And I conceded that perhaps that had been the point of it all.

We were handed a box of prayer cards at the end of the service. They had a pastel-colored angel on the front, with her name and a prayer on the reverse side. I walked out of the small chapel trying to recall if we had selected a grave marker, though the answer was irrelevant. I knew I wouldn't be coming to look for her.

On the ride home, I was angry at Randy for not memorizing the topography of the route. I couldn't comprehend how he could forget something as important as the location of the potholes. The stabbing pain caused by every bump in the road was a quick remedy for any delusion I had concocted of getting out more often. I wondered if maybe it would have been easier for everyone if I had died, if they didn't have to be bothered with me.

In a transparent effort to brighten my mood, Randy drove me one day to see the new house he had bought for us. It was only a few miles from my mom. We'd been considering moving when we found out I was pregnant. We wanted to be closer to her, as she would help us to raise the baby. Instead, in a dark twist of fate, we were moving closer so she could continue to care for me, an adult invalid. I remembered we had looked at a number of houses, though my memories of them were more like dreams now. I thought I recalled while still in the ICU signing power of attorney papers so that we could close on a house. As an attorney, Randy knew that drugged on narcotics post-op, I was not in any state to sign my legal rights away. I stared at him, suddenly doubting his intention.

"Did you have me sign something, when I was drugged?" I asked, sounding more accusatory than I had intended.

"You had just lost the baby, and I couldn't stand the idea that you might lose this house, too, so yes. Even though you weren't in the best shape, I had you sign papers so that we could buy it. We can rip them up now; you don't have to worry."

I allowed that maybe he wasn't a complete sociopath who was trying to take advantage of me. Maybe.

He expanded upon his explanation with some commentary on the "time-sensitive" nature of the real estate market. "If we didn't act, we would have missed the chance," he explained. Wasn't that basically true of everything in life, I wondered? My mind spun in a loop, trying to come up with a single example of something that wasn't time-sensitive. Relationships were time-sensitive, certainly. If you met the right person at the wrong time, it would fail by virtue of timing. Treatment for a disease, however effective if correctly timed, could come too late to help. Children were exquisitely time-sensitive.

"So, which house did we end up buying?" I asked, eager to abandon my existential thought-experiment.

"We got the one that you really loved." He beamed with pride.

"Oh, wow. Great." I forced enthusiasm. I had absolutely no idea which house he was talking about.

We pulled up to the front, and I stared at it. I was afraid to ask questions, knowing I might disclose my total lack of attachment to this particular house.

"It's pretty," I admitted. It was a light gray, with white trim, and a black door. There were two white birch trees in the front yard and neatly trimmed hedgerows of English yews and dwarf boxwoods leading to the front door. The boxwoods wouldn't survive the polar vortex, but the heartier yews did.

"Do you want to go inside? I have the keys," he said proudly as he held them up.

"No." I knew immediately looking at the slope of the driveway and grade of the front walkway that it would be impossible for me to make it to the door.

"Was there another one that I liked too?" I asked, as a memory of a façade of a house different than the one before me entered my mind. I immediately wished I hadn't asked, remembering that he thought he had saved me from a second great loss.

"Yes, the one in the subdivision next door. We were down to those two and this was your favorite," he declared confidently.

I had a distinct feeling he'd bought the wrong house, but would never tell him that. And it was an easy secret to keep, since I didn't really trust my own memory.

"Thank you, for doing all of this," I said instead. And with that he launched into a tirade of how difficult the bank had been, requiring one document after another, and how he had taken his frustration with my illness out on the loan officer one day, declaring he wouldn't provide a single other piece of documentation. He told them they could either give us the house or not, based on what they already had, but he was through faxing documents for their review.

I watched his animated rant from the passenger seat impassively. *What an odd thing to be so upset about,* I thought.

Years later, we casually drove past the other house, each declaring, "I'm so glad we didn't buy that house," though for different reasons. He disliked the lot size and choice of flooring. I simply couldn't picture our lives taking place in that other house after years of living in what proved to so clearly be the right one.

It was there in that gray house that I would definitively and truly heal after the initial weeks spent in my childhood home. The gray house would itself becoming an agent of my healing. It transformed graciously alongside me for years, finding ways to supply what I needed. When I found refuge in painting, Randy constructed an art room in our basement. The wood-hued floors were enlivened by paint splatter, and the large apron sink happily accommodated all manner of mess. When I couldn't sleep I painted what haunted me, and making the suffering visible defused it somehow. When I found writing allowed me to externalize my pain, we designed a welcoming study, with ironic stuffed animal taxidermy and overlapping Persian rugs to retain warmth. It was there that I would spend hours transforming illness into relic, in effect separating it from my lived life. *This thing happened at this time, and this is what it felt like; now it's over, and here, you can hold it. We can both look at it together.* The brightly lit sunroom served as a reminder of the gift and magic of each morning, so we covered the walls in a whimsical toile wallpaper that upon close inspection revealed gnomes napping within topiaries. It was the house we brought our son home to, just before Christmas. The tree in the living room cheery with ornaments, all surrounding a small stuffed Santa at the center.

Some days, if I slept well and timed my medication throughout the night so that I didn't wake in pain, I had ambitions. Grand plans to accomplish something that felt out of reach the day before. One morning in mid-August, I sat on my childhood front porch contemplating the mailbox. It was the kind of summer day that was hot almost before the sun had come up. The kind that made the skin of your thighs stick to the chair and warm puddles of sweat seep from invisible pores behind your knees. The sensory deprivation—a result of being confined to a sick bed in a single room for so long—made the green of the leaves garish. The sun, climbing over the trees in the east, brandished an impossible brightness. I was determined to walk all the way to the mailbox.

The flatness of the concrete camouflaged a near minefield of divots and ridges. I steadied myself. Walking outside required intense concentration. First, it necessitated overriding a dysfunctional message from my central nervous system that lied about my body's actual position in space. If I accepted the message as truth, I would veer to the left. I had still been walking into a fair number of walls. *You are not falling to the right so you don't have to overcorrect to the left,* I consciously reminded myself, attempting to short-circuit the involuntary data feed. *You are centered, walk straight.*

My first few steps were solid, but then a bird darted into my field of vision and I stumbled backward. Its erratic flight made reassuring my brain that I was stationary impossible, as my mind irrationally tried to tether my position in space to that of the bird. Like sitting in a parking lot, and suddenly having the sensation of movement because the car next to you has reversed. I had to reconcile my position with the movement of everything around me.

Deep breath, take two. I spread my arms into a T, as some childhood memory of negotiating balance beams surfaced. I fixed my gaze on the mailbox and sent my left leg forward. After three or four steps I had some forward momentum, and could almost reimagine walking as the involuntary act it had once been. That thought, of all of my past abilities I had taken for granted, made me almost unbearably sad. But I couldn't afford to have tears obscuring my vision. I shook off the thought and marched ahead, determined to get the mail. Halfway down the driveway, I had to shift attention to my breathing. The pocket of fluid had taken up permanent residence in the space my right lung had been accustomed to expanding into. My breathing rate quickened to make up for the shallow depth of each inhalation. The heat in the air made it difficult to draw in my breath. The air felt stagnant, as if it carried no fresh oxygen at all. My heart raced with the effort, and I lowered my arms, unable to hold them up for balance as I had hoped. It was too much effort to bear their weight against gravity. I paused to recover.

Take three. Slower this time, as my thigh muscles were starting to tremble, suggesting they were willing to buckle my knees if I didn't acknowledge their fatigue. A few more steps and I could hold onto the mailbox and rest. A passing neighbor waved, and I was forced to mentally acknowledge I probably had an audience for this pathetic show. I cringed, which when combined with my squinting eyes, I hoped could be construed as a smile. A few more steps. I shuffled and dragged my feet when necessary. Once in arm's reach of the mailbox, I looked back toward the house. I hadn't accounted for the walk back in my risk calculation. I decided to wait.

I took out the mail and sat at the base of the mailbox. The mail was secondary to the primary act of walking, but I sorted through the cards and catalogs and came across a hospital bill. A warm flush spread up my face as I opened it, and a pressure silenced my hearing as if I were ascending in flight. It was a bill for the attempted resuscitation of the baby. I stared at it and shoved it back in the envelope. I contemplated crawling back to the house but, remembering I had neighbors, stood and deliberately and slowly retraced each step.

I was met in the kitchen with congratulatory hugs, and was told, "I bet that felt amazing."

I set the mail on the table, and replied haltingly, "You know, walking is hard." Then added, "For me."

Randy took on the task of reconciling the bill with the lack of a baby. The billing department explained that the bill was generated when we had failed to enroll her in our insurance plan. No one could explain at what exact juncture we should have called our insurance company, seeing as how she'd never technically been alive. The bill was appallingly timed, arriving coincidentally on the baby's due date, an event horizon I was trying hard not to note existed, there being no baby to expect. It took four phone calls to settle the charges. A trivial oversight, by a department ostensibly not involved in patient care, had the potential to bring me to my knees.

The bill felt like a dispatch from a parallel universe. Reminding me of that due date, the possibilities. It was so close, that life with us in the new house I'd yet to live in, with the neatly trimmed hedges and the baby. It was happening in some ghost universe, one where I wasn't in pain. There, the rocker would be used to nurse the baby during quiet nights, not to keep me from drowning. And though the bill reminded me I couldn't be part of it, it seemed also to notify me that I was close enough to it that I could watch it unfold. I could almost wave at it from where I stood.

I learned that everyone had expectations for the trajectory of my recovery. Work colleagues, family and doctors all seemed to share a conviction that I should be improving noticeably every day. Their projections were based mostly on nothing, just vague notions that they thought I'd "be better by now." I didn't know how to try harder to recover. I felt trapped in a body that was traumatized and broken. It seemed better suited to fracture than to bend. The large hematoma, too dangerous to drain, insisted on being very slowly reabsorbed by my body, over a period of twelve months. The pain lasted longer than that, but my willingness to medicate the pain with the mind-dulling narcotics I'd been prescribed wouldn't last the summer.

The plan had been to wean me off the narcotics slowly. I was given a schedule, with written instructions on how to come off of them safely. I would cut back on the dose in small increments, allowing the opiate receptors in my brain to acclimate to the absence of drug. I would take a reduced dose of long-acting morphine in the morning and attempt to push through to evening, sometimes skipping the midday dose. That the root cause of the pain, the balloon of blood compressing my organs, hadn't changed was an inconvenient truth. I wanted off. Pain relief required sacrificing clarity of thought, alertness and energy. And though I never achieved a state of being pain-free, my eyes were always heavy-lidded and my thoughts slow. There were whispers of judgments, fears of attendant addiction. My days had devolved into a dull monotony of pain, pill, sleep, wake, pain, pill, sleep. I was praying for a doorway back into the life I wanted.

Egress came in the form of a side effect. I had taken my evening dose of oxycodone and closed my eyes. I felt an immediate sinking sensation, as if falling through a dream. I felt certain I would die. I opened my eyes and turned on the bedside lamp. I could plainly see I was fine. I was in my bedroom, there was a glass of water on the bedside table, with my glasses and pill bottles. I reread the label and double-checked the dosage. It was a quarter of what I had been taking, and while maybe it bordered on insufficient, it was by no means dangerous. I chalked it up to being overly tired and resolved to sleep. I closed my eyes again, this time leaving the light on in childish deference to the power of light over unknowable monsters.

An immediate, crushing sense of doom flooded in. I knew if I slept I would die. It was as if my body, on a cellular level, had some awareness of a threat I couldn't appreciate. I resolved to stay awake until morning and sort it out in the light of day.

I was not aware of this dysphoric reaction to opiates, though it had been described in the medical literature. It seems the body is wired not only to control subconscious processes like breathing and heart rate, but also to receptively interpret them. The opiates slowed my breathing and heart rate just enough that my body's monitoring sensors became wary. The data were interpreted to mean that soon I might not breathe at all and that my heart could stop. A panic order was issued, which basically stated, "ALERT. Impending doom, details not otherwise specified." And so it went. My only recourse, then, was to stop the medications.

So that's what I did. Propelling me swiftly into withdrawal.

I didn't recognize it as withdrawal; rather, I believed I had contracted some virulent strain of the flu. It was only in retrospect days later that I could align the timeline to my symptoms and understand.

After seventy-two hours without medication, I began shaking with chills, and my muscles ached with a bone-deep soreness. My stomach churned and excreted an acidic taste that I knew heralded vomiting. I headed for the bathroom. My skin was covered in goose bumps. As I leaned over the toilet, rivulets of sweat poured off me. I gagged and coughed with pain as my stomach involuntarily contracted, expelling its contents in spasms of bile and blood. My heart raced. When I could stand, I patted down my face with cold washcloths. I crawled to the couch and positioned a bucket near my head.

Though I had no psychological dependence on the medications, my body had become habituated to them. I had become physiologically dependent. I realized this with a start two days into the "flu." I walked to the medicine cabinet and took out the oxycodone prescription. I held the amber bottle as if it were precious, knowing that I could put a stop to the cold sweats, the pain, the nausea, the shaking chills. The pills rattled against each other like Tic Tacs. I set the bottle down and stared at it. I studied the label, looking for some acknowledgment of corruption. I knew I never wanted to feel this sick again. I estimated that I was probably through the worst of it, and worried that by satiating the need, I would only restart the clock. If my answer in this moment was more medication, another bout of acute withdrawal would always be in my future. I set the small bottle back on the shelf, warily.

The bottle took on a magnetism far greater than its actual physical size should have allowed. It was the center, and I was in orbit around it. I knew how far away from the bottle I was at any given time. And if I dared to venture out, I felt the tug of its tether. *Are you sure you can get by without anything?* it taunted me. *Why don't you put me in your pocket just in case things get really bad?* it suggested. *You don't have to suffer like this,* it re-minded me. Each minute I had to reassert, *No, I don't want to take anything.* The next minute: *Still no, I won't. You might as well stop because I won't listen. You won't win.*

The power of those miniature, compressed disks of white powder shouldn't have shocked me. I had seen addiction ravage the lives of people far stronger than me. What shocked me was that the narrative of dependency could nearly supersede my agency. I did not want to take anything. The drugs made me miserable. But somewhere deep in my brain, the chemical had formed bonds, attaching to a group of neurons, triggering an in-tense reward sensation that demanded to be fulfilled, again and again. Those cells dominated all the others and brazenly wrote the script of my thoughts. To interject an opposing thought was nearly impossible amid the constant single-minded chatter. "Just take one. You're supposed to take them." They would say anything.

I had had enough. I took the bottle out of the cabinet, heart racing. I opened it and looked inside, half expecting the pills to talk to me. I poured them into my cupped hand, appreciating the dissonance between their physical weight and their gravity. I walked to the bathroom, tipped my hand and let them cascade into the toilet. I felt their torment over not being able to control me as I flushed them away. And then they were quiet. Proximity proved necessary for them to have any influence over me. Would that everyone could be that lucky.

After a week or two, I got used to the constant droning hum of discomfort. It became the background noise of my day, rarely loud enough to drown out my thoughts, mostly a distraction. I learned I could find strength in the pain, or push it aside and shun it. I could ignore it or I could focus on it entirely, until I bored of it.

I found that the pain was one thing to contend with, but totally separate from it and equally important was the message I told myself about what the pain itself meant. My experience of the pain depended upon what I agreed to attend to. If a sharp stab came on suddenly, and I felt fearful that it indicated some impending disaster, I became overwhelmed with anxiety, my breath would quicken and, as if on cue, the pain would accentuate and take on a significance and urgency. It could take hours to exit that loop. If I instead reframed the sensation as just another aspect of my healing, and messaged myself that breathing through the feeling was necessary for my recovery, it would pass meekly, robbed of its power.

I learned to look at the pain, rather than hide from it. When I refused to look at it honestly, it grew like a shadow in a childhood bedroom. My pain seemed able to sense fear; fear was the fuel it burned in order to run through me. To disarm it, to look at the pain honestly, took time. I had to learn to inhabit my body. It's a difficult thing to sit with pain and just be. To sit beside it, acknowledge it and be whole in its presence. To experience pain in that way, I had to constantly remind myself that it wasn't *me*. It was just a sensation. I was bigger than the pain and I could withstand it, it wouldn't kill me. I would survive it. I was stronger than the pain. I saw that I had the power to either create closed circuits of panic or build myself exit ramps. I found a way to be safe in my own body.

I learned that what was true of pain was true of most feelings. I didn't have to just submit to them, I was actually central to their construction. I could build a story of sadness and read it to myself, or I could choose not to. I could choose to honestly examine whether I was using the loss as a tether for feelings I didn't know how to part with. I could redefine my identity and claim my desired emotional state. I could choose not to feel guilty for not feeling everything all at once, at the precise moment it was expected of me, because the feelings would continue to come, for years. And with each go-round I better understood how we could peacefully coexist.

I began to feel grateful for each small success. So it seemed right and good that my first elective excursion out should be to church. Whatever had saved me—modern medicine, luck or prayer—deserved to be honored. I would kneel in supplication at an altar and praise everyone and everything who theoretically could have been involved.

I worried I wouldn't be able to stand for the duration of Mass, but everyone reassured me that there were plenty of frail, elderly members of the congregation who sat throughout. I should feel right at home among them, I was told. Which was a perfect comfort, except that I was thirty-three years old.

It still was an incredible, time-consuming labor just to shower and dress, so we arrived late, after Mass had started. We snuck up the side aisle, slowly, attempting not to draw attention, which was an exercise in futility. Everyone had seen us, except for the priest, who still had his back to the congregation. As we took our seats in the pew, I felt stares of gratitude and overheard whispers of wonder. My name had been read on the prayer list for

months, and many of those present had actively prayed for my
well-being.

I hadn't been around that many people at once for months,
and the sensory stimulation was overwhelming. There was so
much to take in. I allowed myself the distraction of focusing
on the beauty of the space. The church was designed to invoke
memories of home for immigrants from many different coun-
tries, so there was a beautiful copper dome, a colorful fresco and
glass windows etched with Roman crosses. It smelled of incense
and candles. A large baptismal fountain, where we would one
day baptize our son, occupied one side of the transept. I felt
humbled and very small in the cavernous space, precisely how
the architects had intended.

Distracted, I missed a cue entirely, and remained standing as
everyone else sat. It was only a moment, but it was long enough
to catch the priest's eye. The same priest whose voice in prayer
woke me that very first day, the same priest who had presided
over the baby's burial, now met my gaze.

"Oh, ladies and gentleman, we have a very special person here
with us today." He went entirely off script. It was a shout-out. I
attempted to shrink into the pew.

"We have someone with us today who walked on water." And
with that declaration, hundreds of heads turned my way.

I looked to Randy, who had the benefit of a Catholic school
education, and whispered, "So, this is embarrassing, and perhaps
not ideal timing to tell you this, but I don't really know the
Bible very well. What does that mean when he says I walked on
water?"

"It's a good thing," he whispered. "Just smile."

"You don't know either, do you?" I taunted him, through my
smile.

". . . like Jesus," the priest added solemnly.

Oh God, he said I'm like Jesus. This was a bad idea. I can't possibly live up to that, I thought silently, as every unkind action or thought I'd ever conceived raced through my head.

"Jesus walked on water," Randy informed me.

"I really think you are piecing this together as you go," I laughed.

"And it was a miracle," he added. "He is saying you are a miracle."

"Right. No pressure there."

Everyone stood and applauded. I smiled and tried to fix my face into an expression of humble gratitude.

After the service, a few friends and relatives came over to congratulate us on my recovery. Our church seemed to be carrying an undue burden of very young people who were very sick that year. We commiserated with friends and the spouses of friends who were there praying for their own miracle. My cousin's wife had been stuck in that terrible non-space of permanent critical illness after delivering her baby. An infection had spread throughout her body and ravaged her heart. She'd die in April of the following year, at thirty-six years old. But at that time there was still hope she could recover. Between catching up on her antibiotic treatment and the chemotherapy regimens of others, I began to sense that I represented something to them. It meant something to them that I had survived. My recovery had empowered their hope with a bright flame of tangible success.

I had a complicated relationship with hope that was powered by religion. Though I had no idea what precise combination of factors had allowed for me to survive the unsurvivable, I weighted science, medical care and surgical skill heavily in my calculation. How luck, religion or God factored in, I couldn't say. I had always had a cynic's distrust of miracles. As a scientist I felt there was a more rational explanation, and that tended to be the one I favored. The intangible presence that I sensed around the edges of my story, that seemed to guide us such that the right thing happened at the right time—well, I was happy to call that luck. I found it difficult to integrate into my sense of self that I represented the power of prayer and hope in the face of futility.

I wasn't always that way. I had been beaten down by the idea, often evoked by families of patients in the ICU, that a miracle would save them. I had seen that belief of an attendant miracle used as a reason to consent to procedures and interventions that could only prolong suffering, could only prolong the inevitability of death. In the context of medical decision making, declaring a belief in a divine intervention is viewed as an expression of unfettered optimism, where doctors wish only for acceptance of the situation at hand. We worry that such hopes are a manifestation of denial or even expressions of disappointment in the limits of medical care.

In medicine, we are ill-equipped to continue to plan when someone tells us, "We're praying for a miracle." We feel utterly helpless. Our rational, cognitive brains tell us there is no use in any further discussion. What use is logic, science or facts if we were going to invoke the supernatural?

If they only understood how hopeless the situation was, we think, they could better prepare, plan, cope. They need to know that it's hopeless. We idiotically tell them again and again that it's hopeless, thinking if we can just "get through to them" they will acquiesce and allow their loved one to die.

Sitting there I began to see it differently. I heard them. They were praying for a miracle not because they didn't understand how sick their spouses were, but rather precisely because they did know how sick they were. Hope was not, as I had believed, an unrealistic, unfettered optimistic emotion. Hope was an orientation, a way of being in the face of a reality that was not of their choosing. Hope was a destination they had arrived at when the situation had been wrestled to the ground and stared at, bravely. Just like the wooden icons painted with the visages of saints they would place at the bedside of their loved ones, hope represented an acknowledgment of the limitations of the reality they found themselves in. It was an invocation. Hope gave them resiliency, a reason to go on, a belief that there could be a future.

Why would I ever begrudge someone hope?

What if hope was the way to face and plan for an admittedly uncertain future?

I rejoined the conversation between my husband and one of his childhood friends whose husband was battling leukemia. I listened as she described the last round of treatment and the terrible toll it had taken on her husband. I listened as she outlined her hopes for the next cycle. I found myself saying, "I really share your hope that he will be cured."

"Thank you."

"I know this is so hard, but I wonder if you have been able to give yourself space to consider what you guys might do if it doesn't work?"

"We've started to talk about maybe enrolling in hospice after this next round. It's just so hard to give up hope, with the kids and everything. But I see how weak he is getting, and I just don't think he can handle much more."

"I think it's really brave that you are letting him talk about possibly dying," I said to her with a genuine gratitude. "No one ever lets anyone talk about death, you know? Even when it's so close you can almost touch it."

Randy shot me a look that said, *I'm not going to take you out of the house ever again if you insist on continuing down this morbid rabbit hole.* He added a not-so-subtle eyebrow lift and head-tilt combination that suggested I might be making her uncomfortable. I shrugged.

In the car on the way home I asked, "Do you think it's a miracle I survived?"

"Yes, I do. You are my miracle," he said without a hint of irony.

"Well, I think if I still do die, which I think I will, you guys should get married." I hadn't realized until the words came out that I still believed I would die.

"Have you lost your mind?" he looked at me sideways. "I really hope this is some weird way of you trying to control a future that feels uncertain, but I certainly do not need you picking out my next wife."

"If I die, you will get married again," I informed him.

"No, I won't," he countered.

"Of course you will!" I argued.

"I don't even understand why we are discussing this. I feel like I just barely got you back. Why are we talking about me losing you again?" He sounded angry but looked ready to cry.

"If I could live another year or two, I think that would be really amazing."

"You are going to live more than a year or two! Why are you saying that?"

I took a breath and answered, honestly, "I don't know, something just tells me I am still going to die."

"Well tell it to stop," he demanded.

"I don't know if I can. It feels real. I'm sorry."

Somewhere inside me, the next catastrophe lurked. And I sensed it. The subtle signals, the imbalance. When I sat quietly and fully inhabited the space of my body, it told me things. I didn't know yet that I could trust those messages enough to act upon them, but I was at least beginning to be able to listen to them and bow at their altar.

. . .

Then, like a sudden rain during a summer storm, my hair fell out, all at once. I was attempting to pull it into a ponytail, and with each attempt to gather it, I had more detached from my scalp and in my hands than was held in the elastic. I stared at myself in the mirror, wondering what this new loss meant. Maybe my body was just diverting energy to more essential processes than hair? I knew that regenerating liver cells as well as healing from the surgery were highly anabolic activities. Maybe I wasn't getting enough calories to do all of that and grow hair? I tried hard not to panic. I'd learn later that this unexpected molting, months removed from the initial insult, was not uncommon. Trauma sometimes "shocks" hair follicles into a dormant state. The follicles would awaken eventually, but for the time being, I looked far sicker than I had when I was truly sick.

Hair ranked low on the list of "Body Parts I Value" when framed against my actual organ failures. I cared far less about my hair than I did about, say, my kidneys or lungs. That didn't mean I didn't call my best friends and cry, asking them to find a wig shop to take me to. I did that, but it wasn't sustainable. Ultimately, I found it difficult to care enough about my lack of hair to do anything about it. I had the fine wisps that remained cut very short and wore a wide headband to hold back the new sprouts as they eventually tried to break through. As ridiculous as I looked, the pity directed at me felt disproportionate to the loss. I became impatient with expressions meant to convey empathy: "Oh, no! You poor thing. You're losing all of your hair."

"It's just hair. I don't understand what the fuss is all about. It doesn't even do anything useful. I can live perfectly well without it," I'd reply.

The trouble with outward manifestations of illness is that they are provocative. People interpreted my lack of hair as an invitation to discuss my relative health in a way that they weren't empowered to when there was no visible indicator of illness. Everyone seemed concerned, and genuinely horrified for me, to have to exist in the world while looking so terrible. Home remedies and supplements were offered as matters of extreme urgency. I was given holy water and biotin capsules by relative strangers. Vitamin packets were pressed into my palms, like communion wafers. *Take this, it will save you.*

When my intestines began protruding through my abdominal layers in fist-sized punches like some grotesque alien baby, I learned I still had some measure of vanity. I met with my surgeon, Dr. G.

"It's a hernia. Actually I can feel more than one defect. Make that hernias, plural." He sighed. "If it doesn't bother you, we should just leave it alone. It's got a broad enough base, I don't think your intestines will get trapped in there," he continued.

"I'm completely deformed and it's disgusting. We have to fix it," I countered.

He was not at all surprised that this had happened. With how severe my illness was, and how little nutritional intake I had for so long, my tissues were just weak. "You know, no one thought you'd survive the operating room that night. I was there when they were closing you and they really just thought they were closing you for an autopsy. They did a whip stitch," he explained, referring to a type of suture that is quick but not intended for healing.

I winced. I'd been in operating rooms like that. I'd witnessed that tipping point, that same silent declaration that the patient wouldn't survive. I'd seen it used as a necessary time-saving mechanism. Situations when you just had to get out of the OR, get the patient to the ICU so you could better stabilize them and bring them back. Either way, meticulous, time-consuming stitches are abandoned in favor of a rapid continuous loop. Tissues aren't approximated carefully, there is little thought of whether the tight ties will strangulate blood flow to the area. You are just closing the patient so they appear closed. For the autopsy, for the next hour of Hail Mary resuscitation efforts, for the funeral, but not for the future. You never imagine sitting across from them in a routine clinic encounter as they complain about ugly but innocuous hernias. Taking the time to close my fascia, the tough but thin covering keeping my organs in place, was not a priority.

"Listen, all I'm saying is let's wait for you to get better. See if things get worse before we try to fix anything. Of course I'll fix it. I'd just rather do it once." He smiled.

I understood clearly he shared my intuition that my body wasn't yet done unraveling. When it did, he'd put me back together again.

He called me at home, a year later, to tell me, "I just reviewed your repeat CT scan. Listen, there are two masses in your liver. We couldn't see them before because of the distortion from the hematoma. But now that it's shrunk . . . well, it looks like one is what ruptured on us last time, but there is another. You need to come downtown right now."

But before that happened, I had returned to medicine.

Six

Shifting Frames

It was autumn by the time I was declared able to work again. Although the accuracy of my own assessment that I was "able to work" is probably debatable. More truthful to say I had simply tired of being my only patient, obsessively tracking lab values and medication regimens. I convinced my doctors that I needed to go back to the hospital if I was to remain sane. I wasn't yet able to drive and was chauffeured by friends, who also lacked the ability to visually map the location of all the potholes in the city. I couldn't imagine the privilege of being so pain-free that I could drive over bumps with impunity. When I first went back, I had very little actual responsibility, which was appropriate. I was at work, maybe to attend a meeting or listen to a presentation, but that was really the extent of my day. It would be two more months before I had the physical endurance and mental stamina to round in the ICU again.

I had gotten sick when I was still a fellow. I had completed the requirements of the three-year training program and had stupidly stockpiled my vacation so that I could study for my upcoming medical board examination before the baby came. The months I spent recovering between spring and the fall were spent very differently than I had planned. But still, I returned to work as an attending physician. That day marked the first time I would be fully responsible for anyone's care. As I stood outside the automatic doors of the ICU and centered myself, I was acutely aware that this moment represented the culmination of all of a lifetime's efforts toward this goal.

The timing of my illness had already superimposed its own narrative on this second chance to fulfill my purpose. I had often wondered what it meant that I had spent so much time preparing to be a physician, only to have the opportunity to apply it nearly extinguished. I struggled to make sense of a trajectory toward nothing. Training that demanded I lock myself away, abdicate all fun and miss family events all in the name of the pursuit of medical knowledge, only to have the path stop dead. The possibility that my formal education had not been as complete as I had believed it to be occurred to me. It was not lost on me that my true education had begun the moment I had gotten sick, and it would likely continue for years to come. Standing outside the unit, I silently hoped for the strength and clarity of thought to unite my experiences as a patient and a physician into a cohesive whole, in a way that would honor all that I had been through.

As the automatic doors swung open to the unit I'd been assigned, I saw the team, dutifully arranged and ready for morning rounds. I took my place before the team, in front of the first patient's room. I introduced myself to the members of the team that appeared to be new faces. I couldn't tell if I was imagining it, but I felt they might be diverting their gazes. Or they seemed willing to meet mine only very briefly. As a group they seemed uncomfortable, staring at their papers or shoes as I tried and failed to put them at ease. I scolded myself; surely I was just being overly sensitive as a new attending. I knew I looked healthy and put together. I'd spent an inordinate amount of time considering how I wanted to dress that first day. I had chosen a navy blazer with bracelet-length sleeves paired with charcoal pants and a flat practical shoe. I didn't quite feel able to wear the white coat yet. The longer I stood there, the more I knew I wasn't imagining it, they were truly behaving strangely. I constructed a series of possible narratives that could potentially explain their behavior. Perhaps they had heard I had been very sick and they weren't sure whether to acknowledge it. Maybe they were concerned I hadn't retained enough of my medical knowledge to be a truly good clinician. Maybe they were just worried I wouldn't be able to make it through rounds. I settled on the belief that they felt unsure about whether to acknowledge my illness. That, I decided, was probably all that I was sensing.

Introductions over, the resident began presenting his first patient. "The patient in C521 is a thirty-four-year-old woman, postpartum day seven, transferred from an outside hospital with liver failure and a presumed diagnosis of HELLP syndrome." He paused to swallow loudly. He raised his eyes from his paper and quickly scanned my face for evidence that he should continue. I have no idea what expression met him. I was completely stranded in a fog of his words. Did I appear disoriented and lost? Or did I present a picture of stoic shock? I felt incredulous; it hardly seemed statistically possible that this could happen on my first day back. That the first patient I would be charged with caring for was in essence a static replica of me from six months prior.

I studied her through the window to the room as he went on describing her liver failure, kidney failure and her attendant issues with blood clotting. Her skin was discolored by a yellowish tint, and she was terribly bloated from the resuscitation efforts at the outside facility. She was connected by a tube to the ventilator, which steadfastly delivered her breath even though she appeared to be cringing against it. Her soft brown hair was gathered in a loose bun on top of her head. Her mother was at her bedside, straightening the collar of her blue hospital gown and patting her bruised and swollen hand.

I looked back at the resident as he reported a torrent of lab values, imaging studies and eventually his assessment and plan. It seemed to me there was something missing in his very comprehensive presentation. Something about it wasn't sitting right with me, though it was difficult to pin down precisely what it was.

I began asking questions, trying to identify the gap. "So, how long after she delivered the baby did she begin to deteriorate?"

"That same day, the afternoon of the birth, she had worsening mental status, but as I mentioned, the signs really began prior to delivery, with her lab derangements," he answered dutifully.

This was a woman who had one single day with her baby and now was perilously close to death, her body cascading before us in an ever-deepening downward spiral, with her mother holding vigil at her bedside, her husband and father in the waiting room. What was missing, I realized, in his reporting of her case, seemed to be any acknowledgment of the absolute shattering horror of this particular sequence of events. They didn't see her as a person. She was a case to them.

I stared at the team. There were five residents, a medical student and a critical care fellow. They, like most of our trainees, had chosen to travel long distances from disparate locations to avail themselves of an "interesting case mix," as it was portrayed in our residency brochures and website. An inner-city hospital with advanced subspecialty services that took care of the sickest of the sick. They wanted to see as much as they could of every type of disease, to soak in the exposure like vacationers in the sun, before launching into practice.

I looked again at the patient, then back at the team.

"What did she name the baby?" I asked them.

They stared at me blankly.

"It seems like something we should know, doesn't it?" I asked curtly. The team looked decidedly uncomfortable now, unsure of what to expect next. I wanted them to see her as the mother of a baby whose name they knew.

"The baby's name is Charlotte," her nurse answered.

"Thank you." I paused.

"So, what else do we need to include in the differential for elevated liver enzymes in a patient who is immediately post-partum?" I asked the resident.

He answered, impassively, reciting a list memorized from years of study.

I continued, with a steely conviction, to drill him with questions. I challenged him to broaden differential for her fulminant liver failure. I redirected his choice of antibiotics, challenged his interpretation of the lab data. I was determined to care for her perfectly, as utterly impossible as that may be. The team rallied in response to my questioning, this being familiar ground to them. They also seemed to let go of their apprehension about how I would handle the coincidence. They seemed to understand that while my illness was similar, I was well in control of my emotions, and could in fact be channeling my experience to elevate her care.

When we were done reviewing her case and formulating a cogent plan, I knocked and entered the room, my team following behind me.

"Hi, I'm Dr. Awdish, and I'll be in charge of your daughter's care while she's here in the ICU," I began.

"Oh, Dr. Awdish, it's so nice to meet you. I heard from a friend of ours who is also a doctor at this hospital that you went through a similar illness, and now you are well! I can't tell you what a comfort that is," she exclaimed.

Her words surprised me. I hadn't thought she might already know. I had been weighing carefully whether to ever share any piece of my experience with her. It wasn't that I needed it to be a secret, it was just that I worried doing so could create an unrealistic expectation of recovery. I was cautiously trying to determine how best to structure the boundary while still offering personal insight and hope. I thought I would learn more about the family, their level of openness and their coping skills before deciding what was best. But then, before I could figure out any of it, the boundary, like a line scratched in the sand, was reclaimed by the shifting tides. Someone had made the choice for me.

Fine, I thought, *time to regroup.* And really, no harm done. I could still navigate this. I just needed to manage expectations while finding ways to thoughtfully insert relevant experiences and simultaneously be a beacon of hope. I could do this.

Then she looked me in the eye and asked with genuine curiosity, "So how old is your baby now?"

I heard a gasp from behind me and remembered I had an audience of trainees and nurses, a pharmacist, and a respiratory therapist. I felt the warm pressure of tears building in my eyes. If someone was going to share my story for me, the least they could have done was share the whole story. My face flushed with irritation and embarrassment.

"Oh, no . . . actually, unfortunately my baby died," I managed, thankful that my back was to the team as I tried to push back my emotions.

"Oh, I am so sorry! I didn't know," she said.

"Of course, no, no, please don't feel sorry. You couldn't have known." I felt worse for her embarrassment than I did for my own. I took a deep breath and on my exhale began again.

"Anyway, let's focus on your daughter. She is who matters now. I want to assure you we are going to take the best possible care of her," I said. That declaration seemed to animate the team, and I observed a pair of them move to her bedside and begin to unceremoniously examine her. One pulled at her eyelids to shine a light at her pupils looking for evidence of swelling in her brain as the other shifted her covers to examine her skin for rashes and pressed the skin of her shins with his thumb to disclose swelling of the tissues. I ran parallel mental tracks; one speaking to her mother, the other lost inside my own head, trying to assure myself that their behavior was acceptable, while feeling distinctly uncomfortable yet unable to articulate why. I couldn't shake the feeling that so much of what we did and how we did it felt like a violation. A violation of her body, of her personal space. All so well intended, but with her unable to participate or grant permission, I felt we were systematically chipping away at her dignity.

We eventually exited her room, ninety minutes after first starting rounds. As we moved on to the second patient, I marveled that I somehow had to find the strength and composure to round on fourteen more critically ill patients.

To say I left rounds that day completely exhausted does not begin to capture the overwhelming, leaden fatigue that draped around my shoulders. My liver felt heavy and pulsatile, my breath felt short, and the pain enacted by speaking so much more than usual was unrelenting. I worried obsessively about my patients; I thought of their families as I drove home, as I showered, as I lay in bed. I sat with my discomfort over the small indignities I had watched inflicted on the patients, and wondered where we had all gone wrong.

I thought about the fourth patient we'd rounded on that long morning, a young man with a habit of injecting heroin who had an unsurprising indolent infection of his heart valve. A by-product of an obviously unsterile technique when he administered the drug. The resident presenting the patient was practically giddy as he described the dark-red, linear streaks in the nail beds of the patient's fingers and toes, known as splinter hemorrhages, and the small densities he could palpate in the pulp of the patient's fingertips known as Osler nodes. His enthusiasm was the result of years of reading and hearing about such findings, only to finally see them manifest in an actual patient.

In medical school we did not study people; rather, we obsessively studied disease states. We memorized their signs and symptoms so that when they appeared in our patients we would recognize them. The disease states were exalted. They represented the mission and the destination. Like explorers, we suffered in pursuit of them, sometimes spending years on their trail. I saw the team now, with their brains laboriously imprinted with sheets upon sheets of the clinical features and laboratory findings of every possible condition, superimpose those sheets like transparencies over their patients, searching for a best fit. Those sheets were the filter through which they viewed the world. The patients were placeholders, positions in space where the diseases would land.

I thought back to all the times on rounds that a patient had been exhibited for the team as a specimen of disease. My mentors would place their stethoscope on the patient, and after locating a characteristic heart murmur, solemnly remove their earbuds and hold the bell of the stethoscope in place on the patient's chest with one hand, urging us to take turns listening with the other. On patients' backs we'd be encouraged to differentiate the sound of fine Velcro-like crackles in fibrotic lungs from the fine wheezes of asthmatic lungs. We stared, curiously examining rashes and skin discoloration with our eyes. We probed and prodded bellies and joints, like scavengers on a hunt. Now I was in charge of a pack of these earnest young physicians and somehow needed to reorient them to the patient beneath all of their entrancing discoveries. I thought of the young OB resident who had asked me to outline for him the still anatomy of my baby's heart on the ultrasound screen. I felt a sense of awakening. Of course that was how he approached the situation; it was all that had ever been modeled for him.

I began to think the timing of my illness was more appropriate than I could have possibly known. As much as I had always believed my training would be completed by some date that could be anticipated on a calendar, I clearly wasn't done. I hadn't seen all that I had needed to see in terms of suffering, identity and illness. It seemed to me a tremendous imbalance, to have spent all of those years focused on acquisition of information without also having cultivated sufficient space for empathy.

I'm sure it seemed to my residents that each time I came to rounds, I brought a new idiosyncratic habit with me. I felt them eye me quizzically as I leaned down to speak into an unconscious patient's ear, "You're doing much better. You have a pneumonia, but the antibiotics are working, and you are getting better."

"I believe he can hear us," I'd explain. "And if it was you, wouldn't you want someone to explain what was happening?"

They would shrug, unable to imagine such a thing.

Another patient, also unable to communicate while attached to the ventilator but more alert, had hands so disfigured by arthritis that she was rendered unable to write even short notes to us. This posed a new challenge. I located her cell phone in her bag of belongings and handed it to her. It was a simple flip phone, unlocked and charged. I programmed my number into her contacts and told her, "You can ask us anything you want."

Her eyes began to tear as she began to type with her thumbs, the only joint not deformed by contractures.

"Can you call my son?" she asked. Then, "What's wrong with me?"

We explained and she listened, inserting questions so fluidly it seemed an ordinary conversation. We called her son.

"That was amazing," the residents exclaimed as we exited the room. I tried to convince them it was anything but amazing. It may have bordered on human, but it was far from amazing.

Sometimes, despite my aggressive scrutiny, or perhaps in spite of it, the team regressed into old behaviors. The lapses that always infuriated me the most were when they spoke about a patient as if the patient couldn't hear what they were saying.

I was observing a resident place a large IV line in a very ill and unconscious pregnant patient, as the fellow instructed him on the technique and steps involved. I was really present to evaluate the fellow's teaching skills as they walked the trainee methodically through, and there he was succeeding. But when they reached a point of comfort with the procedure, where concentration gives way to muscle memory, the conversation devolved and they began to discuss the patient just beneath the sterile gown.

"Do we know who is going to get the baby, when she dies?" the resident asked, with a casualness that suggested he was almost disinterested in the answer.

"*Out!*" I said. They both froze and looked at me, attempting to assess my level of seriousness.

"Stop what you're doing and get out," I instructed the resident. "Your fellow will complete the procedure." They seemed unsure of what to do.

"Now," I added.

I knew from the look on the resident's face as he removed his mask that he was not feeling anything that resembled remorseful accountability. What he was feeling was embarrassed for being called out in front of a peer, and what he was thinking was somewhere between "Oh please," and "OK, she's officially lost it."

We'd reviewed the CT scan of her brain together just hours earlier. The patient had so much swelling, it was unlikely she would survive, much less recall a conversation. I didn't care. I wanted to stop our mindless habit of having casual and thoughtless conversations within earshot of a patient.

While the team was increasingly thoughtful with regard to what they said directly to patients, they lapsed in those times when the involvement of the patient in the conversation was less clear. The conversations that occurred *around* rather than *with* patients; patients who couldn't participate or who had clouded mental acuity due to medication or illness. It was the arrogance in these conversations that galled me, an arrogance amplified by the abject vulnerability of the patient. The conversations presumed the patient's mind was inaccessible or unimportant, and consequently everyone felt they could speak with impunity. In my mind, the carelessness of the resident's conversation revealed what little regard he had for the potential impact of words on the broader context of patient emotion, healing and recovery.

I pulled him aside later, privately, wanting to calmly explain the effect of such a careless statement and to remind him that we must not speak in a way that erodes trust, devalues the patient or delivers news carelessly. We are most at risk of doing this when we do not perceive the patient has an ability to absorb or integrate our words. Those times require intense vigilance to the standards we would adhere to if and when we spoke directly to the patient.

But I didn't have those words then. I didn't know why what I heard him say made me so angry. I only knew that when I was dying, the very last thing I heard was *She's circling the drain here. We're losing her.* And that statement could have been the last thing I ever heard. So I told him that. And I think he understood.

I never ventured very far from being a patient that first year. At most, I'd be back rounding at the hospital for a month or two and something would deteriorate, something would fail and require an intervention. I learned that there is something uniquely awful about being able to anticipate a surgery. Though emergent operations are horrific in their own way, they also eliminate the possibility of maintaining a constant terrorized state of expectancy. With a planned surgery, one has the opportunity to indulge in a protracted state of existential awareness of one's own mortality. "There's a 5 percent chance that in two days I'll die, and a 30 percent chance I'll come out of the surgery with a complication," I'd remind myself.

And so it was with my first scheduled surgery that I behaved in a way I loosely characterize as pathologically controlling. My abdomen, having been so hastily closed that first night, was coming apart. Loops of my intestines were pushing out, and I'd have to knead them back in like balls of dough. I required surgery to place a thin layer of mesh over my intestines to keep them inside. Having a relatively elective surgery meant there was time to do my own research. Not unlike my patients who came in to appointments with printouts of their Google search results, I studied the various types of mesh that could be used to repair my pockmarked abdomen. I found primary sources and cataloged respective rates of infection and incidence of complications.

I filled my surgeon's in-box with just-one-more-quick-question e-mails based on some late-night click on a link. It always seemed to me that the next click might hold the answer I was looking for. I found it difficult to stop.

Dr. G graciously indulged me. After all, I was a colleague, so perhaps I really did want that level of detail. Or maybe he understood that I came by my dysfunction honestly. He had in fact been there with me from the beginning and knew what I had been through. Maybe he believed I was overcompensating for not being able to play a role in my own care that first night. That was actually the explanation I provided him in one of those late-night e-mails, so perhaps he accepted it at face value.

I am not sure I understood what was motivating my behavior. I know I didn't recognize that an emotion was driving my compulsive research. I would not have characterized myself as particularly anxious. In fact, I would have labeled it something else entirely if asked. I was advocating for myself. I was educating myself. I was taking an active role in my care. In retrospect, I can recognize that I was also completely terrified and, not knowing how to quiet my fear, took the only option I thought available to me: to attempt to bludgeon the feeling into submission with data. The problem with responding to emotion with data is that emotion doesn't recognize it. Ironically, I was making the same mistake with myself that physicians make with their patients. I was not naming or tending to my own emotion.

One of the complications I feared the most was what is called an entero-cutaneous fistula. In this nightmare, a loop of my intestine would attach itself to my abdominal wall, and a connection would form between my intestines and the skin. As a result, the contents of my intestines would leak through. There would be a bag to attach to catch the stool as it spilled out. The risk of this happening in my particular case was cited as between

5 and 10 percent. The surgical approach, type of mesh used and a host of other factors all had an impact on increasing or decreasing the possibility of this happening. I wanted to take advantage of every possible opportunity to mitigate the risk. My questions to the surgeon suggested as much.

"Have you decided which mesh you are planning on using? The synthetic seemed to have advantages over the bio-prosthetic, when I was reading, but I know you mentioned you thought bio-prosthetic would be your preference and I don't think I understand why."

He answered patiently, and our conversation looped into discussions of tensile strength and strain, risk of infection and the latest expert consensus from the Hernia Society meetings. They were perfect answers, well thought-out and honest. And yet I still felt terrified.

As physicians, we often don't recognize emotion. And if we don't recognize it, we certainly can't respond to it. We hear our patients ask questions and we believe they want data, facts and explanations. So we dutifully provide them, as we were trained to do. Then we listen as our patient again asks a permutation of the same question, and we wonder if we perhaps weren't clear. It is difficult medical content, after all. Perhaps we'd slipped and used some jargon. So we explain it again. We are trained to do this from the very first day of medical school. Learn the answers, regurgitate when asked. We commit them to memory and feel it is a mark of success when we can provide the correct answer. Being the person who can provide accurate information at the necessary time is a very gratifying and enviable position for us.

Did I actually want to know the relative tensile strength of varying types of mesh? No, I didn't. Did I on some level believe that I needed that information in order to make decisions about my surgery? Yes. On some level I believed that I did. But it was never going to work. I was scared. I knew my surgeon had thoughtfully considered each and every option and had chosen a plan that took so many different variables into account that I wasn't even capable of enumerating what they all were. He is brilliant and trustworthy and thoughtful. But fear doesn't respond to data.

Emotion shuts down the rational, cognitive portion of our brains. Anyone who has attempted to reason with an angry spouse or use logic to get a toddler over a tantrum understands this on a visceral level. Emotion demands to be acknowledged and appeased before it will disengage its controlling grip on the higher centers of cognition.

He looked at me and seemed to know that there was only actually one single answer to any of my questions. "It must be so scary to think about developing a complication like a fistula. I can't tell you how much I don't want that to happen to you."

Yes, it's really scary. I am worried and feel out of control.

It becomes obvious, the necessity of pausing to acknowledge emotion, when one understands the role that our "emotional" brain plays in decision making. The part of the brain that drives our behavior and is responsible for a majority of our choices does not even possess language. The limbic system, which makes rapid yet finely honed judgments about who we can trust and where to place our loyalty, is entirely nonverbal. It relies on a kind of symbolic shorthand to assess threat, gauge appeal and catalog discrepancies. It is the voice of your gut saying, "I'm not sure why, but I just know I can trust him."

And I didn't know why, but I knew I could trust him.

It's a strange thing to enter the hospital that you work at every day as a patient. Everything looks different from that perspective. Even if I entered through the same doors I normally entered through, I found I looked for and noticed different things. It mattered to me as a patient if the staff appeared happy as they walked through the lobby. If a trash can was overfilled, I wondered if there were staffing cuts in departments like environmental services that might impact cleanliness of supplies and, by extension, patient safety. I looked at the nurse's face as she placed my IV for signs of fatigue or distraction. I noticed if multiple people asked the same question about drug allergies and worried it was evidence of poor communication. I had a very low tolerance for evidence of dysfunctional systems. Though as a physician I knew the incredible quality of the care we provided, as a patient, I was always looking for the cracks.

My surgery was far larger in scope than anyone had anticipated. Rather than locating a few isolated defects that the surgeon could quickly repair, he instead found that the entire layer of connective tissue meant to keep my intestines in place was a useless piece of tattered sinew. The graft he placed was six times larger than he'd planned, the incision three times as long. The surgery was twice the duration expected. I came out of the surgery feeling as if I had swallowed a flaming sword and had spent hours lancing myself with its fiery tip, carving circles in my flesh from the inside out.

The anesthesiologist responded quickly, administering more of the pain medication through my IV. He promised rapid relief, but nothing changed. They asked if they should allow family back into the post-op care unit to see me, and I begged them not to. It was all I could do to breathe against the pain. More medication and still no change. Then my mother's voice: "Why is her arm so swollen?" She was the first one to detect the problem. My IV had stopped working. Sometime during the surgery, in fact, it had failed, the tip slipping out of the vein and into the soft, fatty place beneath my skin. When this happened, the drug simply seeped out into the fatty tissue and the medication stopped entering my bloodstream. I still received sedation during the operation, administered through another IV line, but effectively nothing for pain. Instead, the opiate sat uselessly below the surface of my skin. It was no wonder I felt I'd been gored alive, left bloodied and raw.

They quickly got another IV placed, and got pain medication into my system. But we were already so behind it that it took hours to get ahead of the pain. On the recovery floor, I pressed my call light for the nurse repeatedly. She had soon exhausted the post-op orders that had been written and had run out of available options.

"Are you sure your pain is at an 8? I just gave you morphine an hour ago," she questioned me. "They wrote for you to get it every hour, not more often. I'm going to have to call the doctor if you need more."

She *harrumphed* her way to the phone and sent her accusatory remarks to the on-call team, audibly. They arrived, irritated and already biased. The on-call team was a group of residents assigned to cross-cover patients for whom they weren't primarily responsible during the daylight hours, when the primary teams returned. They were tasked with troubleshooting, dealing with acute issues overnight that couldn't wait for morning. They had little knowledge of any of the patients on their service, as signout was generally very concise, reserved for only critical issues. In general, the cases that necessitated substantial discussion between the two teams were the ones that had demonstrated the potential to decompensate or die overnight. I was not one of those patients. They had only the barest of knowledge about me when they were called by the nurse. My age, medical record number, room number, the surgeon who operated on me and the type of surgery would have been on a printout in one of their pockets, but little else.

"How much pain medication do you take at home?" was his first question, shot from just steps inside the doorframe. He appeared tired and irritable.

"I don't take anything at home," I replied, understanding the subtext of his accusation.

"Well, you're requiring more medication than most people would, so that makes me think you do. And we need you to be honest about that, or we aren't going to be able to help you," he added, barely veiling his threat to withhold medication.

I bristled at his condescending tone. "I don't take anything at home," I repeated. I didn't know how to explain away something that I hadn't done.

"Well, I'm going to have to call anesthesia to see you. They deal with . . . patients who are used to the effects of narcotics and need higher doses," he declared and left. He had stopped just short of calling me an addict to my face.

I broke down crying.

"Don't cry, he's not the end of the line." Randy had his phone out, wanting to call my surgeon directly. "Who does he think he is?" Randy was frustrated with him and with me, not understanding why I didn't tell them I was a physician and threaten to go above their heads. I didn't want to play that card. I knew that disclosing that I was a physician would make them no less suspicious that I was abusing narcotics. For all I knew, it may have even been part of their sign-out. Maybe they already knew.

Why was everyone's first assumption that I was a closet addict? The easy answer is because that was their construct. They were biased in the direction of that belief. They perceived patients who asked for "extra" pain control negatively as a group relative to other groups of patients. While they might never verbalize the feeling, and indeed might not even identify as having had that preconception about me, their bias influenced their behavior. While explicit bias requires that a person is aware of their dislike, believes it to be justified and acts on it, implicit bias operates in an unintentional, sometimes subconscious manner. It is activated by situational cues like race, or even profession. It exerts its influence often without our awareness.

Something about my situation triggered a judgment, whether consciously or unconsciously. It's possible that at some point in their training, they felt manipulated into supplying drugs to someone who was just trying to get high off them. Addiction is a pervasive enough issue that they almost certainly would have encountered it at some point in their training. They may have made associations; they may have stereotyped. Explicit bias dictates that they recognized this and believed acting in a defensive and obstructive manner was justified, based on the experiences that led to their biases. Explicit bias allows for overcorrecting as a means of recouping some imagined loss of control, some perceived indignity or slight. If they instead entered the room, saw someone who they knew was a physician, who was not tearful or outwardly anxious and yet describing terrible pain, they could be influenced to withhold medication without even understanding why. That is implicit bias.

When the anesthesiology resident entered my room, I felt immediately relieved. We knew each other, he had worked under me as my resident in the medical intensive care unit. He had soft brown eyes and floppy, straight dark hair that he couldn't keep out of his eyes. Something in how he was constantly smoothing his hair back implied an unending patience. He found me crying in the bed and looked at me with such compassion, I knew he would help me. He immediately promised to do whatever it took to get my pain under control and apologized for how I'd been treated. He looked genuinely mortified that the surgery team had refused to even attempt to control my pain. He asked if I were open to receiving an injection of a numbing medication directly into my spine to get control of the pain quickly. Honestly I would have agreed to anything, including disarticulating the lower half of my body and burying it in a deep hole. I agreed.

Within thirty minutes I was numb from the ribs down to my toes. I understood why in medical school an anesthesiologist told me he felt he had the best job in the hospital: "You show up and people are in pain, and within minutes you've magically made it disappear. They are so grateful. Wherever I go, people are happy to see me. There aren't too many doctors who can say that."

I began to believe I would be able to make it through the night.

It's a terrible feeling to believe you are being taken advantage of by someone for whom you've sacrificed so much of your own life. And there are certainly times, perhaps most commonly associated with treatment of exaggerated or imagined acute pain, when physicians perceive they are being manipulated and used. It's arguably a worse, more isolating feeling to be in legitimate pain and be deprived of relief. This withholding of pain relief by an emotionally guarded physician is damaging to everyone involved, patient and physician alike. The only thing that seemed at all clear was that we all stood to benefit from understanding each other better.

The surgery resident came back and offered an apology the next day, having been reprimanded by someone for not making an effort to control my post-op pain. He appeared genuinely contrite, though his words felt weak. I wished I knew what to say to make him understand what it had felt like to be judged by him, without any evidence.

"You had no right," I began, but couldn't finish the sentence. I only sat shaking my head. I felt I should stand, to meet his eye level, but as I placed weight on my feet, the spinal anesthesia forced me to sit ungracefully as my legs buckled beneath me. The resident lunged toward me and reached out as if to catch my fall. The extent of my helplessness, my inability to even stand without assistance, humbled me quickly. I sighed and began again, with more compassion than anger this time.

"You know, if you trust your patients are telling the truth, you'll be right far more often than you are wrong. They aren't all just trying to get something from you," was all I could say.

Physicians often enter the lives of patients on their absolute worst days. They meet without the benefit of social graces. Patients appear depersonalized in generic hospital uniforms. They lack means to project their identity through dress or choice of hairstyle. They lack ability to control their circumstances. They might be in pain, scared and suffering. They might be angry, frustrated and disenfranchised. They might be worried about bills at home or who will feed the dog. They might be addicts. They might have made terrible choices. They might be easy to judge. They might not have the skills to be kind while in pain; they might never in their lives have had kindness shown to them. They might have been abused or violated by someone they trusted. They might be many things. But one thing is true: they are doing their best. The patient, even the accusatory and fearful patient, is doing their best.

They are doing their best to trust that this person whom they just met, whose name they barely caught during the introduction, will stay up the whole of the night to care for them. They are doing their best to believe that their past choices will not be held against them. They are doing their best to withstand the pain before pushing the call light again. They are doing their best to believe that they are worthy of the compassion and humility of a stranger. A humility that dictates that while we cannot possibly understand every patient's story perfectly, we can trust them to tell it, without imbuing it with our own biases. And when they tell their story, we can receive it, and bear witness to it. And in return for their willingness, however tenuous, to put their faith in us, we can do our best.

Seven

Vulnerable Masses

By the middle of rounds each day, I would feel an unmistakable aching heaviness in my right side. By the end of rounds, it could truly be called pain. At first, I allowed myself to dismiss it, attributing it to either the old, shrinking hematoma or inflammation related to the mesh from the hernia repair. But I knew it was different, and I knew it was new. I also knew admitting it would set off a series of events that I would have no control over. Once I said it out loud, everything would take on a momentum of its own. So I ignored it for as long as possible, which turned out to be three months. Three months of solid denial and pretense. Observant friends would comment, "You're holding your right side, is everything OK?"

The truth was, I didn't know if everything was OK. In fact, I knew something was probably very wrong, but I wasn't yet ready to face it. In an odd way, my medical training had prepared me to ignore my body. Medical training demands a kind of disembodiment by doctors. It begins in Gross Anatomy lab, where bodies are studied but the lives those bodies led and the deaths that followed are not. It continues into a training that dismisses the need for sleep, demanding thirty-six-hour workdays. It is illustrated by the denial of bodily functions in the operating room. A twelve-hour case meant twelve straight hours in which you did not move from the operating room table. You learned not to drink or eat, you learned not to feel hunger or indulge thirst. Corporeal needs were marginalized, ignored and dismissed. To do what needed to be done, we believed we had to be superhuman. And there was, sadly, an implied superiority in those achievements. Doctors, we believed, were just different.

I recognize now that I carried this disembodied persona into my first pregnancy. I saw what was happening in my body as something to be minimized. To be a good doctor to me meant not having my pregnancy interfere with my work, in any way. I ignored signs, like the horrific swelling, that were identifying a problem. I put on compression stockings so that I could still round for hours. I refused to sit, believing it weak and a concession. And so when the aching, right-sided heaviness started up, I was again disadvantaged, having not yet learned to truly and shamelessly inhabit my body.

In an attempt to address what was steadily becoming a real concern, without actually formally pursuing it, I walked down the hallway from my office and asked my friend, a doctor who I had also done fellowship with, if he would take a look at my liver with the ultrasound machine. He was a bright, kind man. He had completed medical school in Nigeria and had an interest in ultrasound, a modality that was very useful in areas of the world that had less access to sophisticated diagnostics like CT scanning and MRI. We had been hired as attendings the same year. I trusted him and knew his judgment would not be clouded by our relationship as colleagues. When we had been trainees together, we had gained proficiency in ultrasound primarily by examining each other's lungs and hearts and vessels in on-call rooms and offices. It didn't strike him as a strange request.

"Sure, I'll grab the machine. Where did you want to do it?" was his only question.

"Just right here is fine," I replied, suggesting I could lie on the floor of another friend's empty office.

I moved a chair and small table out of the way and lay on the rough gray carpet, lifting my shirt to expose my abdomen. He applied the cold gel that aids visualization and knelt beside me, placing the probe just under my rib cage. I waited quietly as he adjusted the probe, moving it from side to side and searching for the location that afforded the best view.

"There's nothing, right?" Some part of me must have thought that a cursory exam by a friend, on the floor of an office, would be unlikely to be revealing. I realized that I was purposefully handicapping myself. I still wasn't ready to face any bad news.

"Hmm . . ." he said.

"What?" I asked, suddenly nervous.

He played with the controls, trying to get a clearer view. He stopped and turned the screen toward me. "See this?" he asked.

"That's the hematoma, I know . . . it's still there," I hurriedly explained. The blood collection from that first night had been steadily shrinking over the past year. It had gone from a ten-pound bowling ball to being about the size of a tennis ball.

"Yes, I agree with you. Which is why I am not sure what this second mass is," he said as he pointed to the screen.

There it was, an ovoid sphere, about three centimeters across, staring back at me from the screen.

"You need a formal ultrasound," he declared, standing up. He added, "I'm putting in the order. I'll call down and see if they can do it now."

I knew he was right. Hours later the ultrasound tech was examining the same area, passing the probe over it again and again, similarly unsure of what she was seeing. She excused herself and left to get the radiologist.

"Listen," the radiologist began. I had learned to dislike that introduction. I found it was effectively shorthand for "I'm about to tell you something that is arguably bad news. But, I'd rather you not react like it is bad news. I'd rather you take it stoically and just maintain your composure."

"When you see the report, you are going to see that I am going to call what we are seeing a mass," she continued. So they had found something.

"It has flow, blood flow going to it that we can see. But just keep in mind, just because it's a mass, doesn't mean that it's necessarily cancer. We're going to recommend further imaging, probably a CT scan or MRI."

I nodded. I understood.

As I walked out of radiology, I realized awkwardly that I'd gotten myself this far, and none of my doctors or family knew. So I began the process of informing them.

I called the surgeon first, who reviewed the ultrasound and agreed that a triple-phase CT scan of my liver was the next logical step. He thought the timing of the injection of the dye in the past could have been the reason we had never seen a mass. He placed the order.

I called Randy, who innocently answered the phone with, "Hey, I was wondering when I'd hear from you. Must be a busy day, huh?"

Poor Randy hated surprises, and knowing I was safe at work had allowed himself the luxury of believing he could ask me how my day had been and not hear anything he would characterize as bad news.

"Well, actually, I was having some pain . . . to be honest, I'd *been* having pain," I began.

"Wait, what kind of pain? Why is this the first I'm hearing about this?" He started to panic.

"It's nothing," I said, which was obviously not true. "Anyway, just listen," I continued, attempting the tactic of the radiologist. I explained that I had a friend look at my liver with ultrasound and he thought he saw something, and so I went for a formal ultrasound and they think they see something, so now I had to have a CT scan. "And that's all," I added, hoping that he wouldn't have any questions.

"But what are they seeing?" He asked the obvious question.

I struggled to think of a word for *mass* that wasn't *mass* or *tumor*. "It's like a collection of tissue, sort of a . . . a ball," I said, struggling.

"Like a mass?" he asked.

"Kind of," I admitted. *Just shoot me,* I thought, frustrated by my own attempt to maintain my composure as I gave news I'd only barely adjusted to. Then I remembered, I had an out. I was the patient, not the physician who had to considerately and compassionately give bad news. "I don't really want to talk about it. I just need to get the CT scan and that's it. Then we'll know more," I declared.

"OK," he said, understanding it was probably best not to push. "Are you going to tell your mom?" It was a trick question. He was entitled to ask that, because he needed to know who knew, so as not to out me. It was casually framed as a simple question. But it had the potential to give him far more information than pressing me on the issue ever would have. For example, if I said no, it meant that it was serious and therefore he should be worried. However, if I said yes, then he knew she wouldn't let me off as easily and would get more details out of me and he would benefit by extension. It was a CIA-level spy tactic.

"I'm not sure yet," I answered honestly, yet strategically. In fairness, I didn't know. It was all moving so fast.

I reported for my CT scan the following day, after completing morning ICU rounds. I took off my white coat and badge and changed into the speckled blue patient gown. I helped the technician identify an amenable vein for an IV, and, once placed, I boosted myself up onto the familiar table.

"Now your doctor ordered this with contrast, so you are going to feel a warm rush throughout your body when it dispenses. It will feel as if you are wetting yourself, but don't worry, you aren't," she said to prepare me. "Try to lay very still, and when I ask you to hold your breath, be even stiller so we can get good pictures, OK?"

I nodded. I knew what was expected of me.

I lay back on the hard metal surface and heard the familiar noise of the table as it clinked and slid me into the doughnut-shaped scanner. I felt the warm flush of contrast as it filled my veins and coursed through my body, making my bladder feel warm and contractile.

"Now hold still, breathe in and hold," she instructed through the speaker.

I marveled that I was able to both lie flat and hold my breath. It was real, tangible progress. To be in the same space a year later, and have those successes, felt like everything. But as the table began to slide me out of the scanner, I felt instead that I was being carried along a conveyor belt, transporting me ever further away from my coat on the wall and from even being a physician. I could see the path ahead clearly; it led down a long, cold hallway. The hallway led to the pre-op area and back into the OR. I sat up and felt an overwhelming urgency to leave the hospital.

I drove home in silence, without radio or phone calls. I tried to listen to the pain and discern what it was trying to tell me. I let the thoughts that held the possibilities ebb and flow, from worst-case scenarios to the bland, boring nothingness I hoped it would be. I trusted myself to sense which would resonate, which would linger without leaving. In the thirty-minute drive, I couldn't come up with a single possibility that was not going to be a serious problem. I would quiet my mind, and in a moment *This is going to be a problem* would float back in. This is a problem. This is a serious problem.

As I walked through the garage door and into my kitchen, I realized in my rush to leave, I'd left my white coat and badge behind. *Perfect,* I thought, *whatever this is it's already making me stupid.* My cell phone rang. It was Dr. G.

"Where are you?" was his first question.

"I just got home," I answered, unsure why we were bothering with small talk.

"Can you come downtown?" he asked, with a noticeable edge in his voice.

"I just left, why would I come back?" I replied, feeling I probably already knew the answer.

"I just finished reviewing your CT scan images with the transplant surgeons," he began.

Transplant? Why were we involving them again? I wondered.

There are moments when you know that the words that come next will change your life forever. The challenge is realizing that your life had changed already—changed some time ago, in fact—and you are only just now finding out the details. But it was all already true. Not hearing it doesn't make it not true.

"Listen, there are two masses in your liver. Tumors. They are called hepatic adenomas. At least we think that's what they are." He paused.

My cognitive brain began riffling through its index, multiple frames per second, in ever-increasing specificity. It located the box labeled TUMORS, then LIVER TUMORS, then more specifically, NON-CANCEROUS LIVER TUMORS THAT AFFECT YOUNG WOMEN. They were embedded within each other like Russian nesting dolls. I pulled up my available knowledge of hepatic adenomas, after discarding the others. I knew they were a very rare form of tumor that had a very rich blood supply and grew in the livers of young women. They grew in response to certain hormones, like estrogen. So pregnancy was a very dangerous time, as they grew and sometimes ruptured. *Oh my God.* "Wait," I said at last. "That's what happened."

"Yes, one is probably what ruptured on us last time, we can tell that because the perimeter looks fuzzy, as if all the blood vessels burst. But there is another one." Another pause. "They were always there. It's just we couldn't see them before because of the distortion from the hematoma. But now that the hematoma shrunk . . ." His voice trailed off.

My first hospitalization appeared before me in sequence, as if I were flipping through a patient's chart. The presenting complaint of severe pain, the blood loss, the lab values, the diagnosis of HELLP syndrome. My brain tried to superimpose this new diagnosis of a ruptured hepatic adenoma at each point in my hospital course. That first wave of pain in the restaurant, could that actually have been the moment the mass ruptured? The liver failure. Rather than being the beginning, could my liver have failed later, a secondary result of compression from the large blood collection? Had we missed the diagnosis all along? Had I misdiagnosed myself?

I realized he was still talking.

"You need to come downtown right now."

"Why now?" I countered, thinking that if they had been there all this past year, why now that we suddenly were aware of their presence did it constitute an emergency? It was always already true. They were always already there. They were the heavy throbbing when I rounded, they were what took my breath away when I tried to walk quickly. They were what pulsed under my ribs at night.

"Well, one has already ruptured on us once and it was pretty bad," he offered.

Yeah, I was there, I kind of remember that.

"And now there is another. It's just waiting," he added.

"Wait, what do you mean there is another one?" I asked. And then I let myself hear what he had been saying all along. I let myself understand. There were always two tumors. One that had ruptured during my pregnancy and one that was still a threat. A very real and very frightening threat.

"The way they handle these things is to embolize them. The guys in radiology shoot little plastic beads into them to cut off their blood supply, and that makes the surgery a little less risky," he said.

"Surgery." It was more of an acknowledgment than a question. Of course there would be more surgery.

"They need to remove the half of your liver with the masses," he said.

"Remove half of my liver," I repeated, as if practicing the words for when I'd have to explain it to others. I tried but couldn't imagine how scary that news would be to my family.

"Tomorrow," I offered. "I'll come down tomorrow, but not tonight."

"You won't come now?" he had to ask again.

"No, tomorrow," I promised.

"OK, but call me if . . ." He didn't have to finish that sentence. He didn't need to tell me what "if" could mean. We'd been through it all before. "And don't eat anything, just in case we have to take you in for surgery emergently."

"Sure. And I know, call if anything changes. Thank you." I hung up, not wanting any more words to come through the phone.

I looked around me and wondered what I should do. I had fifteen minutes until Randy came home, and I'd have to drag him into the abyss with me. I'd inhabited those spaces enough times. Times when I knew of a death or a trauma, and the family was still blithely unaware. I'd seen enough to know there was no benefit to foreshortening the space. No one stood to gain anything if I sped up the truth. I preferred to sit very still and wait. Let him enjoy these last minutes without worry.

I found sitting still difficult. I tried pacing but it felt purposeless and didn't soothe me. I walked instead to the freezer and took out a pint of ice cream. I sat at the counter with the carton in front of me, and dug into it with purpose. I harbored the genuine belief that there was a group of surgeons who were just waiting to pull me into an operating room, and my only form of control at the moment involved never having an empty stomach. Surgeons were terribly afraid of stomach contents, prone to being regurgitated during surgery and entering the lungs. I would eat constantly. That was my very poorly formulated plan, to never have a stomach that was empty enough to allow surgery. I was sticking to it.

It's difficult to eat ice cream when you are crying. It's just not sad food. It's overtly celebratory, always cheerily accompanying cake and summer and birthdays. I put it away and sat at the counter. I took off my wedding ring and turned it in my fingers, an old habit.

Randy, when faced with the prospect of engraving it, had chosen to have it inscribed with the terribly misguided sentiment BECAUSE YOU'RE PERFECT. What he didn't anticipate was that in having the ring resized, his assertion would be unceremoniously amended to instead say BECAUSE YOU'R ERFECT. It was more perfect in its imperfection. Not only was the grammar offensive, but the adjective had been decapitated.

The engraving was set in a time before illness and surgery had left their marks. It was inscribed before my hair fell out, before scars and marks were a permanent feature of my abdominal wall. Perhaps if we had had an expectation of perfection, this all would have been more difficult to handle. Instead I was just slightly deformed, like the truncated adjective that had become an emblem of our life.

He walked through the door and knew immediately that we had a challenge facing us. He looked at my swollen, sodden face and said, "Whatever it is, we've been through worse, and we'll get through this too. Tell me what they found."

I raced through the explanation, which was completely unintelligible through my tears, with Randy waiting patiently for me to loop back to the beginning, hoping he'd catch some of the meaning the second time through, or the third. He held my hand, and as the rate of my breath slowed, he began to piece together the events of the day.

"The thing is, I just found out that I have to have surgery to remove half my liver because if I don't I'll die this time, because there is a tumor that is just like what happened last time, only we didn't know that's what it was, and oh my God it could all happen again. Actually, it could have already all happened again, can you imagine?"

"No, I can't." He was incredulous at the thought that we could have reentered the same bloody loop. "There is no way we would have been as lucky the second time." He clearly believed, as I did, that if the second mass had ruptured, it would have killed me.

I suddenly felt terribly guilty for ignoring the pain for so long. I couldn't have imagined what it represented.

"It's all just . . . the news has, I don't know. It's just completely unnerved me," I said to explain my disarray. "It's like, I feel like I'm starting all over again. I thought I'd gotten somewhere and I'm still at the beginning of everything."

"We'll get through this too. You'll be well again, you'll see." He paused, trying to gauge my willingness to entertain questions. "What's the next step?" he asked cautiously, not wanting to trigger me.

"I guess when I go in tomorrow, I'll find out what the plan is. They wanted me to come down tonight," I admitted.

"I think tomorrow will be here soon enough," he offered.

I shrugged and gently banged my forehead against his chest, wanting to stop my thoughts.

"It's going to be OK," he said, kissing the top of my head and holding it in place. "Just think, they got you through it before, without the benefit of even knowing what was causing the bleeding. Now that they know, it's got to be easier if they have more information, doesn't it?"

"Suppose so," I replied in the most unconvincing way possible.

I couldn't sleep and was back at the hospital before 7:00 a.m. I was scheduled to work and fully planned to round after I saw the scans. I logged into the hospital's record system to look at my CT images myself. I saw immediately I'd been assigned a room on the surgical floor. Morose planning in case the procedure failed, I guessed. I launched a silent protest, subversively eating my breakfast and drinking my coffee as I scrolled through the images. As promised, two masses greeted me, highlighted by the intravenous contrast against the dark backdrop of my liver. I stared at them, wanting to gauge their intention. The little wreakers of havoc. "I see you," I whispered to the screen. "And you don't look so tough."

I had imagined they would appear more obviously evil. Treacherous and spiny, rather than round and sunny. They just didn't look as though they were intending to hurt me. They looked as though they had gotten lost and ended up somewhere they didn't intend to be. And that they now needed help getting out.

I gave in and called my surgeon. "I see them. Where do you want me to go?"

"They're expecting you in interventional radiology. Third floor. Go there," he instructed. I called my division head and asked that he find coverage for my ICU as I walked to the elevators.

For the next three hours, a team of people clad in leaden aprons tried to thread a catheter as fine as a piece of string from my groin into the "feeding vessel" that had sprouted each mass. To get there they mapped the vast network of my body's vessels using contrast and radiation in alternating bursts. We did all of this without any sort of sedation, with my blood pressure running too low to allow for it. I asked them to adjust the angle of their large screens so I could watch the procedure in real time, out of lack of anything else to do. The screens were mounted just above the cool steel table that I lay upon. It was beautiful technology, so precise and elegant. When they accessed the mass, they injected it with millions of tiny plastic spheres intended to deprive it of its blood supply. That was what was referred to as embolization. They succeeded. The masses were strangulated and neutralized. They would never again be allowed to cause me to bleed to death.

Watching it all, I felt an initial sense of letdown that is characteristic of any act of revenge. Whatever we had contrived to do to those tumors, it would never be as awful as what they had done to me. It couldn't be.

"Well, you're safe for now," the radiologist told me in the post-procedure area.

"But these masses," the surgeon added, "I talked it over with the liver surgeons. They think, we all think, we have no way of truly knowing if they are cancerous, unless we take them out. Even if they aren't they carry a small but real risk of becoming malignant. And the risk increases with each subsequent year. You need to let them take them out."

"It's true," the radiologist added. "We do the embolization to help the surgeon. So that you won't bleed out when he does the liver resection. The surgery can be really bloody otherwise."

It was not my favorite visual but it was effective. I agreed, the masses would have to come out.

I sat, gowned, on an exam room table in the liver transplant clinic, shaking my head. Something about the idea of transplantation always frightened me. The complete replacement of an organ by another, the abject dependency on a piece of another human. Life post-transplant seemed almost like an after-life. The transplant recipient representing death resurrected. And while I knew I wasn't there to get a transplant—that I was only there because of the level of skill this group of surgeons possessed—I couldn't shake the sense of inescapability. From the very beginning, when transplant surgery's name was first invoked, it was destined to be. Though it had been over a year since I heard "I've asked Transplant to see you," in this moment, as I sat waiting for them, it seemed totally inevitable.

When the nurse practitioner came in, I was immediately impressed by her level of preparedness. She knew every aspect of my history that was available to her by chart review and discussions with the referring physician. And yet she didn't presume to know my version of the events.

"My goodness, you've been through a lot!" the NP exclaimed on meeting me. "I'm so sorry you've had to go through all of this." She paused, then introduced herself and her role on the team.

"I think I have a sense of what has happened to you over the past year, but will you tell me from your perspective, so that I know I've got things right?" I was struck by how perfect her introduction was. It was knowledgeable yet humble, empathic and well intentioned.

She made it easy to share my history, as she reconciled my narrative with the colder facts and dates in the chart. Her questions were issued with a genuine curiosity about my health and well-being. She paused and looked directly at me.

"I am so sorry you lost the baby," she said.

"It's OK." I gave my reflexive answer, prepared to launch into my preformulated rebuttal that centered upon how fortunate I felt to be alive. It was a rehearsed response intended to put others at ease, and as such didn't actually even attempt to represent the whole story.

"It's not OK," she said, stopping me short. "It will never be OK that you lost the baby."

It was the kindest and most loving thing she could have said. She acknowledged a loss that was abstract to her, but so very real for me. The simplicity of the statement, of telling someone you are sorry for their loss, or that it isn't OK, can feel weak and puny in the face of suffering. We avoid it, feeling impotent, knowing that our sentiment won't fix anything. And we want to fix things. It is so vanishingly rare that what you say can actually fix something for anyone. We cannot change that which is true and sad. But we can acknowledge it. We can humbly witness suffering and offer support.

When she had a solid understanding of my case, she excused herself to bring in the liver surgeon.

When the surgeon entered, it was if he appeared straight out of central casting. Having worked in the same institution, we had occasionally passed each other in the hallways so he was familiar, but we had never formally met. He was immaculate and well dressed, with an easy way about him that put us at ease. He had the same first name as my dad, who had been dead seven years. He sat down and faced us, only looking at the computer when he wanted to check some detail. He was articulate and generous with compliments. He praised my strength, my other physicians and my family for their support. He scrolled through my many CT scans, pointing out small details others had failed to recognize.

"You know, you're very lucky you survived," he told me, as if he were sharing a deep secret. "Ruptured adenomas are almost universally fatal." He pulled up a case-series in the literature, which compared different management algorithms, none seeming to confer more success than any of the others. "See this"—he pointed at the paper—"forty-five cases reported, and most of them didn't make it. That's why we do things differently." He went on to describe how he'd partnered with the interventional radiologists to preemptively ablate the lesions, which I had just had done. From the date of the ablation we would wait six weeks for the tissue to calm down prior to actually undergoing the surgery. It was an innovative, collaborative approach.

He went on to describe other novel strategies, a robotic approach they could sometimes utilize for the liver resection, with small laparoscopic ports for access rather than a large vertical incision. It would be a big surgery, he advised, with a lengthy and difficult recovery, but he would do everything in his power to make it as easy on me as possible. He would worry about every possibility and plan for every contingency so that I wouldn't have to. I absolutely believed him. If he had wanted to take half of Randy's liver out as well, I would have let him.

Despite the shiny trust engendered by the surgical team, the six weeks leading up to the surgery were fraught with worry. Though the team resisted putting a fine point on it, I projected an estimated risk of death associated with the liver resection of around 25 percent. It was likely an overestimate, but this figure hung heavily in the air as I tried to get on with my normal life. It's an odd thing to voluntarily agree to walk into a room that you believe you have only a 75 percent chance of walking out of. But I knew there was a shoreline on the other side that I had to leap across to get to. This surgery would close the chapter on the past year and hopefully leave me well enough to lead a functional life. To be of use.

My worries had worn themselves thin by the day of the surgery. That morning, I felt I had the easiest job of all. I arrived still half-asleep in pre-op, was briefly interviewed by the anesthesiologist, had intravenous access placed and said my goodbyes to my family, who would sit anxiously in the waiting room for the next seven hours. I received a calming sedative as I waited to be wheeled into the OR.

At hour six, Randy left the waiting area to get coffee. In the elevator, he received a phone call from my mom telling him that the waiting room attendant told her to tell him to "return immediately." He naturally believed I had died.

The attendant had actually only wanted him to return because the surgical team had advised her that they were about to come and update him. Six years later, he still hasn't recovered fully from that phone call. If you were to ask him about that day, that one phone call is what he remembers most clearly.

The surgery was far more technically difficult than they had anticipated. Though they had tried to accomplish the resection with a minimally invasive approach, using robotic arms through small ports in my abdomen, they had to convert to a fully open approach with a long 18-inch incision. The bleeding event one year ago had left my liver encased in a thick rind of bony substance, an accretion of calcium-like cement. They had had to chip away at it, millimeter by millimeter, to free the segment of the liver they had come for. There was significant blood loss, and it took some time to gain control of it, but I was alive and being moved from the OR to post-op. My family could see me shortly.

Randy was led back to the curtained post-op area. I felt his hand on mine before I opened my eyes. He was always right there, whenever I awoke. I could count on that. I tried to roll toward him and felt a sharp stinging reminder of the surgery alight in my belly. I moaned.

"Are you in pain?" he asked sweetly.

There was pain, of course, post-operatively. The long incision stung and my abdominal wall felt a deep soreness that came from being spread open by retractors for hours. "A little," I answered.

The pain deepened over the course of the night. Once settled in my room, I was asked to rate it on a scale of 1 to 10, and I replied completely honestly, "It's about a 5 right now."

Randy attempted to explain to the nurses what he understood of my temperament by now. Namely, that I had a skewed pain scale. I had truly experienced shattering pain, and that had cemented my scale in place. The pain I experienced that first night had informed my understanding of what a 10 should signify. Ten to me implied absolutely unsurvivable pain, portending imminent death, with organs being ripped from their moorings. By my self-imposed criteria, a 5 was pretty brutal. But no one else seemed to think so.

"So, it's manageable," the nurse replied.

"I don't know if I would say that." I was confused by her reframing an already subjective measure into words I wouldn't have chosen.

"You said it was a 5," she countered.

"It is," I replied, knowing we were not understanding each other.

"OK, well, 5 isn't that bad now, is it?" she stated, adding, "You did just have surgery, you know."

My face flushed, as I felt the sting of her condescension. I began to get anxious, worried that my pain wouldn't be controlled and by extension, the night would be terrible, like the other nights before. I wondered if I should have just inflated the value.

She approached me with a set of supplies, ready to draw labs.

"No." I held out my hand as a signal to her to stop.

"You are refusing lab draws?" she asked with an accusatory tone.

I shook my head. I didn't have the words or the energy to say that I just needed a moment to regroup, that I couldn't take another stick or multiple sticks trying to get blood when I was already in pain.

"Fine." She gathered her supplies and left the room.

"Your patient is being difficult," she announced to the resident, loudly, within earshot of my room, as she slammed the chart into the slot on the wall.

I didn't understand how things had deteriorated so quickly. I wasn't trying to be difficult. The label stung in a way I hadn't expected.

Difficult. How many times had I used that label to describe a patient or a patient family? More than I'd care to admit. We label patients. We label them as cooperative, or drug-seeking, realistic or difficult. It functioned as an abridged report to our colleagues of what to expect.

"Difficult" was a shorthand for "The patient is not going along with the plan. I have a good solid plan, and they aren't on board." I wondered why we ever presumed that our plan should be the barometer by which we measure compliance. Why our agenda was preformulated and not collaborative. Why we insisted on creating a dynamic in which one person wins and the other loses.

In that bed, in pain, I felt terribly, frighteningly vulnerable, dependent on the care of strangers for my most basic needs as well as the most complex care. I felt powerless in a way that is impossible to imagine, from a privileged position of wholeness and well-being. I know this because after this failure, I pathetically tried to ingratiate myself to the team. I believed that I needed to make them like me in order to care for me. I believed I had to earn pain control through good behavior. I felt I had to prove to them that I was deserving.

Our patients are aware of their labels. One of my patients, a chronic methamphetamine user who had been clean for a number of years, often occupied a bed in our unit. The last time I had seen him, he had just had surgery to remove his gallbladder. I visited him immediately after the procedure and he was in obvious pain.

"Do you need something for pain?" I asked. "You look miserable."

"Nah," he said dejectedly. "With my history, I know I can't ask for anything. They just assume I am drug-seeking."

"No, that isn't true," I offered. I wanted it not to be true.

"It is," he stated, matter-of-factly. "They might give me something because you're here, but once you leave, I'm just another addict looking for a fix."

Addiction isn't the only thing that is sometimes simple and sometimes complicated. Caring for each other is too. What was revealed to me through my pain was a gift. A gift of self-knowledge and past failure. I had gotten so much wrong. How did I not know to stay out of judgment? Why did I ever assume I knew something about my patients just by reviewing their chart? Our assumptions about others said so much more about us than about the people we were judging. We didn't know. It's no one's right to define the parameters or prerequisites of someone else's suffering.

The masses were sliced and sectioned in the lab, stained to evaluate for cancer cells. None were found. My pain came under adequate control, and I was discharged to a recovery with a steep slope toward wellness. One of the unanticipated benefits of having half of my liver chipped out with a chisel was that much of the pain I had endured with just breathing receded. My diaphragm no longer had to move against an unyielding rock. Within six weeks, I achieved something that once seemed entirely out of reach. I would be almost pain-free most days. I began to think beyond the upcoming week when I considered the future. I began to believe I might still be present in a year or two, or five.

"So, just theoretically, if it was never HELLP syndrome, if it was always just the tumors, and now they are gone, does that mean it's possible to safely get pregnant again?" I found myself asking.

None of my doctors particularly enjoyed this question being posed, theoretical or not. I got replies that were noncommittal: "Wow, are you considering that? After everything you've been through?" Or, "My goodness, you're brave."

I wasn't sure if I was considering it. Or that I was brave enough. I was just noticing a window where I thought there had been a wall.

Eight

Censors of Light

The optimism I had about the future dissipated as I again returned to work. I found I was still telling time by last year's calendar. I'd peel up the square on any day, and there was the loss, the due date, the scar. And every day that I walked back into the hospital, I felt I was visiting a memorial. The place I worked was also the place where everything had slipped. I rounded on patients cared for in the room where I had lived, marveling at how different it looked from the outside. Different and yet the same. I met with families in the waiting room where my family had waited to hear if I had survived the emergency surgery. And just like the surgeon who had been surprised to see me take my first steps, I kept encountering my own ghost.

I noticed things I hadn't before, when I was just a doctor. Like the anxious stillness that seemed to be common in waiting rooms, how the normal range of movement there was restricted, even micro. A tremoring leg. Teeth mindlessly edging a nail. Thumbs sightlessly paging through newsfeeds and magazines, rendered blind by the normalcy of the curated content.

Restless family standing to blandly engage the vending machine before accepting an utter lack of appetite. The real movement all happened internally. Every worry, regret and desperate prayer swirling and flashing with the momentum of colliding stars. And the vastness of all of it, of whole lives being revisited and prematurely mourned, the anticipatory grief leaking out, condensed into a tear or a sigh.

I encountered the family of my HELLP syndrome patient in the waiting room of the surgical ICU most days. In her room, an endless loop of Johnny Cash songs played on a stereo. Swelling in her brain had long since crushed the web of neurons that housed memories of the music, or dancing. She remained yellow and bloated, violated by tubes and drains. She had been transferred off my service when she required emergency surgery to clean out her abdomen from the corrosive blood. She'd required the surgery I had feared the most. Her father and husband were no longer waiting for news so much as they were allowing the blunt reality to encase them and resurface them into new, harder versions of themselves. They sat, side by side, like stone statues. She was never going to recover. She would die before Christmas that year, her obituary recalling her daughter and her love of country music.

I would sit and visit with the family, useless but familiar. I'd ask what they were hearing from the team, and they would shake their heads as if to release the memory of the doctors' words from their ears. Instead they would sigh and pull out their phones to share pictures of baby Charlotte, the child she'd never know, suckling on hope and growing steadily in the shadow of her ghost mother. I'd be so thankful that she existed, to anchor them and physically embody a future.

"She's beautiful," I'd comment.

"Isn't she?" they'd reflect back.

"I am so sorry . . ." I'd trail off, thinking I was heartbroken for her, and for them, and that she wouldn't get to know her mom.

I spoke in fragments. I would summarily reject every sentence I drafted and revised in my head. All I could write were apologies. I felt complicit in her death, even before she died. I would hate myself and medicine for years for not being able to save her. Worse yet, they could see my disappointment in my own failure. The vector of my grief was focused on her inner circle.

"We know you did all you could, and you all did so much," they would say to comfort me. "We are so grateful for everything you've done. You have no idea what it meant to us, to have your support though all of this." They were embarrassingly more articulate in their grief than I was.

I couldn't have felt less deserving of their gratitude. It stung like salt on my still-open wounds. Not knowing what to do with my feelings, I built a tower in honor of my patient inside of me, stacking failure upon shame onto blocks of grief and blame. A tower bound to topple.

Externally, I was the walking embodiment of bouncing back, of steadfast resilience. Looking at me, no one would guess what I'd been through. My hair was growing back, and I was fully back at work, standing with a net to catch the next person whose turn it was to take a fall. And yet I'd exit the elevator ten floors early if an instrumental of "Ring of Fire" came on over the speakers. I'd become nauseated by certain combinations of lab values, or groups of organs failing. I was suffering again from nightmares.

Like some cosmically charged magnet, I attracted pregnant, critically ill patients to my unit in numbers that were statistically improbable given random chance alone. They seemed to arrive just as the heaviness of the absent baby began to weigh me down. Just when I would accrue a bare notion of regret, they would roll into my unit. And in a moment, I would wake from the dream of my ghost life.

With each patient, I poured everything I had into their care, despite somehow knowing that failure couldn't be diluted. The loss of my HELLP Syndrome patient proved to be almost unbearably difficult to shoulder. It wasn't just that she was my first official patient as a fully formed critical care physician. It was more than my identification with her because of our shared diagnosis. When I was sick, and so desperately vulnerable, I knew I was completely dependent on others to keep me alive. I worried that if they didn't care enough to do what it took, to do everything perfectly right, that I would die. A death by disconnection and benign neglect. I believed that once I was a doctor again, I could save my patients through sheer force of attention. I promised myself I wouldn't miss any clues or bypass any opportunity to help them inch toward recovery. I had never considered what it might feel like to try that hard, care that much, and still lose.

When I was sick, I believed my team had complete control over my outcome. But here I felt I had no control. I would have done anything to save her, and still I had lost her. I had to acknowledge that in many ways, both symbolic and concrete, I had lost myself. I had failed myself. I had to acknowledge that, despite my best efforts, I would still sometimes fail. I would see that despite what I had told the OB resident, that even when the good outcomes did outnumber the bad, they wouldn't make even the slightest dent in the darkness that bled from the bad ones. That shame is unique in its wholeness, an impenetrable black orb that deflects light.

I don't think I could have named the emotion I felt as I sat with my patient's family as shame. I knew I had a vague sense of worthlessness, combined with guilt. I had heard repeatedly and understood objectively that I was not in any way to blame.

I also understood, objectively, that she had a horrific, crushing disease that few survived, and that no one could have changed her trajectory or prevented her death. I also knew it was my job to alter the trajectory of patients with horrific, crushing diseases. I had failed. I donated to a charity in her honor, in a rudderless search for absolution. Instead of forgiveness, I received large crystal plaques from the HELLP Syndrome Society to commemorate my failure. I knew that my connection to her case was making the loss more difficult, and in this way I felt perhaps I had been reckless. I hadn't maintained the cool clinical distance I'd been instructed to carve out. Could I have? And who would it have served if I had managed to maintain some perfect state of detachment? I'd never know. I'd abandoned my armor at the bottom of the sea when I had to learn to breathe underwater.

That loss, like a funeral veil, imbued everything around me with a dark cast. I would sit silently through M and M, our shorthand for Morbidity and Mortality conference, as we discussed the past month's failures. The department systematically reviewed each case where an error led to a preventable death or morbidity. We critiqued and analyzed the choices and protocols, looking for system-based issues, which if corrected would improve future outcomes.

I'd stare at my colleagues and wonder about everything we weren't discussing. How it felt to be responsible for a bad outcome. How it felt to make such an awful disclosure to the family. How it felt to round on the patient day after day, confronted by the concrete aftermath of your choices. It seemed a terrible blind spot that we did not discuss the toll those errors exacted on us.

Medicine is not oriented to recognize trauma in its own. We

do not debrief our team or even ourselves after a code. We do not pause and assess the emotional well-being of our colleagues after they lose a patient, the way we pause to assess the root cause of errors. We were trained to leave the thin veneer covering our colleagues' emotions undisturbed. We have utterly no idea what to do with shame. We have built no confessionals.

As doctors, we are taught to both conceal our emotions and not to indulge the emotions of others very early in our training. I first heard this characterized in medical school. Our anatomy professor gave a lecture focusing on Sir William Osler, the father of modern medicine. Osler, born in 1849, created the first residency program for specialty training of physicians. He was the first to bring medical students out of the lecture hall and to the bedsides of patients. He is credited with establishing the tradition of clinical training. And though Osler is revered for the value he placed in the patient's voice, the lesson for the day was "Aequanimitas." Osler regarded this trait as the premier quality of a physician. It represented an imperturbability that was described as manifesting in "coolness and presence of mind under all circumstances, calmness amid storm, clearness of judgment in moments of grave peril." It was the stoic posture you held while your colleagues discussed your error. A structured distance from your own emotions. In today's language we'd call it centering yourself, but taken several steps further—fully centered and not ever allowing the emotions of others to jostle you from your position.

The message imparted to us was that in order to have clear judgment, one must maintain distance and coolness. We were taught that to be a good physician, we had to cultivate a certain reserve. We aspired to be good physicians and accepted at face value that lesson, handed down as if a trade secret. They were setting the groundwork for the detachment that was expected of us on the wards.

As a medical student, my pediatrics rotation required that I spend two weeks in the pediatric ICU of an inner-city children's hospital. I found it utterly impossible to be detached or reserved in that unit. Every child there represented a tragedy from that evening's local news: house fires, attempted murder-suicides, meningitis outbreaks. The acuity of the sadness there, the precision of the grief, was impossible for us as students to ignore.

When we expressed sympathy for the suffering of the patients or families, it was shut down by our supervising physicians. "You're supposed to be the doctor," we were told, "you won't be able to care for them, to do what needs to be done if you let yourself feel every sadness that comes through these doors." Despite their fatalism, we suspected they must have once been just as open as we were. So we were left to wonder, had they learned the lesson by feeling every sadness, only to be helpless and paralyzed as a result? Or had they entered training with a wall already constructed? We didn't know. We only knew we couldn't ask.

The demeanor modeled was a coolly distant authority, with little value placed on empathy. "Caring" was the purview of nurses and social workers. The mantra was, if you want to treat disease, become a doctor. If you want to care for patients, become a nurse. Practical, academic rounds continued undeterred by misery or heartbreak.

But we were so young, and we'd yet to be truly indoctrinated to the clinical sterility our short white coats symbolized. Even just wearing the coats felt strange to us. They externally identified us to others as something we knew ourselves not to be. They aligned us with a profession before we had assimilated into the group. They felt more like costumes than clothing. So we gave them utilitarian functionality. We stuffed the pockets full of miniature versions of texts we needed. We armed ourselves with reflex hammers and flashlights. We weren't yet doctors, but we had all the paraphernalia. We could pretend.

When a child with a severely malformed heart died, my classmate and I paused at the end of the bed. She held my wrist as we both struggled to take in the death. Neither of us had ever seen a child die. We had just witnessed the team go to heroic lengths in an effort to save him, and now we were expected to walk away, to let the nurses prepare his body for his parents to view. We were locked together in a moment of shared, solemn grief. The attending walked toward us, after notifying the family of his death, and chastised us harshly.

"Do you know what you're doing?" she asked. I thought I did know, but sensed she didn't want an answer.

"You," she began, pausing to lock each of us in her gaze, "are behaving in a way I would characterize as immature and reckless. If you allowed yourself to get close enough to this child that you need to mourn his death, which, by the way, if you knew anything about medicine, you would know was a complete inevitability . . . if you feel close enough to mourn him then you are irresponsible. Period. How do you expect to care for the other children in your charge?" She paused, and again I understood she did not expect an answer.

"Right. You can't. Make no mistake, you have chosen to put every other child in this unit at risk with your own stupidity."

I caught my friend's eyes and looked away with embarrassment. I struggled to take in what the attending had told us. We were irresponsible and reckless. We were stupid and immature. We lacked judgment and we were making a terrible mistake. Our mistake had horrific consequences. I believed her. I was so sad I couldn't focus on the next patient's needs, except if I viewed them as a distraction from my sadness. So it seemed there could be some truth to her suggestion that our sadness could endanger our other patients. Some truth to the possibility that if we felt our feelings we would kill the people we were supposed to help protect.

At the time, I believed her contempt was directed entirely at us. Looking back, I wonder whether she was scolding herself as well. It seemed impossible to me that she could have succeeded in never feeling any emotional connection to those children or their outcomes. We promised ourselves, when we were in positions of authority, that we would figure out a way to be different. Oppression, by its nature, breeds the power necessary to mount a resistance and to overthrow itself. But that would take years.

In the interim, we learned quickly to shut it down. After all, any and all signs of emotion were immediately met with an assessment of "perhaps this is too much for you. You may not be cut out for this kind of work." We learned that crying happened in closets or on the drive home, but always alone.

We'd duck in after a horrible delivery and we'd cry helplessly. And as we wiped our eyes and attempted to regain our composure, we'd realize there were no safe spaces. Because in the hospital affiliated with our medical school, supply closets were sometimes used as staging areas for those black-and-white shots of dead babies paired with stuffed animals. We would be startled to find the baby at eye-level, propped up on a shelf, while someone gathered the remaining items for the obligatory remembrance box. We'd feel disgusted by the lack of reverence. Paralyzed by the irony that in staging a photo meant to venerate the sanctity of life, we could denigrate the baby and our own humanity in the process. We could find no spaces in which to heal.

I thought of the disillusioned OB resident, crying in the corner of my ICU room, worried that he wasn't cut out for the work. I sunk into the recognition. My room was the safe place he had come to heal. He'd been taught the exact same empty nonsense I had been taught: that there was no room for emotion. We were easy targets. Our need to belong made us each uniquely susceptible. Like any outsider, we found it seductive to think that if we could play by the rules, we could belong, we could be accepted as one of them. We were told the goal was to conquer, suppress and internalize our emotions. We had no idea that there might be an alternative. We did not know we could cultivate a space for those feelings to be unpacked, understood and allowed to foster connection. That there was reciprocity in empathy.

We created illusory selves. We internalized their archaic rules and collectively attempted to forge new respective identities. We took their instructions and wrapped ourselves in them like bandages, leaving our true selves to suffocate beneath. This covering was destined by its own contingency to be unsustainable. For the most part, we'd each find a means of unearthing ourselves later. Our feelings would surface, like bubbles of gas in a liquid. Some of our classmates found reencountering their feelings unbearably difficult and instead attempted to re-drown them in alcohol and addiction. Some left medicine for alternate careers. Some committed suicide.

Because shame and guilt and sorrow always float.

Shame doesn't strike like a fist. It rots its way in. Shame unravels us at our most fragile seams. It burns holes in our façade and allows light to shine on our self-doubt. It whispers to us, reminding us that we are imposters and, by the way, are not actually fooling anyone. It's unique in its devastating ability to make us feel exposed and worthless. Compounding that, our training bludgeons out of us even our ability to have empathy for ourselves. We learn to stop feeling our feelings, just as we are trained to disengage from the feelings around us.

We may try to delete the feeling, like an unflattering photo. We may dig a hole and try to force it in, like a rigored corpse. Some of us may attempt to submerge it, or rebuild the tower of ourselves on top of it. But it remains the foundation, contaminating the groundwater and corroding through every layer.

Physicians are uniquely harsh in our self-assessments. As an internal medicine resident in New York, during my infectious diseases rotation, I was assigned to supervise an intern who was having difficulty performing his assigned duties. He was anxious at baseline and had made a few errors, which resulted in his receiving a poor performance review. His competency was being examined by our program leadership. His every order and presentation were scrutinized for further proof that he was unfit. Anxious and on edge, and knowing he was being watched, he began to unravel. He neglected to act on a positive blood culture result, he wrote a few incorrect orders and misinterpreted some lab values. No one was harmed; each error was caught before it reached the patient. It is difficult to even categorize the mistakes as near misses, but they were each taken very seriously, as a matter of procedure. I was asked daily by a chief resident to elaborate on how he was doing. Each day, I reported that he was decompensating further. He began mumbling to himself. He was sent for a formal psychiatry evaluation. By the end of our month together, the decision had been made at some anonymously high level to hold him back. He was told he would have to begin a structured remediation program and likely repeat his intern year.

He was told that news on the Friday of the long Fourth of July holiday weekend. He called me three times in sequence at 5, 6 and 7 p.m., and I didn't answer the phone out of irritation, guilt and avoidance. Sometime on Sunday, he killed himself three different ways. He didn't believe he deserved to be held back; he believed that his mistakes warranted a sentence of asphyxiation, lethal injection and severed arteries, and he dutifully carried it out. We didn't find him until Tuesday, when he didn't appear to repeat his intern year.

"We killed him," I told my friends when they expressed their horror or pity. They shook their heads, believing my responsibility was misplaced. I was absolutely certain in my conviction. "We killed him with our suspicion and judgment. None of us could have withstood the scrutiny of the lens he was under."

We were predictably told by our mentors, "Listen, clearly he just wasn't cut out for medicine. Some people aren't." There were whispered suggestions of mental illness. The shared narrative of inadequacy and shame was perpetuated. As if resilience were a binary trait that one possessed or lacked. As if resilience didn't require a culture that is committed to fostering dialogue, building spaces for shared disclosure, and empathy. A culture designed to help us heal ourselves so that we may better attend to our patients.

It made no sense: we belonged to a profession that should have anticipated failure at every turn. The complexity of the medical system made failure an inevitability. The human body itself is designed to fail. Senescence is embedded in our genetic code. Our patients would die; it was an unavoidable reality. So if we knew this, then why hadn't we built resiliency into the system? Why was each person's grief treated as an unexpected aberration? A culture that cultivated resilience would be prepared to meet a whole range of experiences, and it would draw upon a community to allow all members to survive.

When a second intern dove out of his apartment window, falling to his death onto the scaffolding beneath, it was his friend and our classmate who ran out to him. He rushed out to feel for a pulse, only to feel exposed bones, extruded by the fall. We received his broken body in our own emergency department. We heard the echoes of our training, reminding us that if we felt the sadness, we wouldn't be able to care for other patients. We were trained to stop feeling death. Even that of our own. I called my mother from the call room and managed, "Another one, another one of us killed himself."

"Oh! How horrible. I don't understand what is going on there. Maybe you should come home," she'd suggest.

But we didn't go home.

Instead, there was a makeshift memorial held in our hospital's lecture hall. Someone read a poem he'd written as a teen. Pictures of him during happier times were projected onto the screen. And then the very next day, in the same seats, at the same time, we attended a Grand Rounds on management of chronic heart failure.

The trouble with not having a safe space within medicine is that for those outside of medicine, our stories are almost too much to bear. I'd try to download my day, in an effort to find solace, but inevitably my sounding board would get caught up in the details of the story. I found if an event was terrible enough that I needed to debrief, it was too awful for anyone to see past the drama to my emotions and needs. I'd become easily annoyed, feeling they were missing the point, perpetuating my sense of isolation.

That was when I took up painting. I found comfort in transferring my disquiet and bad dreams onto canvas. With symbolism and oils I could bury painful narratives under a layer of pigment and find a peace that otherwise eluded me. Somehow during the hours that I held the brushes and allowed impressions to emerge, I'd silently shed many of the conflicted emotions that accompanied each new trauma. Art knows death. It understands that the unbearable happens. It mirrors to us that whatever we are feeling, it has happened before and to others, and they survived it. Or they didn't, but the art survived. The representation of their suffering survived to commune with us. We are not at all novel, art reminds us. We are a very small part of an ongoing and enduring history of suffering and redemption. Art knows subtlety. It knows that our first go at representing anything is almost always flat and insubstantial. In order to really represent an object, we must layer the paints to achieve depth. Our first pass serves only to create a foundation. It's only on reapproach that we can layer in contrast or highlight a previously neglected area. It's only on revisiting anything that we can hope to approach understanding.

I painted young girls cloaked in masks, safe in boats or half-submerged in heavy, opaque blue water. Young boys playing dress-up in military uniforms and taxidermied animal masks, not understanding the true threat of death that war confers, or the danger of disguises. A star-marked sheep emerging into a clearing from one small forest, only to enter a larger, darker one. I painted the coldest winter. A young copper-haired girl sitting, waiting pensively for someone who would never arrive. Blooms of flowers bursting through a skeletal birdcage of ribs.

I'd never actually get over the death of my patient or the suicide of my co-residents, but I learned over time to subvert the shame, both mine and theirs, into a kind of willful dedication to their memory. They stayed with me, reminding me to be more vigilant, more caring and more attentive.

In choosing to carry forward and honor each loss in that way, I felt I was keeping a small piece of them alive. As if I could catch some fragment of the light they'd emitted even through the darkness, like fireflies in a mason jar, and use it to guide the way forward.

As an attending, I went through a period of being almost satirically kind to my teams. I brought them cookies if they were post-call, compliment them at every possible turn, reassure them that they were doing a good job, and remind them that they were worthy of compassion. I'd urge them to identify outlets for their stress. It was a blatant overcompensation. They had no knowledge of the darkness from which that light originated. They saw only blind acceptance, and they knew that regardless of their mistakes, I held them in unconditional positive regard. It was the only way I knew to keep them safe.

What did I want to keep them safe from, but the failures? I didn't know then how transient our successes actually were. Even when everything goes perfectly right and life is restored, is drawn back successfully from the abyss, it's always a temporary state. We cannot define success as beating death because death cannot be beaten. The undeniable fact of death remains, imposing and impending regardless of our temporary victories. How we care for each other during life is the true restoration—the definition of agency. That is the win, the success we must look for and mark and define ourselves by. Our ability to be present with each other through our suffering is what we are meant to do. It is what feeds us when the darkness inevitably looms.

We cannot avoid the darkness, just as we cannot evade suffering.

Loving each other through the darkness is the thing to look for and to mark. It's there, in the shadows, where we find meaning and purpose.

Nine

Revolutions

All told, it took two years from that first night, and multiple surgeries, for me to regain my footing. I can't say "it took me two years to recover," because that implies some aspect of completion, that I arrived at some predetermined destination intact and whole. I didn't and couldn't become myself again, because that self no longer existed. Instead I found that with each incident, each organ failure or surgery, I was reshaped into a new configuration.

That April, two years later, I was well enough to help plant rows of bright pink and red begonias around the perimeter of the boxwood hedges. I enjoyed watering them, and watching them grow, though deer ate half of the garden. At the end of the season, when the plants were uprooted and torn out, I was surprised to find myself upset. "We should have planted bulbs, or some sort of perennial," I told Randy. I disliked that so much care and attention went into something with such a brief lifespan. Though they certainly brought beauty and joy to us, I wanted some version of the same flowers to return to us the next year, as a perennial would. I attached to the idea that from some core central memory, a new burst of life, different and yet the same, would bud each spring.

I identified with the life cycle of tulips and other perennials. Their hopeful rebirth each year, enabled by a graceful return to the ground. Rotting as a means to transform. I knew from my study of cell biology that my body, by cellular makeup, was an entirely different physical structure than it had been when I was a resident or medical student or child. Every past iteration had been supplanted by its replacement. I of course carried forth some aspects of their personalities and the strong memories that imprinted upon them, but the people they were had gone missing. Even today, almost everything I know about myself is already a memory. If death is a state of complete inaccessibility, then in truth we die many deaths.

When I arrived at the hospital in shock, I arrived as a physician. It was my default orientation to the world. I had spent the past fourteen years in pursuit of that goal, and I was completely enmeshed. It formed the core of my approach to any problem, medical and otherwise. It was the framework from which I hung my observations, assessments and plans. Even as I approached the emergency room that first night, my thoughts were the measured, structured thoughts of a physician. I was unable to relate to myself as a patient. Presented with the problem of pain, I responded by listing differential diagnoses and prognosticating for myself. When I found myself dizzy and unable to stand in OB triage, the physician in me perversely enjoyed experiencing shock firsthand. The intensity of my focus on medicine was such that I felt fortunate to have the learning opportunity, to personally engage with the pathophysiology I had studied for so long. I knew I was dying, and I was still awestruck by the science of my decline.

The superficial external indicators of my transformation into a patient came first: the gown, the hospital bed and the medications. I had amassed all the accoutrements of illness. But they felt unmistakably other, in the same way the white physician's coat had years before. I couldn't integrate the gown or the IV into my sense of self; instead I observed them somewhat ironically. They were incongruous with who I believed myself to be. During the first days of my hospitalization, I continued to observe events from the vantage point of a physician. I translated my lab values into a perioperative mortality estimate, as I had been trained to do. I critiqued the decisions that were being made like a supervising physician. I criticized the doctors' plan to send an unstable patient for a CT scan. I believed they weren't aggressive enough getting their crashing patient into the operating room. I didn't warn the family, my family, how grave the situation was. I maintained the measured distance dictated by my training.

My physical body was the first to transform in that space. It swelled and grew grotesquely, like Violet Beauregarde in *Willy Wonka & the Chocolate Factory*, and later shrunk, desiccating almost by the hour. My blood was entirely lost and then replenished by the blood of others. Chunks of organs were chiseled out and humbly regenerated. I lost words and memories, while others remained. The change in my body led to the shift in my perspective. I didn't stop being a physician; rather, being a physician stopped serving me. Without the ability to treat or heal, the orientation became impractical. I had to let those parts fall away in order to grow new, more immediately relevant parts. Anxious parts, parts that understood immobility, pain and helplessness. Like burs and sock-hooks, they stuck to me as I passed through.

When I first returned to work, it was the doctor coat that felt completely foreign. I struggled to wear it, making excuses about the itchy polyester or suggesting that I had spilled coffee on it on the way into work and had abandoned it in the car. For a full year I referred to it as my "doctor costume." I opted for business attire and would wear a blazer or dress.

My heart remained in the patient realm. I felt my patients' fear, I felt the weight of fluid heaviness in their lungs when I studied their chest X-rays, I knew their pain. And far from being the distraction I'd been cautioned against, it felt very right to feel with them. To actually see the people beneath the transparent film of disease. With my illness, everything had fallen away, all notions of the so-called right way to approach patients, the value of austerity.

Who we are when everything is stripped away, in our barest moments, is something we don't routinely examine. When a horrific loss uproots us, we leave pieces of ourselves behind in the soil, the structure on which we built our identity reduced to nothing more than an absent appendage, left behind to rot. We define ourselves, our very identity, by our relationships, and when we lose someone, in the exchange we lose a noun that defined who we once were. We return to our lives as truncated versions of ourselves. We cease being wives, mothers or daughters as we accrue losses. We become the next version. I was not able to be the physician I had been, and I was no longer an expectant mother. I would always be a patient. In the ruined, rotting parts of who I had once been, I found dignity and beauty in the decay.

So it was there, two years later, in my disfigured, amalgamated state, that I first began to feel whole again. I first began to consider another pregnancy.

I made appointments with each of the doctors I trusted, who knew what I had been through, armed with long lists of questions. I asked my questions and verbalized my fears: What was their best estimate of the risk that I would assume if I were to become pregnant again? What was the risk of another adenoma forming in my liver under the influence of estrogen? Could it all happen again? I had long been in the habit of writing lists. Externalizing my memory of trivia and tasks allowed me to focus. I discovered I could externalize many things—even worry. These physicians did far more than engender trust. They were my soil, physically holding my anxiety so that the nidus of hope buried within my debris could grow in the direction of the light. I learned from them that relationships can shape us, that we grow in the shape and form of the cast they generously supply. That we can allow ourselves to be supported by an enveloping mold in the hands of others. Being buttressed by those physicians let me find the strength to trust my body again. I learned I was pregnant the following spring, just as the tulips were beginning to bloom.

My hard-won confidence in my body was not shared by my family or colleagues. And it probably isn't fair to expect that they could have met the announcement with anything but fear. They hadn't had the opportunity to process everything in the same way I had, they didn't have all of the same information I did. Information that suggested I would be OK, that any risk I was facing was no different from the risk of most women. The tumors were gone, and I didn't have a risk of having recurrent HELLP syndrome because I had never had it in the first place. All indications were that I would be fine. No one believed me.

We were not congratulated. The responses we heard in exchange for sharing the news of our pregnancy ranged from "Are you insane?" to "Why couldn't you leave well enough alone?" to

"I don't know if I can handle this" to the obvious "Great, now you really are going to die."

I knew the excessive worry wasn't entirely unjustified, so I reframed it as evidence of love. My illness had hurt everyone who cared about me, and their fear was real. I just couldn't share in it. From the earliest weeks of that pregnancy, I knew two things: I knew it was a boy, and I knew he'd be OK. I had no idea how I knew either of those things, but I told my husband, less than one month in, "I don't want you to worry. He's going to be fine. And I am going to be fine."

"I'm certainly glad you think so, and don't get me wrong, it's a comfort. But I don't know how you could possibly know that," he replied skeptically.

"I just do." I couldn't articulate that somehow all those years of listening to the signals of impending doom or tumor growth had allowed me to just know. Learning to listen had made me able to hear. I explained it in the only way I thought he could understand: "I know it the same way I knew I would marry you from the day we met."

He smiled, and accepted I was making some vague reference to luck and fate and chance.

"You'll see," I reassured him. And try as I might, I couldn't tap into the anxiety. Through some process of transference, it had shifted and was being held by others.

We had met by a trick of fate. Newly relocated to Michigan after completing residency training in New York, I'd brought with me a love of Haruki Murakami, a Japanese fiction writer who at the time would have been considered relatively obscure in the United States. My co-resident, the one who had so tragically dove to his death, had ignited this obsession when he sent me

Murakami's short story "Birthday Girl" on my thirtieth birthday. The most recent book by the author was due to be released that day, and I'd run to the bookstore to purchase it after a yoga class. It hadn't occurred to me that the selection of Japanese fiction in a Midwest bookstore might not match that of Manhattan's bookshops. When I didn't find it on the shelf, I resorted to comforting myself with caffeine in the bookshop café. As I sat down to study, I glanced up and saw the book I had come for, *Kafka on the Shore*, on the table of the man I would marry just over a year later.

It wasn't his book—he preferred Vonnegut and Salinger. Perhaps someone had left it behind? He eyed the cover skeptically when I asked him could I have it.

"You need this copy of Har-oook-ee Mur-ah-kam-ee's *Kafka on the Shore*?" he needled. His deliberate pronunciation meant to imply that my desire for this particular book by this foreign author was nothing more than a fabricated ruse to get to talk to him.

"Yes, actually. You're holding what is probably the only copy in the entire Midwest," I said with a New Yorker's disdain.

"Sure, here you go." He passed it to me, smirking.

My adoration of this particular author did not allow that someone could be so dismissive of his book, so I spent the next fifteen minutes drawing parallels between his writing style and those authors Randy had professed to like. And because he didn't appear convinced, I got up and bought him a copy of a more mainstream book by the author, by way of proof.

"Here. Read this," I ordered.

"Now?" he asked.

"No, not now, but you'll see. I'm right. He's amazing." I sat waiting for him to start reading, though I knew that wasn't likely.

Randy didn't know what to do with the odd woman in the

bookstore staring at him and demanding he read Japanese fiction, so he asked me to lunch.

As we sat in the exam room of the obstetrician years later, I studied his face, trying to remember a time when he had been a stranger. I couldn't. He squeezed my hand tightly.

"It's going to be fine," I told him.

"You keep saying that. I just can't stand the possibility of something happening to you," he replied.

The shape of his jawline from the side brought back a memory of a time when we were sitting in a social worker's faux-wood-paneled office a year before. We had decided to pursue adoption as a means of growing our family, and we were answering a series of generic questions. The social worker, reading off a list, asked Randy, "Why do you want to be a parent?," which struck me at the time as almost too vague to allow for a cogent reply. My mind immediately trended to the existential, the transmission of a worldview and legacy from one generation to the next. I had no idea what I would say. I looked at him, expecting to see a tense jaw or a furrowed brow. But Randy had no such issues with the question, and replied sincerely, "I look forward to waking up, hearing what my kid wants to do that day, and saying, 'OK, let's make it happen.' Whatever it is. I just want to make their little dreams come true. I just think that would be so awesome."

In that moment, all of my thoughts that had been stuck in the precontemplative, even subconscious, realm coalesced. I felt no one deserved to have the experience of being a parent more than he did. I knew I would do anything I could to afford him the experience of being a dad. I acknowledged a deep remorse that though adoption would allow the experience of parenting, it wouldn't allow us the magic of combining our DNA and personalities into a new miniature being. I worried that we were making the choice to adopt out of fear, and I knew in that moment we had to honestly reexamine the possibility of another pregnancy.

We left the social worker's office believing we would adopt. We prepared a binder of sunny, enticing pictures of our lives together. Photos of us engaged in activities children would enjoy, like eating ice cream and making art. We got on the waiting lists and waited, unsure if we were being overly cautious or overly optimistic. We didn't know if my body, after what it had survived, could even become pregnant. We didn't know if a birth mother would choose us. We debated and wondered and then decided we would trust in something bigger than ourselves to determine our path. We would stand in the presence of our lives and embrace whatever approached us. I stood in church and promised silently, *Whatever baby you decide to bring to me, I will know is it is meant to be mine.* And we became pregnant before we could adopt.

And so it came to be that we were sitting in an obstetrician's office rather than a social worker's. The obstetrician entered and sighed as he sat, smiling at us and our chart in series. He looked exactly the way you hoped an obstetrician would look, late-middle-aged with grayed temples and sharp glasses. He had clear blue eyes that conveyed an intent to get things right. His shoulders were slightly hunched and his brow furrowed despite the smile.

"I know, we're here really early in the pregnancy," I explained, thinking his sigh was a message meant to convey that we were too excited, too early. "And I know that there isn't anything much to do so early, but . . . well, you know what happened last time, and, well, we're probably crazy now. Which is why we are here, I guess. For reassurance."

"Yeah. That's OK. You're at about six weeks, right? That's fine," he reassured us.

Smiling at me sadly, he then said, "I might not be seeing pregnant patients for much longer. I've been trying to cut back on my hours. If I could get down to eighty hours a week, that would be really great. I talked to my chairman; I told him I just couldn't keep up with the pace anymore. I love the work; I am just trying to find some semblance of balance."

He described the toll his job had taken on his family. His difficulty in his first marriage, the kind of husband he wanted to be but wasn't. The way they blamed each other for their failures. The stigma and the blame of the cases that ended poorly. The variety of unhealthy coping mechanisms he'd sometimes employed to get through. How he was exercising more and it was helping. He cited chewing gum as his only vice.

"It is hard work being a parent," he admitted. "And a spouse. And it is hard work being a doctor. We carry around a lot of fear and anxiety and shame, don't we?"

I nodded. Randy's head ping-ponged between us, unsure as to whether he was understanding what he was seeing.

"Yeah, I know. So, you're six weeks pregnant, and that's wonderful. We'll check some blood work and you'll have an ultrasound in two more weeks. Maybe we'll get lucky and see a heartbeat. That would be nice." He smiled. "It's just that I want you to know, it never gets any easier, you know? But it will be fine. One way or another, it will be fine."

I felt suddenly certain I would cry. His suffering was palpable, and I knew by extension he more than understood our special kind of crazy. And I trusted him that no matter what, it would be fine. Either way, we'd be OK.

Anxious patients can be frustrating. Their endless lists of questions are easy to view as some passive-aggressive indictment of our capabilities. Physicians often become defensive, or worse, patronizing. Hearing "don't worry" or "just rest" is, more often than not, frankly insulting. And I had heard that repeatedly. But then there were physicians like him, physicians who had had their hearts broken. He understood implicitly where I was and how I had gotten there. He had been humbled by his own suffering.

He spent the next six months in partnership with us, accessible and present. He validated our occasional fears and meticulously followed through on his promises. And just as he had assured us, it was mostly fine. It wasn't until the twenty-seventh week that we realized there was a serious problem.

As was true of every other stitch placed that first night, the ones placed in my uterine wall were intended only to vaguely approximate tissue, not to facilitate healing or entertain the possibility of future pregnancies. As the baby grew, and the wall stretched, it became perilously thin.

He called me an hour after my routine ultrasound was completed.

"Hi, where are you?" he asked.

Oh, how I hated that question. "I'm here, in the hospital, I just had my ultrasound, but you probably already knew that. I was just headed back to the ICU." I realized I was rambling, possibly as a means of stalling the news.

"Good." He was not deterred. "I want you to go to OB triage, and tell them I said to put you in a bed on the prenatal ward, and give you a steroid shot to help the baby's lungs mature. Do that right now, OK?"

"Why? What's wrong?" I asked, struggling to catch my mind up with the apparent urgency of the situation.

"The wall of your uterus, in the area of the scar, it's just that there's no muscle there. It's about two millimeters thick and it should be two centimeters at least. You are at risk of uterine rupture and you need to be on bed rest immediately, that's all."

My initial reaction was pure self-pity. I wondered silently and aloud why it was so difficult for me to get past this stupid seventh month of pregnancy. The disappointed voice didn't last long. It was quietly and tenderly replaced by a comforting line from "Birthday Girl": "No matter what happens to a person, he or she will always be who they were meant to be."

"It's going to be OK," he assured me. "I'll ask the neonatologist to come by. We'll handle everything. They're used to early babies."

"I know you will, but it's too early," I told him, remembering the awful translucence of the first baby's miniature body from the black-and-white photo.

"Maybe we can get a few more weeks out of you, we'll see. But either way, it will be OK. I want you to remember that." And with that he hung up.

I sat, phone in hand, wondering who to call first.

I was checked in and handed a gown. A papery ID band that recalled entry to childhood carnivals was secured tightly around my wrist. As I looked down at the gown and neon socks with built-in traction stripes, I recognized myself as a patient. Then a long needle was plunged into my backside as if to accentuate the conversion. Randy arrived, shaking his head, incredulous we were here again so soon.

The neonatologist laid out the possibilities for us. "At twenty-seven weeks, it's certain the baby would need breathing support. By thirty-two weeks this decreases significantly. The risk of bleeding into the brain, or intraventricular hemorrhage, is decreased by the steroid, but still a very real complication, and the incidence similarly decreases with age," he said. "Usually by twenty-seven weeks, it's rare to lose the baby. We can do what we need to and keep them alive, it is more a question of disability."

I smiled at his confidence, knowing we'd lost the last baby at exactly twenty-seven weeks.

I listened to each risk estimate he put forth, each horrific possible scenario, with a certainty that it would be OK. It wasn't that I didn't value their carefully formulated risk estimates, it was just that in the same way my body had warned me of its own impending demise, it was now covertly reassuring me that it would be fine.

Whatever the challenge or disability or setback, I would be who I was meant to be. And something told me I was meant to be this baby's mother.

I made myself at home on the antepartum ward. I was kept entertained with a steady supply of books, food and company. Randy came every morning on his way to work and every evening on his drive home, as if the hospital were a refueling station on his daily commute. He brought in bouquets of brightly colored tulips to cheer the room. They served as a visual reminder of rebirth allowed by each change of season. My mom would arrive laden down with bags of soft pastel reams of wool and warm food. She patiently taught me to knit, effortlessly crafting beautiful receiving blankets by way of example. I knitted misshapen hats and booties from online patterns. The days passed peacefully, with a comforting rhythm that allowed for testing, but also space to not feel as if I were a patient every minute of the day.

My friends and colleagues stopped by to check on me; as I was conveniently located within our shared workplace, it made a good break in the day. They seemed consistently surprised to find me perfectly well. Behind their cheery greetings, there was often a fine trail of sorrow trailing behind them. Bad outcomes, elusive diagnoses and mistakes that left them tinged with guilt followed them into the room. In that quiet space, where absolutely nothing new happened to me from day to day, there was space to fill. They were offered tea or homemade cookies by my mom and the disclosures would follow, liberated by the shared time, carbohydrates and caffeine. Though they arrived most often in pairs, in my memory we're all in the room together, at the same time, sitting in a circle. Drinking strong tea or coffee out of small Styrofoam cups. There would be a period of silence and someone would start talking.

> *I have a kid in my unit, he's not quite brain-dead, but anything that would have defined him as himself is clearly never coming back. But he can breathe above the ventilator and blinks once in a while. But the family just can't accept it. They keep saying they are hoping for a miracle, so now the poor kid will get placed in a nursing home for the rest of his life. And I just feel horrible about it. Like I somehow should have stopped this from happening. But I didn't know how. How could I have done that differently?*

I came to recognize these admissions as a form of purging. These were the thoughts that haunted us. They nearly always came out rapidly, with almost pressured speech. Always en bloc, without even a pause. The questions posed within them were entirely rhetorical. Asked of themselves, of the room and of me, without any expectation of an answer. They were our collective memories, shared in traditional storytelling format. Uniting us as a group by reflecting our shared experiences back to us. As if we had hit our limit of individual understanding, and by sharing our experiences with our little community, we hoped to understand them through the combined wisdom of our group.

We rarely responded to each other, opting instead to share another event or struggle. At times the disclosures were framed as irritations or annoyances, when really it was a deep remorse over a flawed system that we felt powerless in the face of.

> *So, my team told the patient that Nephrology wouldn't offer dialysis because of how sick he was and that the patient should really have comfort measures only. Then, Nephrology comes by and says they will dialyze the patient. So we look as if we aren't communicating, which I guess we aren't, and everyone is confused. And now the family doesn't trust us, or our suggestion that the patient enroll in hospice.*

Rather than any awkwardness, the silence in between disclosures was a kind of tacit support. It said, *Yes, I know how that feels, and it's terrible. I have felt how you feel and I have no answers.* I saw how, lacking other options, we internalized so much of the anger that was directed at us. We believed being conciliatory and acquiescing in the face of confrontation was the professional thing to do. Friends who were physicians at neighboring hospitals would visit, and I would be struck by the commonality of our experience, regardless of venue.

> *The team wasn't sure of the code status of the patient, so they did thirty minutes of CPR and intubated the poor ninety-six-year-old man, and his daughter comes in this morning just livid, not understanding how this could happen. What could I say but "I'm sorry"? Because honestly, I don't understand how it happened either.*

There was a range of distress expressed that went from compassion fatigue to addiction to full-fledged burnout.

> *I'm finding it hard, seeing so much sadness every day, to even feel it anymore. And I've been drinking so much more lately, and I know it's not good, but honestly it's the only way I can fall asleep.*

> *I am seriously considering switching training programs or getting an MBA. This just isn't what I thought it would be like, clinically. I don't feel as if I am making a difference for anyone in any meaningful way.*

And at times, we reflected on utterly heartbreaking moments that somehow were supposed to be just part of a day's work.

> *The patient wouldn't accept a blood transfusion, so I told her, "That's fine, we'll deliver the baby and I'll hand it to you and you'll have maybe one or two hours with your baby, and then you'll have to say good-bye." And she looked at me and said, "You mean I'll die?" And I had to tell her, "Yes, without blood, you will die, but I will honor your wishes that you do not accept a blood transfusion, even if I don't agree."*

We had no idea what to do with our own feelings over the losses we carried.

> *Today I had to watch a seven-year-old say good-bye to his mom, because she won't be getting a liver transplant. He looked at me and said, "Are you going to fix my mom so she can come home?" I mean, what am I supposed*

*to do with that? I'm scared to go home because I know as
soon as I see my kid who is about the same age I'm going to
lose it.*

There was heartbreak and mountains of guilt and the desperate wish for some mechanism, any mechanism, to augment our resilience. As a physician, I understood how perilously close we always were to failing someone. Even when we intended to do no harm, it seemed we lacked the necessary tools to heal without layering in some added suffering.

I didn't realize during these visits what we were doing in sharing these stories. I didn't know that we were exploring the relationship between memory and trauma. But because the site of the trauma was always in our workspace, and would necessitate being revisited rather than sanctified, we had to find a different way to venerate the loss. While the rooms our patients inhabited were the sites of shared trauma, they could not assume the connotation of a consecrated space; they had to be reused. It's interesting: in turning over the rooms to the next patient or the next procedure, we were obliterating the memory of the sacred. In communities that experience a shared loss, obliteration is usually reserved for tragedies that are a source of shame. Did we realize we were obliterating our losses? Was it because we lacked a marker for the trauma that we absorbed it into our beings? Having no physical place to memorialize them, we collectively took them on as our own. We held them in our chests and in our stomachs and in our hands.

I saw how much we all hurt in the same vulnerable places. The shame of doing your best and never having it be good enough left its mark on each of us. And though we'd grown accustomed to never discussing it, there was a grace and a mercy to be found in sharing our pain. It transcended the individual trauma, united us as a sacred group. By organizing and understanding the events within a social context, we organized and mapped our memories in the kind light of shared understanding. I knew then that the deficits I had witnessed as a patient and my struggles as a physician were not in any way unique to me. And I knew that while we had no solution between us, we were a community.

"You have a really hard job," my mom would say, looking up from her knitting needles, addressing those visiting in the same way, almost independent of what they had said. And we'd nod. She was acclimated to the sadness of our stories as well as the harshness of our own lens. There was no judgment and no attribution of blame, only acceptance. It was such a simple validation, and yet for us, in those moments of risk and exposure, it was what we needed. We had sanctified and found refuge in such an unlikely place—a room on the obstetrical floor, just meters from where I had first died. And perhaps what was the most surprising was how little it took to heal our spirit. A safe space, shared disclosure within a trusted community, and we could each breathe again. We could reenter our world.

The bonds formed in that room outlasted my stay there. Even years later, when we encountered each other in elevators and hallways, we would skip the superficial and say exactly what we were thinking.

"Did you hear about the suicide over at the medical school?" my colleague asked as we walked in to a meeting. I had.

"I've been thinking about running a seminar for medical students on shame. Would you be interested in helping?" he asked, his eyes cloudy with sadness. I would.

We found each other when we had a case that unhinged us. We didn't hide. We texted each other after a code: *I need to debrief,* and we would come together and we would listen.

Our circles gradually expanded, bringing more people into

the protective fold. We brainstormed and collaborated, finding agency in our shared grief. We developed seminars and communication workshops, armed ourselves and other physicians with the tools necessary to navigate difficult conversations. We gave lectures on empathy, we shared poetry by e-mail and tried reflective writing. We admitted we needed each other. We became a community.

Before we managed to put any of that in place, I was offered a reminder of why it was so necessary. Four weeks into my stay on the antenatal ward, things deteriorated, and my uterus threatened to rupture. It began subtly contracting, challenging the thin wall, leading the obstetrician on call to come in to introduce himself, just in case. His insistence upon addressing me from just inside the doorframe immediately irritated me. He appeared tired and vaguely bored. He asked me no questions but instead began by saying, "I know the plan is to take you to the OR in the morning, but if things get worse, I just wanted to have met you." I considered his statement and was confused by it. He wanted to have met me, as if that were the only prerequisite necessary to operate on someone.

"OK, so you've seen my scans?" I asked.

"No, I haven't, but it's fine. There's nothing to worry about," he said, attempting to reassure me.

I found it insulting and condescending to assume that he could reassure me simply by stating that he wasn't worried. I thought maybe he needed more data to decide if he should be worried or not. "So, the placenta is actually laying exactly over the area in which you would make your incision." I paused, waiting for some reaction. I got nothing in return, so I continued. "Did you know I had a vertical incision during my crash C-section before?" I again gave him an opportunity to respond. He stared at me silently. "So, hypothetically, if you found that scar intra-operatively and decided to make the same incision, you'd cut through the placenta. Did you know that? No, how could you if you hadn't seen the scans? Do you know my history at all?" I was angry.

Randy observed my tirade calmly, seeing clearly I had found my voice and could advocate for myself.

When the obstetrician finally spoke, there was no concilia-tory acknowledgment or apology. Instead he was full of arro-gance and self-importance. "Listen, you can't be a passenger and pilot at the same time. And just so we're clear, I'm the pilot." It was the first time he made eye contact with me, and it was clear he was using it to intimidate me.

I allowed five seconds to silently pass, and I held his gaze while I weighed my options. Fire him and have no one on staff to de-liver me that night if needed, or accept his dismissive posturing and swallow my discomfort.

"You will not operate on me, and you can leave." I was done. I was done tolerating patronizing physicians. I was done being made to feel as if I should accept that I could not trust the per-son whom my life depended upon. I called my OB and begged him to promise me that this doctor would not be in the OR, no matter what.

"I do not want that man operating on me." I was indignant. "I'm not trying to be difficult, but I honestly don't think I could do it. I don't trust him."

"If I have to come in from home, I will. I will be the one to deliver your baby," he promised. He confided, later, how con-cerned he was that he would not be alert enough to drive in if I needed him before morning. He was on call the previous night and had not slept in forty-eight hours. He hoped I would get through the night, and he could get sufficient rest to safely deliver our baby the following morning.

And he did. At 7:45 a.m. he delivered by C-section a premature but healthy 3-pound, 11-ounce baby boy. The moment I first heard his screechy, vigorous cry I let out a breath I felt I must have been holding for at least two years.

He was here.

And in that moment, I was transformed again, this time into a mother.

Ten

Deliverance

The tiny baby was examined, bundled and held near my face for a moment before being transferred to the Neonatal Intensive Care Unit. He was not breathing well at all. The delivery had been difficult. When my uterine wall was exposed, they found it thin enough to see through, like a transparent film of red velum.

Understanding the potential trauma conferred by a high-risk delivery, my obstetrician had attempted to prepare Randy for every contingency prior to going into the operating room. "If you hear me say kind of lightly, 'Hey, why don't you go to the waiting room?' it means things are OK, but I don't want you to worry. And if you stay, I know you'll see and hear things that will make you worry. But on the other hand, if you hear me say in a serious tone, 'I think you need to go to the waiting room *now*,' I want you to leave the OR and go to the waiting room. It means I don't want you to see what might happen. It means I think we are in trouble and you don't need to see. Do you understand?" He modulated his tone, demonstrating what urgency would sound like, versus a casual sort of request. We were primed for drama, and we both half expected to hear him say that Randy needed to leave immediately. We understood that if we heard that, he would be performing an emergency hysterectomy due to impossible-to-control blood loss, and that I could still die.

He never needed to use his secret code, but what we did hear him say repeatedly with an escalating sense of urgency was, "I need working suction. I need working suction. Why isn't the suction working?" I had lost a liter of blood, briskly, which obscured the operating field, but he managed skillfully to gain control of the bleeding.

The spinal anesthesia had the effect of making me feel as if my diaphragm were paralyzed and I couldn't breathe effectively. With my body flat and my arms secured to the table with heavy straps, my mind insisted on recalling that the mechanism of death in crucifixion was suffocation. It was a dry sort of drowning, a useless effort to draw in air. I thought of my friend trying to breathe against the wind as he fell from his apartment window to his death. I felt my heart race and beat heavily in my ears. I was reassured by the anesthesiologist that I was not in danger, even as they placed supplemental oxygen on my face.

I was grateful when the spinal anesthesia began to wear off, though it meant I began to feel each stitch as it was placed. I felt the needle puncture my skin, felt the thick cord-like suture pull through, and the needle pierce the other side. I could appreciate the tension placed on the string as my tissues were brought together. It wasn't painful, but the surreal experience of being awake as someone stitches you back together was disorienting. I waited it out as six or seven sutures were placed, before I announced casually to the surgeon, "You know I can feel your stitches." He redoubled his efforts to close me quickly.

In the controlled chaos, the baby had managed to get two

big inhalations of amniotic fluid into his premature lungs. I saw the harmful effects of this when I was moved and situated on the postpartum floor. Randy arrived and proudly showed me cell phone video of the baby in the sterile NICU incubator, and all I could think was *He needs to be on a ventilator.* "Why isn't he on a ventilator?" I asked, watching the spaces between his ribs retract with the effort of breathing and his lips go blue, understanding the extent of his respiratory distress.

He was placed on breathing support within the hour and given a viscous injection called surfactant into his airway twice, in an effort to help his lungs inflate. I was wheeled from my room to stare at this miniature being, red and feisty, connected by threadlike wires and electrodes to monitoring equipment. He had an impossibly thin line entering through his umbilical cord site. He had tiny goggles to protect his eyes from the UV light they were administering to help with his jaundice. His feedings were measured in milliliters and his weight gain in grams. Everything struck me as incredibly minute and precise, like wiring a dollhouse for electricity.

Though I didn't continually draw associations between the prior pregnancy and this one, it became clear that the NICU nurses did. Like a colony with a shared memory, they all seemed to be aware that I had lost the first baby, a few of them having been present at the emergency C-section. They generally seemed unsure that I would want to be reminded of that event, and they were mostly right in their conclusion, though their logic was flawed. I felt by focusing on the prior loss that they were missing some broader perspective. They saw only the delivery of a premature twenty-seven-week baby that didn't survive their efforts to resuscitate her. That event, admittedly awful if judged independently, couldn't be viewed in isolation. It deserved to be enveloped by the larger context of my critical illness. It was there that it gained meaning. I had survived both. I was whole and I was well and I was profoundly grateful. I couldn't see talking about one without also acknowledging the other.

When an NICU nurse tentatively mentioned to me that she had been there at the first delivery and began retelling the events from her perspective, I recognized immediately she had been the one who had been so disappointed when I wouldn't hold the dead baby.

"That was a bad night," she said tentatively.

Yes, I remembered, *it was a bad night.*

"This is going to be better," she reassured me. I attempted to judge the extent to which she believed her own statement by studying her expression. But like a flight attendant during heavy turbulence, she did not allow her face to betray her worry.

Perhaps unsurprisingly, she was the one who advocated, early and often, for me to hold this baby, even though he seemed remarkably fragile to me and I was sure it was a terrible idea. She warned that his skin was still delicate and I shouldn't apply any transverse pressure as his skin could tear. This description, of course, reminded me of the awful decomposing baby. She maintained that despite the fragility of his skin, holding him would be good for me and for him. It struck me as so odd that the same generic sentiment that a mother should hold her baby, if at all possible, could be projected onto such a different situation.

Holding him was logistically challenging and required an orchestrated effort to accomplish safely, all of which the nurse did uncomplainingly and with great efficiency. She untangled and secured his various wires and tubes, instructed me on how to sterilize myself thoroughly. It was then that I was handed the lightest possible version of a human. He felt like a bird in my hands, as if his bones must be hollow and that he might at any moment take flight.

She was right, of course, that it was tremendously beneficial and reassuring for me to hold him to my chest and feel the weight of his being in that tangible way. He was our levity and our gravity, lightening our burden while simultaneously firmly anchoring us to the earth and to each other.

"Hey buddy," I whispered to him. "We've been waiting for you." In that moment I understood our mutual dependence. I felt our small family being bound together and entwined by graceful, invisible stems. I understood that my body no longer defined the outer perimeter of my being. There was a part of me that occupied a space in the world that wasn't contiguous with my physical self. We would forever inhabit each other's orbit, held together by gravity, love and other unseen forces.

We somehow managed to avoid the many truly terrible events that can befall NICU babies. Debilitating hemorrhages into soft brains, heart defects that aren't compatible with life—truly gut-wrenching, scarring, life-altering horrors. We had none of that, thankfully. What we had were trivial, minute dramas that played out mostly in our heads, fueled by anxiety and the perceived tenuousness of a life so small.

We learned, for example, that premature babies have such poorly developed centers of respiration that they frequently stop breathing, events referred to as apneas. When they stop breathing, their heart rate declines sharply. NICU nurses are adept at responding to this, and often the baby will simply need stimulation to begin to breathe. They will jostle them, rub them and press firmly on their feet, and often that's enough to bring them back, to remind them they need to breathe. Sometimes the nurses uttered things under their breath like, "You aren't going to crump on me, little guy, are you?" I silently wished they wouldn't say such things, as this added weight to our fears that something serious was about to happen. Because while typically harmless, some apneas are in fact evidence of an infection or something worse.

When he was finally taken off the mechanical breathing support and left with only a miniature oxygen cannula, I would sit and watch as multiple times an hour he would have these long pauses in his breathing, and his heart rate would drop. Each time, it seemed I was watching him nearly die. I knew cognitively that wasn't the case, that this was common and expected, and in many ways part of the maturation process. We understood this in large part because this was anticipated for us. The beauty of the NICU is that for the patients there, the problems are somewhat limited in scope. They are all, to some extent, premature babies. While they each have some element of uniqueness, and varying degrees of illness, the problems they might have can be anticipated in a way that is not possible in the adult ICU. Many of them have a somewhat predictable course. This allows for true prognostication. The doctors and nurses were able to tell us, "Because of _____, we are worried X could happen. If X happens, we will respond by doing Y."

This engendered a kind of trust I hadn't known was possible. The very transparent discussions, the follow-through, the constant communication and disclosure created a cocoon of safety around us. I was able to leave him there at night and know I could absolutely trust them to care for him, to anticipate and respond to issues, and to communicate the results to me.

Despite this, there were moments of true anxiety. And those moments were enough to cast a dark shadow over that time. One of his apnea episodes was particularly refractory, and he was placed back on breathing support and given antibiotics in acknowledgment that his deterioration might be due to an infection. In that moment I wished more than anything that I could be the "sick" person again. Watching helplessly as he deteriorated was far harder on me than anything I had been through. I was embarrassedly aware of the privileged position I had occupied and how difficult it must have been for my family, watching me struggle through illness and setback after surgery.

I stared at the Santa ornament hanging on one corner of his small incubator, willing it to be a talisman, or at the very least to only be an ornament. I tried visualizing it hanging on our future trees, imagining its importance diluted by hundreds of other ornaments crowding the branches. I wondered why it had to be the exact same size as the teddy bears that accompanied the dead baby pictures. I didn't think I could survive leaving the hospital again with a box of haunted objects.

The nurses sensed my apprehension, my fear that we wouldn't be taking this baby home either. Though they couldn't concretely reassure me, as they never wanted to give the suggestion of false hope, they shared anecdotes and axioms. "There is something you can just tell about babies that are going to stay, they have this energy to fight right from the beginning. We look for that, and when we see it, it's very reassuring." They described babies born without that energy, without that light behind their eyes that declared an intention to remain. "The ones that are going to leave, it's almost like they were never even here. There is just something that somehow didn't make it into them in their journey to us, some spark that just didn't take."

I studied him in the light of these bits of insight. I thought I saw lots of energy, lots of light emanating from him. He was red and feisty and seemed tougher than his size would allow. He recovered from the setback. In fact, he improved steadily and was quickly transferred to the step-down portion of the NICU, to learn to eat and grow. For weeks he was unable to coordinate the combination of sucking, swallowing and breathing necessary to thrive. Then one day, just before Christmas, he finally figured it out. We learned then that we could take him home.

His nurses sent us off with warm hugs and genuine wishes. One nurse told me, "I will never forget waiting for him to be delivered, and you were on the table. The doctor kept asking for suction, because the suction in the operating room wasn't working. And I hear this voice just sort of quietly but firmly say, 'Can someone please fix the suction for him?' and I looked around to see who it was and it was you! And then towards the end of the surgery, you just calmly said, 'You know I can feel your stitches.' And I remember thinking, my goodness, if this woman can be so calm in this situation, she will be able to handle anything parenthood throws at her!"

"Hmm, did I seem calm? That's funny because inside I definitely was not feeling calm," I admitted.

"Then you are ready for motherhood, my dear!" she laughed.

She had been his primary nurse, which meant that if she was working, she was assigned to care for him. This paradigm allowed some continuity and a relationship to form. At that point, when we were leaving the NICU, I truly felt we shared the role of mother. She had done so much to care for him.

Ironically, though we had months to prepare to take him home, we had resisted fully preparing. We'd achieved a moderate level of superstition after having to return the first set of baby furniture, and we were reluctant to prepare his room. We had friends who understood our struggle and comforted us with stories meant to relate their state of utter unpreparedness when they brought their baby home.

My friend Dana, who had been with me the night I died, told us, "The truth is, you need a couple onesies, some diapers and a few bottles. That's it." She'd adopted her two children and was similarly unwilling to populate a home with baby equipment that might never be used. "The problem with this plan, however," she warned us, "is that once you do get home, you will almost certainly at some point find yourself parked in a Babies"R"Us parking lot, eating Taco Bell with one hand while frantically trying to figure out what items you actually do need to keep the baby alive."

Another friend kept his baby in a detached dresser drawer, cushioned with blankets, for the first two months until he and his wife had each slept enough to shop for a crib without arguing. He justified this by reminding us that he was raised in a Third World country and he understood this was not the standard for US parents.

I had eventually conceded that we should buy furniture, accepting that in all likelihood we would bring this baby home. Even with his physical presence in the world, it somehow still felt like a tremendous leap of faith to do so. We bought an ivory crib, a dresser with antique brass pulls that doubled as a changing table, and a tall French blue armoire. We retained the rocker and ottoman from our first ill-fated shopping trip, it having come in so handy when I was sick. We attempted to redecorate it with a blue throw pillow and the one blanket I'd managed to successfully knit while in the hospital draped over the back of the chair. On the wall hung three paintings I had made. One, an impossibly large elephant in a tutu balancing on a miniature ball. The second a circus ringmaster in the form of a monkey in a tuxedo with top hat and cane. And the third a large bear in a birthday hat riding a very small bike on a high wire. I wanted to imprint on his tiny memory the certainty that even the most improbable, fantastical things could happen if you allowed yourself to believe.

The first night home, I sat in the rocker to feed him. I laid the blanket I knitted over my lap and marveled at how, though it was a finished blanket, you could still see every loop and pull-through of the yarn. The process of its creation was evident, even long after it had been completed. I sat supporting the baby's neck with my hand the way I'd been instructed to in the NICU. Randy stood, frozen and speechless, leading me to believe I was doing something wrong with regard to positioning or feeding.

"What?" I asked. "What's wrong?" I saw tears building in his eyes.

There was a long stretch of silence before he began. "I used to watch you sleep in that rocker. Did you know I'd stay up all night worried you might die if I didn't? I'd listen to your breathing and be so scared I was going to lose you." He shook his head at the intensity of the memory.

I thought I understood. He was looking at me feeding our child in the rocker, but seeing my ghost. "But I'm OK now. You don't have to worry."

"No, I know. I'm not worried or sad," he said, wiping away his tears. "I'm happy. It's just one of those times when you really have a dream come true. Back then, I don't think I even dared to wish I would one day see you rocking our baby in this rocker. I just wanted you to be OK."

"But here we are." I smiled.

"Here we are indeed." He smiled back at me.

I sat and rocked our baby, reflecting upon how each child is a kind of distillation of every generation past, a concentrated extraction of DNA, of history and habits, of personality traits and aspirations. The old spirits evaporate, leaving only the residual essence of their shared history. He had my father's name, Marwan, which was also my liver surgeon's name, as his middle name. His first name was purposefully simple—Walt. Though we alternatingly attributed it to wanting a name that conferred a sense of kindness, or an evening newscaster's earnestness, or a Disney-like belief in magic, it also honored my love of poetry.

"I swear to you," I whispered to him, reciting from Walt Whitman, "there are divine things more beautiful than words can tell."

I had found all of my lost words, and still found them lacking. I couldn't articulate the magic that I felt in that room, with our little family crowded on that rocker. I knew that one day, despite what I knew of how words could utterly fail you at times, I would want to tell him how he was the physical embodiment of so much love and the distillation of our silent wishes and prayers.

Eleven

Relapse

Because of his severe prematurity, walking and other gross motor skills came late for Walt. His coordination was poor for the first two years, though in large part we chose not to acknowledge this reality. We instead made a series of compensations, including obsessively walking behind him to catch his falls. I photoshopped a lot of drool out of otherwise charming pictures. Unlike adults, who learn to hide so much, children have the remarkable gift of being unified in feeling and in body. They innocently express what they feel. If Walt was frustrated with the discoordination of his walking, he showed frustration; if he was sad because falling hurt, he cried. This honesty was so pure, and stood in contrast to the adults around him who seemed not to know what to do with feelings except to hide them. Vulnerability is not our default state, and most of us spend years creating layers of protection to shield us from judgment. So much so that when we encounter disability or even vulnerability in others we believe the proper thing to do is to pretend we don't see it.

By age three, he seemed to have shed the disabilities of prematurity for good, and we planned an elaborate circus-themed birthday party to celebrate. He and his friends were taught trapeze skills by a Ukrainian family and put on a show for the adults. There were unicycles, balance beams and a circus ringmaster. The children were decorated in brightly colored face paint and costumed themselves in ornate tutus and top hats. Balancing atop wobbly balls, they smiled proudly, aware of the magnificence of their newly acquired skills.

The instructors made the impossible seem effortless, while the children grunted and wiggled through their successes. Still, we were all impressed by the level of concentration and centeredness even the smallest among them demonstrated as they traversed the thinnest ropes and bravely mounted the unicycles. They seemed to naturally reframe their fear as excitement and channel their energy into sharp focus. That is the special magic children possess: their willingness to thoroughly invest in whatever reality they find themselves in.

Not long after his third birthday, the record-setting cold winter blew in, covering everything in an icy shell. There were four-foot-tall snowbanks and gusts of wind that simultaneously froze and burned any exposed skin in minutes. Looking out at the arrested world from inside the house, one could appreciate a static sort of beauty. It was the beauty of implied harmony, a neighborhood united under a single glittering blue-white surface. Charmed as I was by the transformative power of a massive snowfall, I still couldn't deny a sense of malice. Though I hated feeling physically cold, I stood on our front porch to assess the nature of the risk. I immediately recalled the last time I had felt a cold that extreme. As my breath crystalized and my eyelashes froze, I felt an overwhelming sense of dread.

I had just cause to be fearful. I had been having abdominal pain and it was escalating. It was happening frequently enough that I had actually gained the ability to discriminate three different types of pain. There was the tearing pain that happened sometimes as I bent down to pick up Walt. The surgical repair of my abdominal wall years before had been disrupted by the C-section for Walt's delivery. The constant lifting of Walt had added to the disruption and there were holes in my abdominal wall again. It would require surgical repair and more mesh to be placed. I learned to recognize the taut pull and sharp warning that preceded the tearing, and I understood I was to freeze in place if I felt that warning. I also learned not to lift children, despite the obvious temptation.

That surgery and all the others needed to explore my abdominal pain left fine webs of tissue called adhesions throughout my belly. My intestines would get hung up in webs and bands, and loops of my bowel would twist and choke, causing the second kind of pain. It was not a distractible kind of pain. It was more of a desperate, breathless agony that comes from dying tissue and torsion. When that pain struck, I was unable to either move or speak. Its presence dominated every moment of every thought until it passed.

The third pain was a consequence of the surgery that had been necessary to remove the half of my liver with the masses. The surgery had left a tight narrowing or stricture in the duct tasked with draining bile from my liver. The small orifice would get clogged with a sludgy debris of bile salts and stones. This created a backlog in my liver and a sort of stagnant, dull pain that would transform into infection as the bacteria in my gut spread upward into my liver. I was admitted to the hospital almost once a month that year and underwent a number of procedures in an attempt to fix what was wrong. With each episode of abdominal pain and each hospitalization that followed, I felt my chances of functional long-term survival decreasing.

I became morosely pragmatic. Even before the pain escalated that frozen winter, I had created a network of support around Walt in a futile attempt to make myself as extraneous as possible given my role as his mother. It was a transparent compensation for the fear that I would one day be forcibly removed from his life. I was trying to create a construct so that if I died or when I was hospitalized, his life would continue as normal, with my mom and Randy and a network of family and friends affording consistency. In pursuit of this absurd goal, I made sure I had no institutional knowledge that was solely mine. I externalized my memory of our relationship into photos and scrapbooks, writing down each conversation and sharing the funny stories so that I would never be the solitary keeper of our shared history. I pathologically avoided doing necessary tasks like shopping for new clothes or his favorite snacks, so that Randy or my mom would always know what he liked and needed.

I wondered a lot that year if he would retain any memory of me if I were to die. I thought of the scant memories I had from the years before I was four and acknowledged I probably hadn't imprinted upon him at all. At least not in any meaningful way. I believed that in his memory, my entire existence would be reduced to the nostalgia of a warm vanilla scent, or a sense of déjà vu at the pitch of someone's seemingly familiar laugh. Close friends recognized the elaborate birthday parties as love letters, shameless attempts to affix early memories upon his young brain. None of my compensations provided actual comfort, though. Instead I was reminded daily of the absolute power of death's chill to erase the visible world entirely. I found it a dark irony that just as Walt was getting stronger and healthier, I was getting sicker and weaker.

Whenever Randy saw the pain mounting, noticing me pacing or holding my right side, he would ask, "Do we need to go to the hospital?"

"I don't think so," I would answer unconvincingly. I would smile a smile that was meant to suggest everything was fine, and there was no need to worry, that this pain wasn't the pain that would bring about the end. This pain was a nuisance, and we should pretend it wasn't happening.

The answer should have always been yes, but I hedged. I believed I had learned to judge the difference between the episodes that would pass (and could be managed at home simply by resting my gut and taking in nothing by mouth for days) and the ones that required the intensive care unit, hospitalizations and procedures.

I was frankly tired of being in the hospital, having found myself there so many times already. But more often than not it proved to be unavoidable. At times I misjudged the seriousness and waited too long before presenting to the emergency department. I responded to these mistakes by overcorrecting, wanting to prove I was a "good" patient. It seemed impossible to find precisely the right moment. But I learned that if I came in early, at the first hint of a problem, rather than being credited with making a good decision, I was regarded with a thinly veiled skepticism. That subtle dismissiveness left me feeling ashamed, and thus I was more likely to wait until I knew I had no choice.

We do that, when the symptoms are vague and the lab results and imaging studies are normal, we believe the patient must have some other motivation, some secondary gain or emotional need that is placated by medical attention. It's an uncomfortable position as a physician: to believe a patient wants to be sick when they are not. It's difficult for us to conceive of desiring sickness when surrounded by so many patients desperate for a cure. We have a tendency to wall off these malingering patients within the confines of a box called mental illness. We naturally distance ourselves from them, believing we are pawns in some incoherent game without rules. In our more generous moments, we sometimes allow for the possibility that the test results have not yet had a chance to catch up to what is an invisible but real and mounting illness. And in those situations, we may observe them a bit longer, even as we doubt them.

As a physician in my own hospital, I was generally given the benefit of the doubt when I presented too early, and they placed me in the observation unit so I could be monitored for deterioration or discharged if it amounted to nothing. I was of course never discharged from observation.

I had a series of procedures over the next year to redress the cause of my recurrent abdominal pain. Doctors first tried to dilate the tight area of my biliary duct to allow the bile to drain rather than stagnate and cause infection. They attempted to spread the tight muscle apart and stretch it wider with an expandable balloon. When the duct closed on itself again, declaring that first procedure a failure, they instead cut the area with a scalpel, a procedure called a sphincterotomy. When that caused aggressive scar tissue to create an even tighter stricture, they used the balloon again and this time left a trio of stents in place to allow the tissue to heal around it, and hopefully remain open. The stents instead would clog and I'd become violently ill, requiring them to be removed.

From the moment the stents were first placed, I could feel them spreading open the bile duct in my liver. It was not an unmanageable sensation, but it was always present. The closest I could come to describing it is to say it was as though the dentist needed me to hold my mouth wide open so that he could have both hands fully engaged in a tooth extraction for days on end. It was too much of an imposition for too long of a duration. It became the steady machinelike murmur of discomfort that followed me through my day. And because it was always and unrelentingly present, I lost my acuity indicator for impending disaster. After a few days of rest following the procedure, I believed I was well enough to go into work. I knew well how to marginalize unwelcome feelings and discomfort. I would ignore it and get back to being of use. I had no way of knowing that the next warning would be overt shock.

I was driving in when suddenly my eyelids felt incredibly heavy, as if they might not open again if I blinked. I began to experience the same disorientation that had struck that first night in OB triage, which caught me completely off guard. As I struggled to park the car, the woozy drunken sensation steadily creeped in, and when I finally reached the elevator banks, I told the first person I encountered, "I think I'm becoming septic."

Sepsis refers to an infection that has completely overwhelmed the body, resulting in low blood pressure and organs not getting the blood flow needed to sustain them. When recognized early, and afforded the benefit of the best, most aggressive care, it kills about a third of those it strikes. By the time there is clinical evidence of shock, mortality climbs to well above 50 percent. When the symptoms are ignored, or dismissed, it is uniformly fatal.

I was taken to the Emergency Department and placed on a gurney; labs were quickly sent off by the nurse. An ultrasound that my surgeon had ordered previously was completed while I waited for the doctor. I felt marginally better when lying down, as my low blood pressure didn't have to work against gravity to deliver blood to my brain. I channeled my energy and tried to focus so that I could text Randy. I wrote that I was in the ER, and that he should come to the hospital on his way in to work downtown and I would update him. I recognized most people would not text this kind of information to their spouse, but it was our normal, and I had no cell signal in the Emergency Department to allow me to place an actual phone call anyway.

The emergency physician walked in to see his patient with suspected sepsis and abdominal pain texting. I didn't recognize him and he didn't know me. He was apparently new to the hospital. To add to the confusion, we had just switched to a new electronic medical record system, so most of my history was buried in an old system that he didn't know how to access. He cocked his head suspiciously. "Well, I just reviewed your blood work and we're not really seeing anything on the studies, so . . ." he paused, uncertain of what to say next. He waited for me to fill in his blank.

I explained my rationale for coming in and my history. How I had felt that spacey feeling before and it preceded me dying. That I thought I was doing the right thing by coming in before things truly deteriorated. I explained how quickly I'd seen the situation shift from one that was manageable to one that was truly desperate. It was a balancing act and I was trying to do the right thing. He shrugged and said he'd put me in for an observation bed, but he thought I was fine. He added that he didn't think I would meet insurance criteria for admission.

Doctors bring their own ghosts to every encounter, and they come in many different forms. A well-appearing patient who is perceived as monopolizing attention and time for nothing could elicit feelings of resentfulness. This is especially likely to occur if the doctor is predisposed by feelings of being overworked or missing his family. A patient who recalls to mind a past manipulation, or expresses a suggestion of blame, will elicit defensiveness. Even a patient who is reminiscent of a past failure can inspire fear and a desire to avoid reengaging in the same scenario.

We weren't trained to recognize ghosts, either in ourselves or others. We don't know what haunts our mentors and friends. We might get a glimpse every once in a while of the depths of someone's personal pain, when a fragment floats to the surface. We might hear, "These cases are the absolute worst" or "I hope this doesn't end like last time" or "If she dies on me, I swear I'm done with medicine." These feelings do not exist in isolation. They are not inert. They permeate our thoughts and influence our decisions. They become the subtext, the gravel of the path where we'll drive again and again, wearing ruts into the road before eventually laying down tracks. They are our vulnerability, our weak spots. They are the wax binding the feathers of our wings together. The wax that too easily melts when next we approach the sun's fiery orbit.

Like any weakness, they can be transfigured into a source of strength. If recognized, contemplated and bravely wrestled with, the ghosts can gain substance. They can materialize, even become allies. Difficult cases, losses can drive research and revelation. Rather than inspiring fear, those heartbreaking cases can transform lives, become the raison d'être. But if the feelings are ignored, as we were trained to do, they are a wall that blocks out sound.

On the observation ward, the nurse's aide came in to take my blood pressure and it barely registered. She shrugged and went to get another machine, believing the problem was with the equipment. As she walked out I began shaking violently with chills, a physical manifestation of an overwhelming infection. My heart raced, and my hands and feet went cold.

When the next blood pressure cuff also couldn't register my blood pressure, I asked to speak to the physician.

He walked in and I explained through chattering teeth, "I am cold and shaking and my blood pressure wouldn't register and I think I need to be transferred to the ICU." I believed the situation was rapidly becoming critical, and for the sake of brevity, I gave him just the basic details. I believed that was all he needed to hear to agree with me.

He looked at me and smiled. "Maybe you're just anxious. It can be hard being sick, especially as a young woman."

I realized he was responding to the tears that I hadn't realized were streaming down my face. He saw a girl in bed crying, saying she was cold and possibly worried about the quality of the equipment on that floor. He took my belief that I should be transferred to the ICU as a request to move to a place where I might feel safer. While he was correct in his assessment that I was profoundly frightened, I was not generically anxious; rather, I was terrified because I knew exactly what lay ahead. While it can be immensely valuable to name the feelings of the patient, it is somewhat less valuable to attribute physical manifestations of illness to a presumed feeling. Disregarding my symptoms as representative of anxiety was a misappropriation of empathy. By naming my emotion, incorrectly, he was in effect invalidating my own assessment and usurping my agency.

Sepsis is notoriously difficult to recognize early. A variety of algorithms have been introduced specifically to address this issue. Our hospital had been a leader in revolutionizing early treatment of sepsis and improving mortality. But on the granular, micro-level of a single patient, we could still be blind. His dismissiveness ignited an anger in me I didn't have the energy for. I tried explaining, loudly, that the combination of high heart rate, shaking chills and abdominal pain should probably elicit a different or at least broader differential in his mind than anxiety. Even in women. Within an hour I was sicker than he could have imagined, having not recognized the occult nature of my septic shock.

William Osler famously said, "Listen to your patient, he is telling you the diagnosis." It is almost always true, the patient is almost always telling you the diagnosis, but listening is harder than it seems. The story the patient relays can be circuitous, or filled with content we believe to be extraneous. We might feel pressed for time and wish that our patients could somehow just tell us what we need to know, despite knowing that no patient can do that; they can only tell us what they know. We listen imperfectly, through a fog of ghosts and competing priorities.

Once in the ICU, large-bore intravenous lines were placed to allow for the simultaneous administration of antibiotics, fluids and other medications called vasopressors, which squeezed my peripheral circulation to allow for some semblance of a blood pressure. I continued to shake violently with chills, my teeth chattering against each other with such force, I felt certain they would crumble.

"Are you cold?" Randy would ask, knowing the cold made me miserable.

"It's the infection," I would answer, understanding the severity implied by the rigors.

I was boarded for a procedure to remove the stents the following morning. The procedure required being placed on a ventilator and being given general anesthesia so that a camera could be placed in my esophagus, allowing the retrieval. This required being positioned face down for between one and three hours, depending on the complexity and complications encountered. I met the anesthesiologist in the pre-op area, a middle-aged, soft-spoken man with a surgical mask hanging around his neck. He recognized me from a lecture I had given to their department.

"Oh, I am sorry to see you here," he said. He then turned to the nurse anesthetist who would be assisting him during the procedure. "Were you at Dr. Awdish's talk last week?" he asked. His colleague shook her head no.

"Oh, it was a terrific reminder about how sometimes—especially in our field—we say things around patients that we don't think they can hear." He seemed genuinely to see the value in the lecture I'd given. I'd projected statements I had heard in the operating room, that no one would have thought I could re-member, like, *We're losing her. She's circling the drain here.*

"Thank you," I said, beginning to get uncomfortable. Is this what it was going to be like for me from now on, I wondered? Every time I needed medical care being reminded of all the times I lectured on what not to do? I began to question my strat-egy of attempting to change the culture of the hospital in which I was still a patient as well as a physician.

"No, thank you. It's important work you're doing." He smiled before turning to my chart. "So, it says here you get nauseated sometimes with anesthesia. You've been through a few of these procedures; what drugs work best for you?"

"Oh, I don't know exactly the combination they used last time, but that seemed to work well," I said. "I know they gave me a little steroid to help with the nausea, but that's all I remember."

"Ok, we'll do the same thing this time then! I don't want you to worry, it will be fine!" he reassured me.

I resurfaced from the anesthesia out of a dream of drowning. The water was heavy, almost leaden, and I could see nothing through it though my eyes were open. I was surrounded by a murky, opaque, Prussian-blue sea. In my paintings I never allowed that the water of my dreams could be translucent. I'm sure this depiction was construed by others as a novice's best effort. Water's density in my paintings was more easily interpreted as a lack of refined skill, rather than what it was: a clear vision, a memory committed to canvas. Even once fully awake, I found it impossibly difficult to breathe, as if my airway and lungs themselves had brought back that leaden water from my dreams.

"I can't breathe," I alerted the nurse anesthetist who was by my side.

She looked at me and suggested, "You might just be congested from being face down for so long. Maybe a nasal spray will help?"

I knew plainly that she was wrong, but not how to convince her. I'd experienced nasal congestion, and this struggle to breathe bore absolutely no resemblance to that minor nuisance. I tried to shake off the fog of the anesthesia-induced sleep, to be more alert and articulate. I wondered if my spacey fatigue was disadvantaging me. I studied the monitoring equipment attached to me: my oxygen level was fine, heart rate was a little fast, but otherwise no obvious issues.

The nurse and the anesthesiologist listened to my lungs, one on each side of my body, and shook their heads. He told me, "Well, you sound clear and your vitals look good. We'll send you back to the ICU, and I bet you'll feel better soon." As he walked away, I heard him remark to his nurse, "We gave her exactly the same combination as last time, so I don't see why it should have gone any differently."

It occurred to me that he may have believed I was blaming him for my difficulty breathing. And, feeling blamed, he would have become defensive, a reaction to thinking I was accusing him somehow of causing my problem. I had in no way meant to imply that I blamed him or his choices for how I was feeling. I had no idea what to say or do next.

By the time I was in the elevator headed back to the ICU, I was becoming itchy and sensed my lips swelling by the second, as if being injected with collagen fillers in a plastic surgeon's office.

I pointed at my face, finding it increasingly difficult to move my tongue. "Lips swollen?" I asked Randy.

"Yes, they look huge. Is that just from the scope they placed in your mouth?" he asked.

"I wish," I replied, my voice sounding raspy and faint. I was having a full-fledged anaphylactic reaction to one of the antibiotics that had been administered during the procedure. As the severity of my distress escalated, I became more annoyed. I thought it would be exceedingly stupid and anticlimactic if after everything I'd been through I died of an allergic reaction in an elevator. Surely, if I had demonstrated anything in the past five years it was that I was more difficult to kill than that.

I realized we had lost the window of time when I could be treated for an allergic reaction in the post-anesthesia care unit. Somehow miscommunication and defensiveness had muddied their assessment, which left me stuck in that elevator having an allergic reaction, far from anyone who could help.

The transporter responded by wheeling me quickly down the series of long hallways to the ICU, where the team was waiting for me. Immediately upon seeing my swollen face and difficulty breathing, the Ear Nose and Throat physician on call was paged to examine my airway with a fiber-optic scope she passed through my right nostril. It's an odd thing to have to tolerate when you can't breathe as it is, and someone places a camera through your nostril and further blocks your airway. Fortunately she was very quick.

"Yep, it's swollen. Definitely probably an allergic reaction," she confirmed. "Benadryl, steroids and Zantac," she recommended. "And discontinue the antibiotic," she added, stating the obvious.

Pharmacists rushed in to try to pinpoint the antibiotic that had caused the reaction by graphing the temporal relationship between administration of the drug and my reaction. I was getting three different antibiotics in an attempt to kill a wide variety of organisms that could be implicated, which naturally confounded the issue. It was vitally important that we identify which drug was the culprit, as I still needed to be able to receive antibiotics for the sepsis. They offered the most likely offender, with a caveat that they couldn't be sure and I'd have to be monitored closely with any future doses.

Breathing treatments were administered in an effort to improve laminar flow through airways made narrow by the swelling. I closed my eyes so as not to have to watch a roomful of people look as panicked as I felt. I tried to calm my breathing and focused on silencing the fearful thoughts. As I distanced myself from the agitated energy around me, I was able to consciously step into an internal stillness. It was a practice I had learned in yoga class and encouraged my patients to try. Purposefully slowing the breath, using the long stretches of inhalations and exhalations to signal the body that it could relax. Disarming the "alarm" system with elongated breaths that implied a state of calm long before I arrived at one. I gathered stillness toward me, drawing it in with my breath, and exhaled the unwanted frenetic energy away from me. I reminded myself that cultivating stillness was most necessary when it seemed most improbable. Even in the destructive power of a hurricane, there is a center, and within it there is perfect peace. I recalled the perfect peace

I had once felt in the operating room as my body unraveled. A peace that was at once diffuse and expansive as well as intact and whole, just like the breath. Long minutes passed as I tuned out all that was happening around me.

I opened my eyes and smiled. I saw the fear in the room and resolved to share the peace I had found. I said in short bursts, "Well, the good news is . . . I think . . . I've officially had . . . every form . . . of shock now: hemorrhagic . . . cardiogenic . . . septic and . . . anaphylactic shock . . . I'm done."

My joke broke the tension in the room and I saw the team around me visibly exhale. I saw their masks fall, and recognized I had scared them. They were watching their friend and colleague suffocating in front of them and trying to judge when and how best to act to save my life. I knew the stress they were under and further understood that it was exacerbated by a lack of any systematic approach or even any language to alleviate stress and accommodate resilience. There was no training within our medical education that addressed how to cultivate a space for ourselves, a space of stillness within a storm.

"There's still neurogenic," my friend joked, winking at me. "Don't give up yet."

I shook my head, incredulous at the dark humor we some-times employed to get through difficult times. I thought of the transplant resident who joked about needing to somehow find me a new liver. I thought of another physician who smiled while walking in to assess me and said, "You're not going to die on me, are you?" I wondered if perhaps each attempt at humor was an indirect indicator of fear, a joke as a subtle bow to a nearby ghost, an admission of vulnerability. By discouraging other out-ward manifestations of emotions, had we been left with humor as our only sanctioned outlet? In lieu of actually feeling our feelings, had we subverted them into quick, pithy one-liners to deflect emotion? I worried that if we couldn't recognize and respond to our own emotions, what possible hope did we have of helping others to navigate the complex emotional sea of illness and recovery?

I hoped that humor was more of a way station than a displacement. That it represented a bookmark meant to be revisited when we could stop and examine our emotions. That it was a space from which paths led out in all directions, into transformation and acceptance of our own limitations.

"It looks like your breathing is getting better," the ICU fellow reassured me. "And I think I can see the swelling starting to come down. The medicine is working. I want you to know, I'm not leaving. I'm going to be here all night. We won't leave your side until you can breathe. You are safe."

He was part of a new generation of physicians that was being deliberately trained in empathy, trained to recognize the emotions of others and reflect them back. I took a deep breath by way of testing his observation. The tide was receding. Though I knew I wasn't entirely out of danger, I felt comforted by his words and by his reflection of the situation back to me. His messaging spoke to his assessment of my fear, his ability to empathize with me and his understanding of what I needed to feel secure.

What was immediately stunning was the hard-won sense of trust his few sentences brought into that ICU room. I thought in those words there was more actual doctoring than in the prior twenty-four hours combined.

It was so surreal that I had actually run the communication training program that he had taken during his orientation. I knew the steps that had been outlined to him. And yet, even as he demonstrated the skills, it felt completely genuine, almost effortless. I understood his simple statement required a situational knowledge of how it must feel to be unable to breathe. It required an emotional humility to suspect that I was fearful and would benefit from being reassured. It required that he allow himself to feel with me. It required a self-knowledge of what feelings he was bringing into the room so he didn't dump in. I looked at a medical student standing in the corner and wondered if he recognized the skill involved. I wondered if after witnessing such an exchange he would be able to break it down into replicable, manageable chunks, or whether to him it just looked like magic.

I had the opportunity to ask him two weeks later when I rejoined the team as the attending. I pulled the medical student aside after rounds and acknowledged that it might feel awkward for him to have me as his attending after witnessing me so ill as a patient.

"No, not at all," he answered genuinely. "Just because you're a doctor doesn't mean you are different than anyone else. We all will be patients at some point."

I smiled. "When I was scared, when I couldn't breathe, I thought the fellow did a really good job of reassuring me, and I noticed you in the room. I wonder if you remember what he said?"

"I think he just offered support, said things were getting better and he wouldn't leave until you were safe. Something like that."

"Yeah, actually, that's exactly right," I said.

"I know you're really interested in communication, so I wanted to share something I think you'd find cool," he said. "Our med school stopped doing traditional interviews, you know, where they ask you about your research experience and aspirations to be a physician. Instead, now we have to sit in a room, our chair back-to-back with another candidate. One of us has a LEGO structure that is already built in front of them and the other candidate just has the LEGO pieces. And we are judged on whether we can communicate effectively enough to recreate the piece. Isn't that cool?"

"That's incredibly cool."

"It is, but at the time it was really challenging. I mean you really realize how deliberately you have to choose your words," he said. "And you have to listen to really hear what is being said."

I thought about how often I listened to truly hear rather than thinking about advancing my agenda, or mentally rehearsing the next thing I wanted to say. How often does anyone listen generously, without ears pretuned to what they hope the answer will be? We hope it's just nasal congestion and not something we've done. We hope the baby's heart is still beating even though we can't see it on the ultrasound. We hope the patient isn't so sick that nothing we do will save them. We hope the swelling in our patient's brain will lessen so she can see her child. We hope that the events of the day will allow each of us, physician and patient, to leave the hospital free of permanent scars.

Our preformulated agenda is often nothing more than another mechanism of self-protection. We might be simply hoping for a good outcome, both for the patient and for ourselves. We enter conversations with patients and families with each of our personal ghosts trailing behind us. We enter them not always aware of our capacity to bear more grief. We are not adept at gauging our resilience or counting the shadows in the room. I wondered if the new skills I was seeing in the fellow and hearing from the medical student were indications of a shift. If training was changing, perhaps we would soften at the door of a patient's room rather than steel ourselves. Perhaps we would stop believing we had to make impossible things look effortless. We could believe instead that we were there to truly listen.

. . .

My breathing continued to improve, and my room slowly emp-
tied of doctors, nurses and students. It wasn't until I was nearly
alone with just Randy resting in the chair that I realized I was in
the room that we generally regarded as being cursed with terrible
luck. In an ICU used to so much death and sadness, it isn't easy
for one room to stand out, but this one did. For the past week
it had been the site of so much heartbreak. I looked around for
evidence, some permanent mark or acknowledgment, but found
none. I thought about the last patient who had been in the room,
the last time I had been here.

He was a young man whose body was riddled with cancer,
so much so that his muscles had been cannibalized to feed the
tumor and only a gaunt skeletal frame remained. We had discussed his case on rounds, the failure of this third round of salvage chemotherapy, the failed surgery, the progression. We were
burdened by the knowledge of what his future held. The conversations that should have occurred far upstream of the ICU
had been tabled, out of respect for the age of his children and
his ardent hope of a future. But we had found ourselves against
a wall. It was a different place than he had been before, and it
was a hopeless place.

I had believed we owed it to him to guide him, given our
knowledge, to talk honestly about what lay ahead. We needed
to know what he hoped his remaining days would hold. We
wanted to discuss the option of hospice and palliative care.
We all knew the inevitability of his death, and by extension, how
awful it would feel to perform CPR knowing we couldn't save
him. We knew what it would feel like to have his ribs break
beneath our hands, and his lifeless eyes bulge with our efforts.
How it would feel to have our shoes soaked in his blood that

already would not clot. We were traumatized in advance of our efforts by ghosts that had yet to arrive. I prayed, as much for him as for our team, that he would not want us to put his body through those paces.

The palliative care team was going to be present to aid in the discussion of end-of-life issues. I steadied myself for the discussion, mindful of my feelings, my own internal dialogue. The doctor first asked the patient, gently, what he understood of the situation, knowing that this last round of salvage chemo had failed. She asked with humility, as we all wondered if he had allowed himself to approach the edges of his mortality. We listened as he told us he had always hoped to live to see his oldest child graduate from high school. I smiled at the sacredness of that wish, grateful that it could be shared, that there was trust enough to allow it to be expressed. The palliative care doctor frowned, knowing that child's graduation was still eighteen months away. The patient turned his head, and his eyes fogged with tears, embarrassed by the grandness of his wish. We broke his heart and told him that wish could not be made to come true, that we were looking at weeks and not months. He sighed and shrugged, as if he knew it was too much to hope for.

We talked about getting him home. He didn't want his children to see him die at home. We offered to hold a makeshift graduation in the hospital and offered to contact the school and ask if they would be willing to generate a diploma in advance of graduation. He smiled, glad for the compromise. We left the room, feeling as if we'd done something useful. Though we couldn't fix the disease, we had found a way to bring meaning to his final days. We felt connected, and for a moment that felt like everything. We'd navigated some tightrope with him on our shoulders, and we hadn't fallen. We hadn't hurt each other.

He died anyway that night, before we could arrange anything. He died before he was ready, before he had decided not to have us attempt resuscitation. And his ribs broke, and his blood soaked our shoes. And as I told his family I prayed they wouldn't look down. That they wouldn't notice my shoes were squeaking, as if I'd just walked in from a winter storm.

"Are you worried?" Randy asked, turning his body so he could look in my eyes. "You're awfully quiet."

"Just thinking about a patient that was in this room," I answered honestly.

"Hmm. Do I want to know?" he asked.

"Probably not," I answered and sighed.

"Did that patient die?" Randy asked.

"Yep. Sure did," I answered, remembering the sound of the audible bleeding as blood hit the floor.

"Do you want to talk about it?" he nudged.

I sighed and shook my head. What could I say? That trying to do good can sometimes hurt so much that you break inside and you don't know if you can go on doing good anymore? That we see terrible, awful, bloody things and it hurts? And we don't feel we have a right to hurt, because we are in the outer circles of the diagram and everyone around us is right in the center of it and it hurts so much more for them. So feeling anything that resembles sadness or grief feels terribly selfish and entitled. That though we don't feel sorry for ourselves, because we know it's not our sadness, it sometimes just feels as if we are seeing all the sadness in the world at once and we just need a second to breathe, but we haven't built in a mechanism to allow us to breathe, or pause, or feel all the feelings. That when we feel them it guts us, and we hate it, so we joke or we drink or we run or we harden. And that it worried me that that was all any of us knew how to do, to joke or drink, or run, or harden. That I wanted to learn how we could truly be there for everyone's hurt but not to have it transfer onto us like some sort of prickly dark matter. That sometimes I felt I got a glimpse of what that could look like, to heal and not to be haunted.

"We wanted . . . to help him," I said.

"Of course you did. You do help! You all do amazing things," he said, attempting to reassure me as I broke down crying.

"I thought I was going to die in the stupid elevator." I added a half-laugh to my cry.

"No one was going to let you die."

"That's the thing, we can't stop it. We don't 'let' people die, they just die. We can't stop it." I thought of my team after our patient's death, their faces as sad and raw as circus clowns who had just wiped off their painted-on masks.

"It's not your fault, I didn't mean that," he said, recognizing we were not having the same conversation.

"I know you didn't. It just . . . I don't think anyone understands." I tried to think of how to explain what those losses were like. "Sometimes, sometimes it feels as if we're all juggling so many balls and if any one falls and breaks it's actually someone, and we can't ever fix it. And sometimes it's actually you yourself that you let fall. Like maybe you can save the others, but to do that you have to accept you'll be broken by it."

"You feel broken?" he asked.

"Oh, we're all broken, in some way. Broken and haunted." Even as I admitted that I knew it wasn't the whole truth. I realized I wasn't capturing something intangible about why we kept coming back for more.

"There is more though. It's not all sad." I struggled to put into words how it felt in those times when I truly believed in medicine. I thought of one of my patients who had survived lung cancer twice. She had wanted only two things: to make it through Christmas with her grandchildren and not to be a pulmonary cripple, dependent on oxygen for every movement. She was very clear and articulate in expressing what she valued, and because of that, we were able to formulate a plan together. We decided we couldn't operate on the second tumor, even though it would improve her likelihood of survival, as it would leave her with too little lung remaining to function the way she wanted to function. We planned instead on radiation. I did very little but to listen and outline the possible avenues available to her while giving her a sense of what each path would look like when all was said and done. In the end we chose a plan together that aligned with her values. I held my breath with her through the radiation treatments, hoping they would be enough to get us through to the end of December. I woke up at night worried we were being too cautious, not aggressive enough. I reminded myself this was what she wanted, but I couldn't fall back asleep.

She did make it through Christmas; in fact, she cooked the whole meal. She prepared a turkey with stuffing and mashed potatoes, and a sweet potato casserole and green beans and two different pies. She bought gifts for her grandchildren and she was there when they opened them. The letters she had written to them in case she wasn't remained in a drawer. When I received her Christmas card in the mail, with a picture of her standing with her grandchildren, it was the best thank-you I could possibly have wished for.

"There is magic too," I said, attempting to distill my memory into some cogent statement. I wanted to explain that when I was able to truly be present, there was a sacredness in what we did every day that was intense and intimate and perfect. It was those times, they were so fleeting, but everything about life was wrapped up in those moments . . . love and respect and humanity and science. It was all there. And it was better than anything.

"So the good outweighs the bad," he summarized in his own linear way.

I sighed and nodded, and we both smiled, happy that I had decided to embrace his reductive version of a far more complicated notion. "The good outweighs the bad, yes." I thought that was a fair enough representation of something I would never be able to articulate, but that every cell in my body understood. My cells had the advantage of not being constrained by actual words.

I thought of how remarkable it was that he was always there, to the right of my hospital bed, holding or rubbing my hand. Whether I was suffering in pain, or with loss or grief, he was always right there. He lacked the ability to heal that the others around me were graced with, and yet his presence had been the most healing aspect of all. I realized that his willingness to witness my suffering had changed it somehow. He held what he saw and was never repulsed by it. He didn't attempt to evade it, but he also didn't intrude on the parts that were wholly mine. Because he understood there were parts I was possessive of, accepted that while I wanted him to know what I felt, I also needed him to know my pain was unique to me. Not all of it could be shared. He believed in humility, in asking questions. It struck him as a fragile pretext to assume anything, so he always asked. He taught me to believe in the healing power of *us*.

As physicians we so often feel we aren't enough. We've seen too much. We know the disease is stronger than the cure, we feel the deck is stacked and that we can't possibly win. We frame our losses and successes in terms of the disease, which is a mistake. The language alone implies a battle and a clear outcome, a victor and a loser. If we are honest and allow ourselves to see death for what it is, an inescapable inevitability, then our story can change. In that light we can accept that our greatest gift is not in fact healing, because all healing is transient. Our greatest gift is, in fact, our ability to be absolutely present with suffering. To allow it to transform us, and, by holding the suffering of others, transform it for them as well.

As young physicians, we had each imagined ourselves as barriers perched at the top of a steep cliff, our patients hurling themselves toward the abyss below. We were, in this version, the catchers, and when successful, we were the saviors, the heroes. We didn't talk about the inevitability of the fall. Our back was always to the void. And this orientation suited us just fine; we didn't want to face the gaping hole that swallowed each of our losses. We would stand and catch our patients and throw them back a few feet, and not let them look down. We didn't want them to see what we had seen. We didn't want them to see the magnitude of our capacity to fail.

If we instead had faith in the meaning of our presence, we could turn and stand at the edge of the chasm and face it together. We could acknowledge its vastness and darkness. We could speak openly about our fears. We could offer insights of what we'd witnessed when others faced this same darkness. Our orientation would change. We could look in the same direction. We could have faith that our presence was meaningful, that in many ways it was everything.

It took me ten years to figure out I should stand and face the same direction as my patients. It took that long to lose my vision of myself as someone who could help others defy death. It took losing colleagues to guilt and addiction to learn to soften, to bend rather than break. To value community and shared grief. Imagine if we trained physicians from the very beginning to know their value came from partnering with and being present for their patients. Imagine if we augmented their knowledge base with a resilience that came from a revised understanding of their role in their patients' lives. The burden of guilt we could lift.

That orientation—turning together to face what our patients face—is what allows us to not only bear witness, guide our patients and treat disease, but also to bring more compassion to each moment, a compassion that extends even to ourselves.

In believing that his love was enough, that his presence at my bedside was needed, Randy showed me what could be.

I didn't dream of drowning that night. Instead I dreamt I was walking a tightrope, anchored on the edges of two cliffs, above a murky, opaque, Prussian-blue sea.

Twelve

Broken Vessels

I worried that after what we had been through, we risked being overly protective of our son and never allowing him to experience the sorts of hardships that conferred a toughness, a grit below the surface of his character. I didn't know how to not do that to him, so I set about trying to at least name what I wanted him to become.

We were determined to raise a kind, adventurous, autonomous child, one who saw the value in art, who was willing to take risks and to fail, and who knew the meaning of perseverance. From there, we worked backward. If we wanted that to be true, we had to create an environment that presupposed our vision of who he could be. We had to live as if it were actually already true. So it followed that he would have to know from the earliest age that he could trust his own judgment. To ensure that he would trust himself, we would have to demonstrate that we trusted him and allow him to take calculated risks. We would permit him to fail on a small scale and reward the attempt, not the outcome. So that by the age of four, if he asked, "Can I walk to the creek?," I had conditioned myself to answer, "Sure, I trust you," even if my first thought was of him drowning in the shallow water. And we pretended not to watch as, empowered by our trust, he changed his shoes in search of better traction on the slippery rocks. He judged his distance from the house and assessed whether we could still see him before running ahead.

He made good choices. Or he made small, bad choices, and the lessons he learned were valuable. He collected things, small bits and pieces of matter that are only a treasure to a child. He would take a small, special stone out while he played in the leaves, despite our observation that it might be difficult to keep track of. The precious thing would predictably become lost in the pile, and he would feel the loss and understand it was his choice to take that risk. We allowed him to be hurt. And though the temptation was to fix it for him, we resisted. We rewarded failure. Practicing yoga together, I'd congratulate him if he fell. "That was amazing! You took such a big risk that you ended up falling. I am never more proud of you than I am when you fall."

I wanted to enliven him with an intense curiosity about all things but especially the world around him, so while I made dinner, he would make art or conduct science experiments. Armed with baking soda and vinegar, he would inflate balloons with carbon dioxide gas until they exploded. Randy would return home to piles of powder fueling volcanic eruptions or finger paint covering the kitchen counter, and I'd smile and say, "The mess you see is the price you pay for dinner and curiosity." He would nod and say, "All right then," and roll up his sleeves to help tidy the mess.

I wanted him to know the power of perseverance and armed him with magic tricks that required hours of practice to master. Magic was the perfect tool in that I couldn't do it for him; he had to learn how to perform the illusion convincingly, independent of any adult help. The reward, of truly surprising an adult with a trick that elicited genuine awe and applause, was something he learned to want, to work toward.

So perhaps it isn't surprising that our curious, brave and adventurous child broke his arm the summer he was five. He jumped from the highest platform of a schoolyard playscape and landed squarely on his left forearm. It was the kind of fall you felt through the mulched ground more than heard. He cried, briefly, before sniffing the tears back and shrugging it off. In the fall, he fractured the elbow of his left arm. His reaction was so mild that over the next few days I didn't even consider that it could be broken. I thought rather that he was just a bit bruised and favoring it slightly. Though he was generally unwilling to turn it and winced if it was mistakenly touched, he still went to his Saturday swim lesson and practiced karate. I mentioned the fall to his pediatrician at his well-child visit over a week later, almost dismissively, as an FYI.

"He fell pretty hard at the playground last week, complained for two days, but seems fine. And also he gets a rash if he eats too much red dye," I offered, having recently witnessed the outcome of a Strawberry Quik binge.

He held my gaze as he manipulated his left elbow, nodding solemnly as Walt winced. "It's the real deal," he said, with a sideways glance. I read his look as, "How could you not know that?" He looked at his watch and ushered us toward radiology to get imaging before the radiology department closed.

I had been completely blind to the extent of his injury. Why?

I was simply unable to be objective as it related to him. I wanted him to be fine, so my observations of him were filtered through a lens of what supported my desired truth. He hadn't cried for very long. Children cried excessively when they broke arms, that was a thing. The next day seemed better and by the second day, he barely mentioned it. That didn't seem to be the natural history of a fracture. Wouldn't it hurt more, and for far longer? I was choosing to pay attention to the information that supported my belief while ignoring any information that challenged it. It was classic confirmation bias. I didn't want anything to be wrong with him. And not wanting it to be true colored my view of the situation. I came to the situation with an agenda, which didn't allow me to objectively observe and embrace the truth as it actually was. I was only able to see how I wanted it to be.

As I looked at his X-ray, I felt shame. I hadn't allowed myself to be present with the reality of his pain.

The doctor brought in the temporary casting materials and a sling. He wet the material, which would polymerize and form a support for his arm, then wrapped it in an elastic bandage. It would stay in place until we could see the orthopedic surgeon. As Walt patiently held his arm in position, I explained that the doctor had found a fracture in his bone.

"It's broken?" he looked at it, appearing surprised.

"Seems so." I showed him the fine crack on the X-ray and the piece of bone that had chipped off in the fall.

"And this will fix it?" he asked of the cast.

"Yes, it will hold it in place while your body heals itself," I said. Then, wanting him to understand how bizarrely magical and resilient the human body was, I added, "And the really amazing thing is, when it heals, it will be the strongest part of your arm, because the places we've broken form strong new bone." I paused and looked at him to see if he understood.

"Show me again where it's broken?" he asked.

"See that line on the X-ray? Seeing that very fine shadow is how the doctor knew there was a fracture. It was hard to tell from the outside." I acknowledged my own blind spot. "We had to look deep inside to see the broken spot. Once we knew it was broken, healing could begin. If we hadn't done that, it wouldn't have healed properly."

His pediatrician looked at me sideways, clearly understanding I was no longer talking about his fracture.

I wanted him to understand the truth as I believed it. While I had failed to know that he had broken his arm, there was no shame in it being broken. It is possible to be both broken and incredibly strong. We can be wounded and in that space find more cohesion and wholeness than we knew possible. But only if we are willing to acknowledge and confront the cracks.

"Cool," he said excitedly. "Will it be as strong as Darth Vader's robot arm?"

The pediatrician saved me from answering by going through discharge instructions as he demonstrated how to connect the sling.

I looked at my son, admiring his tough-looking cast, and wondered what lesson he would take away from all of this. So much insight had come to me through my illness. It's impossible to think of who I would have been without that education. In fact, it's with a kind of tortured agony that I look back on our graduation from medical school, the fact that we thought it represented some culmination of knowledge, some imagined completion of training. For a time, we indulged the notion of ourselves as protectors perched atop a cliff. We were so arrogantly confident, so sure we were going to change the world. We had no understanding of the nuances of medicine, the meaning of suffering or the comfort we'd have to seek in the shadows of spaces between truths. We had no idea how much we still needed to sit in contemplation of the abyss. How intimately we had to know the darkness our patients faced before we could ever hope to partner with them. How much we needed each other.

We were not well prepared to be physicians to our patients.

Perhaps it speaks poorly of me that I needed to become a patient to see cracks in our façade. Did I not have enough empathy or perspective to understand the magnitude of the suffering that was all around me until it affected me directly? It's possible. But that doesn't resonate with who I understand myself to be. Closer to the truth is that I'm not entirely to blame. I came to medicine with an open heart, and somewhere during my training I was taught to wall it off. We all were. We were implicitly and explicitly instructed on the absolute necessity of partitions, measured distance and aequanimitas.

We were taught not only that it would save us, but that if we didn't somehow find a way to do it, we would kill those we were put there to protect. Our feelings were a direct threat to our patients. It was impossible to evaluate, diagnose and treat patients if we felt something as they decompensated in front of us, struggled with cancer diagnoses in our office, and lost their dignity to disease.

It was a lie.

It is entirely possible to feel someone's pain, acknowledge their suffering, hold it in our hands and support them with our presence without depleting ourselves, without clouding our judgment. But only if we are honest about our own feelings. Physicians are prone to all the same human emotions of pride and guilt and denial and shame that distort our reason. We are just trained to believe we can surmount them. Emotions tended to can be claimed. Those we deny will always float. Allowing space for our feelings when we've been trained to deny them is not selfish, it's necessary, both for ourselves and for our patients.

When chaos and uncertainty swirl around us, and the darkness envelops us, having someone by our side who has seen the darkness before, who can map our path toward the light, who can be our eyes as we fumble in the dark, that person is a gift.

When we allow our human channels to remain open, we better understand emotion because we've bravely confronted our own. Only then we can see where we are needed and the spaces we must move in to fill. Only then can we can help each other pass through the storm intact. Only then can we understand the value of our presence during the storm.

When people talk about an illness or a terminal diagnosis as being a gift, it's easy to dismiss them as naïve idealists intent on finding the bright spot in what is an obvious cavern of hopelessness. The notion itself is a paradox. And as with most paradoxes they are difficult for our minds to make them fit neatly together. We try, and fail, so we ricochet back and forth between the poles, wanting to choose between this one or that one. Is this news as horrible as it seems, or is there more? Could there be a larger, more meaningful explanation that has yet to surface? We might patiently hold each possibility in contemplation and attempt to assess if one is a better fit. We might push them toward each other, willing them both to be true despite their discordance, and becoming frustrated when they just won't approximate neatly. We might try to chip away at one to see if the edges will sit more comfortably with the other. Perhaps we try to convince ourselves that an immeasurable amount of value will eventually come out of a finite amount of suffering. We find ourselves unconvinced. We are, it seems, just uncomfortable with contradictory truths. That inherent discomfort forces us to devalue one position or the other.

I know I resisted silver linings. They felt like clumsy attempts to dismiss my suffering and force me to focus in the direction of some imagined grace. I lost a baby that was very much wanted, as well as any semblance of health for nearly eight years. I couldn't know then the purpose and direction my illness would grant me. That my loss would prevent other losses, and though no one would ever know that baby or who she would become, that I would learn even from her absence. Others would learn from what happened as well. Even in the dark void that constituted her life, there was light, a purpose. My experience of her loss opened the lid on a vast network of connectedness and healing that was completely hidden from view. I had to accept that my body and her body, through their weaknesses and susceptibilities, could actually provide access to truths my rational mind would otherwise reject.

I knew it was neither practical nor at all desirable for everyone to have the kind of experience I had been through, and yet, like some religious pilgrim, I wanted everyone to see what I had seen and to know what I knew to be true. When I rounded in the ICU, I shared my experience as a patient with my teams as a way of orienting them to my expectations for empathy and their sacred responsibility to their patients. I enlisted like-minded colleagues to run our workshops on communication skills training. I insisted, always, that we could be better. I took every opportunity to lecture on the importance of empathy. So when our hospital asked me to present the "patient perspective" of septic shock at our regional World Sepsis Day Conference, I accepted. The meeting we were hosting was meant to increase recognition of the disease as well as the toll it took on our patients. As I prepared slides for my presentation, I thought about the lessons I had learned as a patient and what I hoped to communicate to the audience.

We were a hospital that understood sepsis. Much of the research on the optimal care of septic patients had been conducted in our hospital emergency department. Dr. Emanuel (Manny) Rivers and his colleagues had redefined the management of septic patients and had unquestionably improved outcomes by sharing their vision of early, goal-directed therapy. He sat in the

audience along with physicians who had operated on me, drained
fluid off my lungs and watched me die in their operating room.
There was no question: it was through their efforts and teams of
others that I was alive and standing before them, able to tell my
story. Despite my immense gratitude for their efforts, I found I
didn't believe that their talent, dedication and clinical success
was in any way the whole story. The story was in the darkness.

I presented my hospitalizations, laden with successful clinical outcomes, in sequence. The terrible hemorrhagic shock, the
loss of the baby, the suicidal spiral of my blood unable to clot
from the hypothermia, the massive transfusions, the kidney and
liver failure, the ventilator dependence, the stroke, the tumors, the
embolization and resections, the sepsis. I interspersed the heroic
clinical narrative with slides that showed the words I heard, as
a patient, at each step of the way. White words on a black background, projected into a silent auditorium.

> *Can you show me where you see that?*
> *She's circling the drain.*
> *She's been trying to die on us.*
> *That was a really bad night for me.*
> *Your kidneys aren't cooperating.*
> *It wasn't my call.*
> *You should hold the baby. I don't mean to get graphic, but
> after a few days in the morgue their skin starts to break
> down.*
> *At least you didn't die.*
> *How much pain medication do you take at home?*
> *Are you sure your pain is an 8? I just gave you morphine an
> hour ago.*
> *Maybe you're just anxious.*

There I was, onstage, representing what I was—a visible, tangible post-sepsis success story, one that was disfigured by all the ways we fail our patients on a daily basis. Two seemingly contradictory truths. And as we revisited my hospital course together, the auditorium gasped in disbelief in unison, understanding how we failed. How we do so many impossible things, so perfectly right, that it can sometimes seem effortless. How we succeed only to fail in the smallest, simplest of ways. How we damage our patients and wreck ourselves in the process. How we didn't know how to reorient ourselves to face the same direction as our patients. How we didn't know how to be present with emotion, be it our own emotions or those of our patients. In that moment I could see we all wanted to do better.

I knew that together, we *could* do better.

Sometimes when you bring a problem into the light, you find the answers are different than you expected, that indeed the problem itself is different than you had believed it to be. What you had thought was the problem was just an indication of a deeper, more amorphous issue. Amorphous and yet so tenacious it clings to you, grows into you until it's no longer clear where it ends and where you begin. You find you can't peel it off without fundamentally changing each of your respective structures. I was still taking those first tenuous steps, trying to truly see and acknowledge the giant, daunting, ingrained nature of the problem. Trying to understand the culture that entrained the behaviors, that created a system that bred more of the same, year after year. To understand how it had altered me, and how I could in turn shape it.

Medicine is a culture that does not indulge suffering, though it is everywhere. It is there in every patient, every family member, and within ourselves and our colleagues. The omnipresence of the suffering makes it the easiest thing to ignore. It is the most important thing to attend to and we are constantly dismissing it, pushing it aside, whether it's our own suffering, or the patient's suffering, or our family's suffering. We push it aside to get to the patient.

The thoughtfully designed curriculum that gifted us cadavers to dissect and learn on also disembodied us from ourselves. The lesson was: Honor these bodies before you, they are sacred and magical. And to do this, you must utterly neglect your own body, your own emotions, and your wholeness. Esteem your mentors, hold them in such high regard that you dismiss your own truths. Be so enamored with the diseases that you present the patients burdened by them to your teams as incarnations of classic texts. That is the best way to honor the patient bearing the disease: to learn from their sacrifice. Distance yourself from your own feelings, lest they contaminate the field. The system is configured to produce a predictable product, and the dysfunctional product is then tasked with roles it is not trained to manage. This misalignment perpetuates feelings of isolation. It is an ironic paradox that medicine has become. We disembody doctors and expect them to somehow transcend that handicap and be present in their bodies, empathic and connected. Physicians who have had to learn to disengage from their own emotions to function naturally divert their gaze around the emotions in the room.

It isn't just that the system creates an environment that leads to a lack of empathy. Physicians look past suffering partly because we don't believe we have power over it. Because in the face of pain and suffering, our presence alone feels puny and weak and not at all like the powerful version of ourselves we'd envisioned when we signed up to be healers of disease. Yet if we can disclose our weaknesses and even our failures, there can be forgiveness and grace. Even when we are breaking, we are already in the process of coming together, healing to become stronger. In the same place you see the fracture on the X-ray, if you look closely, you can also see the sclerotic bone that represents healing.

If we could admit that as physicians we held only one piece of the whole . . . if we could pull together not only our medical knowledge but also the patient voice, the knowledge of the body and our communal knowledge, maybe we could redefine wholeness. I looked at the front row, at my colleagues who had been there from the very beginning, the small group of physicians who had commiserated in my room on the obstetrical floor and who had begun championing change. They smiled and nodded, and I understood that in that moment, our community was growing. I looked past them to the sparks of light coming back at me from iPhones and the greenish light of the hospital-issued pagers the residents still carried. A memory flooded in, something I had not thought of in years.

It was a myth told to me by one of my elderly patients during my residency in New York. I'll tell you the story the way I remember him telling it to me.

He began by demanding I sit.

"Why do you always look like you are in such a hurry?" I winced at his accurate representation of my day and the suggestion that I might not have time to spend with him. I dutifully sat.

"Good. Now we can talk. So how are you?" he asked.

"What's important is how you are doing. You are the patient, after all." I attempted to pivot the conversation back to him.

"Yes, I am your patient, and as such, I can't hope to be any more well than my doctor, so that's why I ask, how are you doing today?" He winked at me.

"I'm fine," I offered, shifting uncomfortably at the implication that my emotional state impacted him.

"You don't sleep," he reminded me. "This," he paused, emphasizing the word, "*this* is a problem." His gray skin tone, wild white hair and his accent recalled old black-and-white videos I'd seen of Albert Einstein when I was in school.

"It's just the way it is, it's the training. It is how we are meant to learn. It's important," I said. "Everyone before us did it and it made them better doctors," I added unconvincingly.

"Listen, you want to talk important . . . let me tell you something important," he said with an intensity.

I leaned in, believing he was going to share a new symptom he was having, some new portent of his inescapable death.

"This is what's important. I am going to tell you a story. Are you ready?" he asked, and I nodded. "In the beginning, there was only God," he began, holding me in his gaze.

I sat back and tried not to visibly sigh. This was not the revelation I had been hoping for.

"And in the beginning, God's presence filled the universe. And then He decided to bring this world into being. So he drew in His breath, and from that contraction darkness was created." As my patient explained this, he too drew in his breath, puffing out his chest and growing taller. "And then light came and filled the darkness"—he spread his arms wide across the span of his bed—"and filled ten holy vessels with primordial light."

I felt myself relax slightly, vaguely entertained by his investment and animated retelling of the story. His aged, arthritic hands bounced around, shaping the ten vessels. He mouthed the numbers as he silently shaped them: "One, two, three . . .

"These vessels, though. Well, there was a problem. They were too fragile to contain such a divine and powerful light. They broke open, and all the light scattered like stars." His fingers darted about the room, in the direction of the fragmented light.

I smiled at the idea of a primordial light fracturing into stars.

The one part of religion that had always appealed to me was the allegorical nature of the stories. If I found myself thinking, *These are just the stories people told themselves before they had science to explain the universe,* then I couldn't engage with them. But if I reminded myself that these stories were in essence metaphors, then rather than become infuriated by the lack of scientific rigor, or the impossible nature of the stories being spun, I found I could suspend disbelief. The idea of a guiding metaphor gave me something to look for. It was a roadmap. The tales were a representation of more tangible values; I was to divine the hidden meanings. I enjoyed imagining what I was meant to glean, what wisdom I could take forth that would be of use to me from these ancient tales.

"Scattered like stars," I repeated after him.

"The wound is the gift, you see?" he implored me.

The wound is the gift.

"We have to make the light whole again," he told me with great sincerity and a sense of urgency. "That is why we are here, to gather the sparks and repair the world."

I held his hand, understanding he thought his death was near.

"You are enough," he said. "Now, go. Gather the sparks," he demanded, gesturing to the hallway.

I wasn't sure what he wanted me to do, but he seemed insistent I leave, so I took my exit from his room, feeling it was all a bit surreal.

I looked out at the audience and saw sparks. And I began to wonder: if we believed that, if we believed our purpose was to gather the sparks, what would that look like?

What if the question I had been posing was entirely wrong? What if it was not How do we get from here to there, but rather, How do we live? How do we live in such a way that honors all aspects of knowledge? Not just medical knowledge, but the body's knowledge and the truths that can only be delivered through the patient's perspective, and our communal knowledge of suffering and identity? If each of those bits is a piece of the light, if each one is a spark, we could unite them to become whole.

My presentation was changing in my mind as I gave it. I should have perhaps expected that; I knew that teaching was inherently reciprocal. We learn early on that we gain as much wisdom from our students as they do from us. We learn as we prepare lectures, as we contemplate unexpected questions and embrace new angles on old ideas. We confront our own biases, laid bare by the face of innocence. To teach something, you first have to truly master it yourself, and that requires a kind of self-discovery, an immersion that ignites the first sparks of knowledge before we are ever in front of a student. I knew that to be true, and yet I wasn't expecting to learn anything as I delivered my prepared lecture that day. I believed I had an experience and point of view that I wanted to impart to the audience. In doing so, I found the audience had the answer I didn't know I was looking for. They allowed me to look into the darkness of the auditorium and *see*. See that the darkness in the end would bring forth the light.

My presentation had nothing to do with sepsis or hematomas. It never did. It was about uniting the patient story with medical knowledge and a larger, supportive community so that together we could heal the world we had proximity to. Because although the healing potential of medical knowledge is remarkable, it cannot function in a vacuum.

I walked off the stage to a line of people waiting to tell me I was brave. I didn't feel brave. I felt tentative and scared, wondering if I would be understood. I felt like an ambassador sent from some faraway planet who wanted to explain what it looked like in the places they would never see, but not knowing if we had a common enough language for me to express myself effectively.

In the hallways after the lecture, I became the recipient of the stories of others. Notes were jotted down and passed to me as if secrets: *Here, you can read this later, I just want you to know you aren't alone.*

> Three years ago, my mom was diagnosed with an aggressive Stage IV breast cancer. She had metastases everywhere, her liver and spine were riddled. And she was scared, she felt she didn't know what questions to ask, so I went with her. Her son the doctor was there to help. And I listened during the visit, I didn't want to be pushy, you know? Overbearing physicians and all of that. And I asked him, "So what are we looking at here? What's the prognosis?" And the guy looked at me and said, "Seriously? You're a doctor, you know how this goes. You really want me to spell it out for you?" And my mom just started crying. She's been dead for a year, and I swear to God, I can't think of her without hearing what that doctor said.

Messages filled my e-mail inbox. The subject line usually said, "Your talk" or "Sepsis Day." One read,

> When I had a heart attack last year, the cardiologist doing the catheterization told my wife, "I found the blockage in his artery. We call it the widow-maker." As an internist I had probably heard that phrase a thousand times before, and I never thought much of it. Like, ha

ha, yeah it usually affects young-ish guys and it usually kills them, so we call it the widow-maker. But saying that to my wife, telling her in that way, it just terrified her, you know? In some ways that sentence scarred her more than the heart attack itself. She hasn't let me go golfing since.

An elderly colleague stopped me in the hallway one day and told me:

I didn't really tell anyone about this, but I was in the emergency department a few weeks ago, with an intestinal blockage. It was pretty painful and I was scared . . . I'm older now, you know. No one is surprised when you die at my age. And my wife doesn't drive so I was there alone. And this doctor sat down next to me, I'm sure he was busy, but he sat down next to me and he held my hand. And it comforted me more than I can explain. I was so moved by that small act. But you know what? It also made me think, in all these years of being a doctor, why had I never just sat down and held someone's hand? It could have made all the difference for someone, but I just didn't know. Until that moment, I didn't see the value. I didn't think that was my job.

I always printed the e-mails rather than read them on the screen. If someone told me their story out loud, I jotted it down later in a journal. I saved the notes. There was something powerful in that act of making the suffering visible. Maybe I believed that if it was visible, if it was made physically tangible, it could better be known. I could be a better witness to it.

Other stories emerged, from colleagues who understood

where they had failed. Stories that emboldened them to want to change the system. Stories rooted in shame that they couldn't find a place for. Stories that intersected with my own.

One described an encounter in the ICU with the father of a twelve-year-old girl who had had an asthma attack and required life-support. The physician knew that the girl was brain-dead, that there was no hope of a functional recovery, and stood before the crying father, speechless.

> I was looking at him, and I just saw myself, you know? My daughter has asthma and her mom and I had just gotten divorced. And this girl had been riding her bike when she had an attack and the dad didn't know. He just thought she was out playing. By the time he got there it was too late. He told me his ex-wife was on her way, and he just needed to know how bad it was. And as he asked me that, I was thinking that this was the worst thing I could imagine a father going through. I saw myself in him and it really shook me up. So, all I could manage was, "It's as bad as it gets." And the guy nodded, and he kissed her and he left. He just walked out of the ICU. I got the sense he didn't want to be there when his ex-wife showed up. So, I found out later from his ex-wife that he went home and killed himself. He shot himself in the head. I've never talked about this before, but I know it's my fault. If I had known what to say, or if I had been able to stop thinking of myself for a minute and be there for him, maybe he would still be alive. I couldn't save his daughter, but he didn't have to die. That's on me.

It struck me as these submerged stories resurfaced that in the same way physicians had denied the primacy of the patient voice, medicine had also silenced physicians. We'd been trained to believe that the burdens we carried, the suffering we witnessed was meant to be borne in silence. We were further taught to establish clinical distance, to don white coats that declared we were on the side of health. It was an intentional delineation of ourselves as separate, and therefore safe. We made this declaration not only to our patients, but also to ourselves. Because in order to practice medicine we needed to see ourselves as somehow separate and therefore not susceptible. If we believed we were the same as our patients, with the same propensity for illness, we would be forced to confront our own mortality. It's a difficult thing to know that much of the suffering we witness will in some form touch us as well. All of the illness and dependency and death. But it seemed to me in retrospect that the anchors intended to moor us had actually pulled us under.

The notes seemed to acknowledge that we were, in fact, all the same. Maybe the mechanism of injury was different, but we were all facing the same abyss. And taken together, our isolated voices, the shared disclosures and e-mails, the voices of the patients, they were actually able to amplify each other, even in the darkness. And they were all begging for change.

One card appeared in my hospital mailbox and transported me immediately back to the ICU, to the patient who had asked each person to write a message of hope for her wall. I remembered clearly standing with the team as we rounded on the patient who had been waiting months for a lung transplant. The card said only,

Dr. Awdish, I want you to know that I filled out the index card. I didn't do it the day you told me to, or the day after. I don't know why but I just couldn't. I'm sorry. But when she had her transplant, when I saw her up and walking again, I did. I couldn't bring myself to give it to her. I was too embarrassed and I didn't think she would remember me anyway. So I wanted you to have it. It's kind of written for both of you anyway.

The 3x5 index card, which was enclosed, said simply, "Thank you for teaching me that there is always room for hope."

I stood in my office staring at it as the words became obscured by my tears.

We were the light needed to heal each other.

People get shattered in many ways, and they heal through different means as well. Each of my wounds had healed differently. I have one scar that is a pale, thin, perfectly straight line. It is eight inches long and runs from just under my breastbone to my navel. It recalls a wound intentionally created with a surgeon's scalpel, the one they made to remove half of my diseased liver. The edges the scalpel produced were sharp and clean, and could be brought together neatly. It healed well. In medicine we call it "healing by primary intention."

Some wounds are too large and can't be closed that way. Wounds created by trauma don't have sharp clean edges. The deep craters of tissue loss have wide perimeters that can't be pulled neatly together. These injuries heal slowly as new tissue is generated to fill the space, layer by layer. These sorts of injuries leave behind larger, rougher scars. Scars befitting a city decimated by civil war. This healing, which we call "healing by secondary intention," is more like a mourning process than a surgery. It requires a rallying of resources, both internal and external. The significance of the loss is acknowledged and announced, and a support system arrives to attempt to fill the vacancy. And though everyone present feels deeply inadequate as an individual, together they are able to provide the necessary support. They form a network that can support regrowth into the newly empty space. It is a rebuilding rather than a reclaiming.

All great losses heal this way.

We would heal through secondary intention. The people behind those notes and e-mails, and those in the hallways, would band together and fill the empty spaces. They became our allies and advocates. We enlisted patients and their families, and embedded their voice in every effort. We learned together how to honor our respective brokenness, the vastness of the wound and the primacy of the patient's perspective. We work each day to add another layer, to make hope visible, to make the space whole again.

It's a very different course than the one I set out on all those years ago when I believed healing to be clean, academic and straightforward. It's far more humble, and honest, informed by an ocean's weight of suffering. And despite a sense of forward progress, I know the strength of the tide and the constant threat of the undertow. We've all felt it now. And though we are building the ship as we sail it, it is finally being built. Because no one else should have to drown.

WE CAN DO BETTER—
COMMUNICATION TIPS

Conversations that occur in doctors' offices or at a hospital bedside are some of the most critical any of us will ever have. The effectiveness of those discussions has a direct, measurable impact on individual patient health outcomes. Something as simple as providing quality information about a new medication has the ability to influence whether patients actually take the drug. It's well understood that activated, engaged patients are more likely to participate in health-promoting activities. Yet both doctors and patients lack the tools necessary to ensure that the needs of each side are met. We even lack a common language. Physicians spend years learning to translate common symptoms into archaic terminology only to be tasked with explaining medical issues *without* using jargon. We can do better.

These encounters are too important for us to passively allow them to simply happen to us. Patients and physicians alike have to take ownership and be deliberate partners in their construction. From before the visit to long after, there are a number of steps we can take to ensure we have given ourselves the best possible chance of success.

BEFORE THE ENCOUNTER: PHYSICIAN
Arrive present

The emotional state of the physician impacts everyone in the room. While it is important to take the temperature of the room, it is equally important to know what emotions you are bringing in with you. Think of yourself as a thermostat. You have the ability to return the temperature of the room to neutral. Your emotions should never add to the heat; they should only equilibrate the room.

Check in

Take a moment to check in with yourself—are you hungry, thirsty, tired, or otherwise distracted? Given the demands on physicians, it is likely that you are all of the above. What can you do to tend to yourself in a minute or less that will help you be more present for the encounter? A well-timed snack, a peek at a picture that reminds you of what you are looking forward to at home later, or even just a deep, cleansing breath can center and calm your nervous system. It can deactivate the flight-or-flight mode physicians often find themselves in and allow you to focus on the patient. Allow yourself the gift of being able to truly see.

Know the history

There is little that is more influential in building trust than truly knowing the patient's history. An elderly patient who has just been discharged from the ICU undoubtedly requires more care coordination and an in-depth knowledge of the events of the hospitalization, but that same approach is just as beneficial for a routine outpatient. Even a few moments spent reviewing a patient's list of medications or your last office notes will help to set a positive tone for the visit and demonstrate your commitment to properly coordinating their care.

BEFORE THE ENCOUNTER: PATIENT
Bring support

Consider bringing someone with you as an extra pair of ears for especially high-stakes appointments. Give them a task beforehand, and be explicit about your needs or expectations: "It will help me if you write down as much as possible about what the doctor says so I can read it later if I forget." Or, "I need you to be sure I remember to ask this one particular question, so if I don't, please ask for me."

Make a list

Ensure you make the most of your visit by writing down your questions, concerns, and any of the issues you hope to be addressed well before your visit. Remember in school when you were taught to brainstorm—not to filter your thoughts but just write? Do that, then sit back and look at what you've written. What stands out to you as important? What questions can be asked of other members of the care team, perhaps the nurse? What are the things you might be afraid to ask? Reflect on your answers and then start a new list, prioritizing each item, and determine which items must be addressed in order to feel the visit was effective.

Keep a journal of your symptoms

If one of the items is a new symptom, start a journal of your symptoms. In order to determine the most likely cause of your symptoms, your doctor will ask a series of questions that is part of the patient assessment tool OPQRST. Structure your journal with these questions in mind:

Onset: When did you first notice the symptom? Your doctor is listening with ears attuned to acuity, because a symptom that began ten years ago is far less likely to harm you than one that came on suddenly last week. Be honest with yourself and your doctor. If it started six months ago, but you were afraid it signified something serious or embarrassing and didn't mention it before, admit that. It will help your physician to know that this is difficult for you to discuss.

Provocative Factors: What were you doing when the symptom started? Be specific. Sometimes this tells us everything. Someone who never has chest pain at rest but always has chest pain while climbing stairs may have a very serious blockage in the arteries that supply the heart muscle. Similarly, if the pain in your shoulder began when you were playing softball, it tells your physician something about the likelihood of injury.

Quality: Can you describe how the symptom felt? Symptoms are often the most difficult to describe, so think of defining characteristics. If you are experiencing pain, is it sharp or dull? More of a pressure or a burning sensation? If you had to make someone else imagine what it felt like, what words would you use?

Radiation: Does the symptom ever change or move within your body? This is something that is easier to figure out outside the doctor's office, when it's quieter and you can notice details. Sometimes we are so distracted by the primary symptom that we fail to notice there is more to it. Has the burning in the center of your stomach moved up to your throat? Maybe the dull ache in your right side sometimes travels to the middle of your back. Have you noticed a change with certain positions? Is it better or worse when you lie down? Pay attention to your body, as these are clues that can help your doctor tremendously.

Severity: When is the symptom at its absolute worst, and how severe is it? This may vary and change over time, so it's good to think of the range of severity. If you find it hard to quantify, think of the following questions. How does it impact your life? What does it stop you from doing?

Temporal Factors: Does anything make it better? Say, avoiding spicy foods? Taking an over-the-counter allergy pill? What have you already tried? Does anything make it worse? What makes it go away completely? Does it ever go away completely? Can you associate it in time with anything? Meals? Time of day? Does it ever wake you up at night? Look for patterns. If you notice one, write it down and share it with your physician.

BEGINNING THE VISIT
Agenda setting: Physician

We each have defined goals for patient visits. Many are based on best practices and guidelines that are designed to improve the relative health of large populations of people. It can be easy to fall into believing that we know what the goal of an encounter is without negotiating the agenda with the patient. But to engage any patient in health outcomes, we first must find out what is important to the patient. We can then use this data to help create an agenda for the encounter. Begin with an open-ended question and then listen to the patient's answer. My usual greeting ties this all in: "I was reviewing your records in preparation for today's appointment, and I have a few things I am hoping to discuss, but first I'd like to hear what is on your mind. What brought you in today?" It can feel like a loss of control, as if the patient's stream of concerns will never end, but studies show most patients will keep their response to less than two minutes if left uninterrupted.

Ask, and ask again: Physician

Don't assume everything is on the table when the patient stops speaking. The most pressing concerns are often the last to be stated. When there is a pause, ask for more—"Is there anything else?"—to ensure you've got a complete picture. This will allow you to prioritize. "It sounds like your knee pain is really limiting your ability to get out of the house, and that concerns me, so I'd like to be sure we address that today. But I also want to talk a bit about your annual health maintenance. Would that be okay?" Always check in to allow the patient to feel they have agency and choice in their care.

Agenda setting: Patient

It's time to pull out the list. READ the list to the doctor. Don't censor yourself; simply read those top issues that you had identified prior to the encounter.

Possible starter sentences:

- "What I hope to accomplish today is to gain a better understanding of my recent diagnosis."
- "I am hoping to learn from you what steps I can take at home to reduce the impact of this disease."
- "Can you explain how you will know that the treatment we decided to try is working?"

Understand that the physician may have a different priority. Something that the doctor has identified as a "red flag" symptom may redirect the entire encounter, but know that this is being done for your own safety and well-being. But, even in situations when your health is stable, it's important to know where the doctor feels the focus should be. If the doctor doesn't provide his or her own agenda for the visit, try asking questions like "What about my current health concerns you the most?" Or "If I were to focus on changing one thing in order to positively impact my health, what do you think it should be?"

DURING THE ENCOUNTER: PHYSICIAN
Empathy

Emotions can be difficult to decode. Even benign symptoms can trigger intense anxiety. I don't know of a single physician who, when stricken with a terrible headache, hasn't for at least a moment thought, "I wonder if this is a brain tumor or an aneurysm that's ruptured?"

Explore: It helps to ask the patient what they are worried about. For example: "I have some ideas based on what you're telling me, but what do you think is going on here?"

Check in: Consider whether news you thought was relatively minor seemed to overwhelm the patient: "I want to make sure I hear what you're thinking. How do things look from your point of view?"

Name the emotion: When you do see emotion, try naming it: "It seems as if you are feeling anxious." Find out what feels authentic to you; everyone's communication style is different.

Provide support: A gateway, if you are less comfortable expressing emotion, is to offer genuine statements of support and reassurance. "It must be overwhelming to think about. I want you to know I'll be here with you to figure out our next steps."

Assess understanding

Opportunities for misunderstanding can occur on both sides of the exam table. To avoid this, take the following steps:

Restate and reframe: An easy way to ensure that your message has been understood is to ask, "Could you tell me how you might explain what I've just told you to your family when you get home?" This will allow you to gauge both what content has been absorbed and how the patient may be framing it to themselves.

Check in: How is their perspective? Is it accurate? What meaning has the patient attributed to a diagnosis, test or treatment plan?

If, for example, you are discussing the need for a procedure—say, an ultrasound examination of the heart to better characterize chest pain—and you ask the patient for their thoughts on having the procedure and the patient says, "It sounds like I'd better get my affairs in order," there is a clear disconnect. On the other hand, if the patient replies, "I think it is time to be proactive; I've been putting off finding out the cause of the chest pain for too long," you are better aligned.

Respect: Regardless of what is said, respect the patient's viewpoint, and add to it if necessary. "That's a really good restatement of the issue. Can I add one detail that I think is important?"

Expectations

When setting treatment goals, know that the desired endpoint might look very different from the patient's perspective. Ask the patient "What would you most like to achieve?" To us, heart failure management may simply mean a certain number of pounds of water weight lost to offload pressure on the heart. To a patient, it may mean being able to go back to church because the swelling has decreased and she can get her shoes on again. That is a shared goal, just articulated differently. Use it to effect change.

DURING THE ENCOUNTER: PATIENT
State your fears

If you are concerned about something and feel it isn't coming across or that your concerns are being minimized, be deliberate and direct. For example, tell the doctor, "I am worried that this pain represents something serious, like a tumor." Fears left silent will fester and feed on themselves. Fears expressed can be calmed.

Restate for clarity

If you are unsure of something, ask about it. If the physician lapses into medical jargon, try saying, "Can I try this in my own words so I make sure I understand?" Or rephrase what you hear: "What I hear you saying is . . . is that right?" This allows the doctor to understand how effective their communication has been and where gaps remain.

Next steps

Make sure you are clear about next steps. This may require direct a question, such as: "What symptom changes would warrant a follow-up visit?" If you are having testing, ask how the results will be communicated: "How will I learn about the results of the testing? Will a letter be sent or will someone call? When can I expect to hear?" Not doing so may mean unnecessary anxiety. This is true of either a clinic visit or an inpatient hospital stay. One of the most anxiety-producing aspects of being an inpatient is the loss of control, the unknown. Ideally your care team will anticipate this and inform you of what lies ahead, but if they don't, ask. "What tests are planned for today? What are you hoping to learn from the results?"

Have an action plan

If you have a condition that flares up or is subject to exacerbation, you have the advantage of being able to plan ahead. By developing an action plan with your physician, you will be able to better self-manage certain recurring issues. For example, some patients with heart failure who weigh themselves daily are instructed to take an additional dose of their water pill if they have gained two pounds of fluid weight. Some asthmatic patients know that if they are using their rescue inhaler more frequently, they made need to start an oral steroid pill. To the extent that plans can be worked out in advance, you can stay ahead of problems that may arise while still having the comfort of knowing that each step you are taking is supported by your physician and care team.

USE ALL AVAILABLE RESOURCES: PHYSICIANS AND PATIENTS
Technology

Take advantage of whatever communication resources are provided to you. Many electronic medical records have a patient portal through which you can directly communicate. Use it to ask the question you forgot to ask during a visit or follow up on test results. Your physician may be happy to e-mail responses to questions. The knowledge that communication channels remain open after the encounter can alleviate some of the pressure of the visit and allow for a trusting relationship to develop over time.

Human Resources

Some clinics have care teams staffed with nurses, social workers or even pharmacists. Patients, learn what services your clinic offers and who best to direct your questions to both during and after office hours. Find your community. This may mean joining a local patient support group or (if you suffer from a rare disease) an online forum that is supported by a national organization. Physicians, find out about the support system your patient relies upon for help. Is it a family member or a neighbor who drops in to check on your patient? Are there community services in the area that you could engage to fill the spaces between visits? It is only by building a community that is engaged and active that we can hope to effect true change.

Acknowledgments

I've written a book that is about the darkness, the shadows, and the times when we failed. Implicit in the fact that I was even able to write this is the truth that my life was saved on more than one occasion by teams of people who are experts in their field. I will forever be indebted to each of them, and I hope that my efforts to change our profession for the better are seen as what they are—an effort to honor your life's work, the passion you bring to it, and our shared commitment that we can always be better.

To Tony—You are the hero of this story.

To Marwan—You are everything I aspire to be. Resilient and wise and humble and generous. You are ALL OF THE THINGS.

To Maria Z.—You truly showed me another way. It is so clear that medicine is your calling, and you exemplify compassion. You know I adore you.

To Dave—You showed me what bravery looked like. What showing up every day for your patients looks like. And how to know when it was time to blow everything up and start over.

To Jacqueline—I have no idea how you knew I could write a book, but thank you for finding me. Your e-mail changed my life.

To Karen—Thank you for believing in this project, for being its tireless, passionate advocate, and for getting half the world on board! And above all, thank you for making me believe I was a writer, when I was quite insistent I was not.

To Father George—Thank you for your endless support. During every crisis, you were a tremendous comfort to us. And for enthusiastically sharing our joys as well.

To the Pulmonary and Critical Care Department (especially Geneva, Razaq, Mike E., Paul, Bruno, Jenn, Lisa, Ron, Joey)— Thank you for your support during this time; the coverage you provided when I was endlessly sick; the leadership, mentorship and friendship; the sideline consults, the guidance and the treatment. You're like family.

To Hector—You taught me everything I know. And I entertain you by eating bananas with a knife. So I'm pretty sure we're even.

To Rose and Vanessa and Kelley and Vicki and Michelle (and the whole CE team)—Thank you for partnering with me in the actual, tangible, hard work of improving patient care. I'm so proud of what we are doing together.

To Kristen, Erin, CLEAR facilitators and actors—What you do is MAGIC. Kristen, thank you for bringing the VitalTalk format to our institution. It has been a game-changer.

Tricia and Jillian and Erin and Kelsey and April and Susan and Debbie and Barbara and truly all of the nurses—Your presence through those days meant more to us than you'll ever know. I learned more about how to be there for my patients from watching you than I can ever hope to explain.

To Rosemary—I will forever be grateful that a chance

encounter in a grocery store brought you into my life. You made this book better. You led me to an introduction that was so elusive, for so long. You are a gifted and generous teacher.

To Maria—You are my Guru. Your wisdom and compassion are boundless. You have made me into a smarter, braver version of myself through your friendship and coaching. I wish everyone had an opportunity to learn from you.

To Cara—Thank you for teaching me to trust the reader. You were a Godsend. And I don't know which aspect of you I adore more: Talented editor, with amazing insight? Or late-night dance partner and karaoke singer? I hope our yearly trips together continue for-EVAH!

To Jim—You can say things to me that no one else can. And you are ALWAYS right. I don't think I'm overstating it when I say this book would have been unreadable without your insights. Thank you for reading the horrid early drafts.

To Mechelle—Thank you for insisting Jim re-befriend me. And your endless encouragement.

To friends that I trusted with the awful early drafts (Bryan, Lisa, Sara, Lynn, Kelly)—Thank you for your guidance and encouragement to keep going. You helped me to find my voice.

To Sara—Thank you for being my partner. Your dedication to our work has allowed me to do more than I ever could have alone.

To Dana—Thank you for being there for ALL OF IT, the pain and the healing and the work that followed. Thank you for asking the hard questions and for always prefacing them with, "OK, so . . . loaded question, but . . ." For wearing the Spanx, for the -erfect wedding toast (even though everyone kept talking), and for telling me I am your favorite human. And I totally forgive you for making me walk up the hill.

To our families and friends who visited, fed EVERYONE and

provided comfort (esp. the Awdish/Ayoub/Kouza/Chammout/Sharrak/Shaya families)—Thank you. Though I couldn't participate at the time, knowing you were there was a great comfort.

To Kamal—Thank you for dropping everything and driving to get to me. You have always been there for me when I needed you. And I'm so glad we share so many memories that no one else understands.

To Nellie—Thank you for teaching me to look for the light, in every situation, to be grateful always, and that GIRLS CAN DO ANYTHING BOYS CAN DO. Everything I am is because of you and Dad.

To Randy—Just like everything else in our lives . . . this book is proof of your love and your willingness to sacrifice for us. And yes, you can use this as a testimonial if you ever have to date again. But I hope you never have to use it. Because nothing would make me happier than living our -erfect life together forever.